CLOSER devotional

A 366-day discipleship tool challenging you to apply biblical knowledge to daily life

By Louis W. Heard

Copyright © 2016 by Louis W. Heard

Closer Devotional
A 366-day discipleship tool challenging you to apply biblical knowledge to daily life
by Louis W. Heard

Printed in the United States of America.

Edited by Xulon Press

ISBN 9781498480123

All rights reserved solely by the author. The author guarantees all contents are original and do not infringe upon the legal rights of any other person or work. No part of this book may be reproduced in any form without the permission of the author. The views expressed in this book are not necessarily those of the publisher.

Unless otherwise indicated, Scripture quotations taken from the English Standard Version (ESV). Copyright © 2001 by Crossway, a publishing ministry of Good News Publishers. Used by permission. All rights reserved.

www.xulonpress.com

Dedication

This book is dedicated to my wife, Cathy, and our four kids: Haley, Noah, Eden, and Levi. I hope it shapes the lives of many, but ultimately I pray it continues to stir in my family a deeper yearning for Jesus. May the words of this book, inspired by *the Book*, encourage my descendants and beyond for generations to come.

Acknowledgments

A special thank you is extended to the wonderful people of Emmanuel Baptist Church in Tucson, Arizona, and Grace Baptist Church in Fort Worth, Texas. When I started writing in 2008 and throughout the creation of this book, I've had the distinct honor of pastoring these two God-fearing congregations. Many of the daily entries came as a direct result of preaching sermons and having personal interactions with the amazing people of these churches. Only as a result of God's mercy can one man stand before others and speak His Word. From one sinner saved by grace to another, may God bless you all as you continue to draw *closer* to Him.

Another thank you is extended to Brian Armas of *Lightfly Creative* for designing such an eye-catching cover.

Thank you Cindi Chase, Jil'lana Heard and Kristi Stevens for reviewing the manuscript and providing some suggested changes.

Finally, thank you *Xulon Press* for making the process of publishing as easy and clear as possible. May God be glorified as a result of all the effort placed in this book.

Preface

As a lead pastor desiring to see Christ-followers mature in faith, I grow weary of watching faithful believers slip away over time. It's disheartening because I see that they have the knowledge of Christ, but slowly lose fervor, which ultimately leads to a lack of influence in the world and a disconnect with God. What I find even more demoralizing is that I see myself slip into some of those same patterns! When this happens to me, I realize it's not my biblical *knowledge* that has failed me but the practical *application* of that knowledge. I long to be close to God, but like many others, I need a plan. This frustration set me on a quest.

I started the process of seeking a discipleship tool that could help me better apply Scripture and draw closer to my transcendent, spiritual God. When I couldn't find one to quench my spiritual needs, I began creating a personal discipleship tool that would increase the practical application of the truths I believe. I thought this would set my heart ablaze, and in theory, I seemed to be on target.

After a few years of working on this book, I had almost completed it when I discovered a deeper problem. Indeed, I needed to apply better the truths I had learned, but I realized my focus and motivation had been off course. I thought if I simply increased my application of God's truths and worked harder for God, I'd find satisfaction. That wasn't the case. Instead, I discovered that working harder *for* God didn't necessarily mean I was communing *with* God. I had been little more than a lifeless robot obeying orders. I perceived God more as my boss than my Father, who yearns to *abide with* me. Something had to change!

For centuries the Westminster Catechism has taught Protestants that "man's chief end is to glorify God, <u>and</u> to enjoy Him forever." In my shortcoming, I have often omitted the second part of this creed. I've been on mission to glorify God, but I haven't made enjoying Him forever the chief way to accomplish glory. Thus, I've missed realizing that the crown yearning of God is to simply commune *with* us! Martha humbly learned this when she was gently rebuked by the Savior for working when Mary eagerly sat with Him.

This truth has been the key in redirecting my motivation for creating this discipleship tool. It's also led to a challenging paradox. If we're supposed to obey God through diligent service (somewhat like Martha or a robot obeying commands), can we also have a meaningful, vibrant relationship with God (like Mary or a child adoring his dad)? Can these two realities of the Christian faith coexist? Can I obey God (work *for* Him) *and* be in a close relationship with Him (commune *with* Him)?

This paradox has led me to yet another question that is essential for finding a suitable answer. Can the secret of a fulfilling life be found in the combination of these two truths? If we accept *communing* with God as the **end** goal, and view our *work* for God as a **means** to that end, could they work together masterfully? Could this be the key to Christian maturity? I believe so. Now, it should be noted that salvation is a free gift. There is no way you can attain salvation through works. Instead, your works give evidence of your faith. As a result, the spiritual works of your life will glorify God in two ways: 1) Your works provide a strong witness of Jesus' character and mission; 2) Your works draw you closer to God in sweet fellowship.

With this in mind and by the direction of the Holy Spirit, I've assembled this book as a tool to not only refocus your mind on the knowledge you've gained, but also move you beyond *intellectual* knowledge to *experiential* knowledge, resulting in the greatest satisfaction of communing with God! This tool will radically challenge your personal faith so that you'll have no choice but to draw closer to God every day in complete, utter dependence with the ultimate goal of abiding with Him. I'm confident this book will draw you into a deeper relationship with God if you wholeheartedly commit to it.

This book isn't merely a daily devotional of happy thoughts to carry you through the day. It's a tool meant to challenge your spirit by calling you to action. You'll be requested each day to complete a *Closer Challenge*. A *Closer Challenge* is a request that moves you from intellectual knowledge to experiential knowledge. These moments can appear risky and may even induce fear because they propel your faith into action. But lean into the fear and embrace the great adventure ahead!

The truth is, after a few entries, you may feel as if you're not ready for this book because it will call you to act in ways that are uncommon to the flesh. However, I urge you to endure! And as you do, don't merely use the insights as clever, pithy devotional thoughts. Fully follow the instructions *each* day. That's the way you will experience a closer walk with God. This book is not meant to vastly increase your mental understanding. Its purpose is to awaken your spirit to action resulting in the crown yearning of God for His creation: *Drawing closer to you*!

So, as you prepare to start this journey, here's how I would suggest you use this discipleship tool. Read it as you would a devotional each morning, for you will be called to finish a task that day. In addition, it should be noted that *time* must be set aside every day to deepen *any* relationship, especially with God! As you follow through with each daily entry, journal the results of your *Closer Challenges*. I advise you to walk through this discipleship tool with a Christian partner. You'll need this person's assistance and accountability. (See Appendix 1 for my One on One Disciple-Making Plan. Use Appendix 2 for Topical References.) Pastors, use this book as a discipleship tool in your churches. Have your whole church or a small group work through the book. Each month, host a gathering to share stories. The spiritual transformations made by using this book can become even more life-changing when stories are shared as encouragement with others. You can also share your spiritual progress and life experiences on my Facebook *like* Page. [www.facebook.com/louiswheard] Your testimonials can be a great source of inspiration for others as we wrestle through these challenges together. When on social media, use the hashtag **#CloserDevo** to assemble and reveal more stories of life-change.

My prayer is that you'll see Jesus in a fresh way every day, moving you to the most precious and satisfying calling of your life: to **commune with** and **draw closer** to God!

Louis W. Heard

"...whoever looks intently into the perfect law that gives freedom, and continues in it—not forgetting what they have heard, but doing it—they will be blessed in what they do."

James 1:25

January 1

God is Not Far Away!

Acts 17:26-27

For centuries, mankind has sought the meaning for existence. From philosophers to everyday folks, people have debated whether or not God is real. And if there is an Intelligent Designer who has properly brought everything into order, does He want to know us? Does He actually care for His creation? According to the Bible, the answer is a resounding yes! From the Garden of Eden when God breathed life into Adam's nostrils (Genesis 2:7) to the final assembly at the New Jerusalem (Revelation 21:3), the Bible teaches that God is on a hot pursuit to dwell in a close relationship with mankind. And it's also our innate pursuit to do likewise with Him.

When the Apostle Paul was reasoning with a group of Jewish and Greek philosophers at a synagogue in Athens, he shared with them God's desire to be close. In response to their belief in an "unknown god," Paul attempted to persuade them that God can be known, and then Paul provided the way to know Him. Seek Him, feel your way toward Him, and you will find Him. (Acts 17:26) And then with some of the most encouraging words in all Scripture, Paul declared that God was in fact not far away! (Acts 17:27) He is *close* to you. As you begin this journey of drawing closer to God this year, you must believe God is not far away. If you cling to this truth, the treasure of knowing God in a closer, deeper way awaits you!

Closer Challenge: Do you really believe God desires to be close to you? If so, you will receive the blessing of God's presence in your life. **Today,** as you begin the journey of drawing closer to God this year, drop to your knees in this moment and pray this simple prayer: "Father, I trust that You are not far from me. This year, I commit my life to seeking You, feeling my way toward You, and finding You. Show me that You are close." With this commitment, be prepared to experience God in ways you never have before. A great journey awaits you as you follow the *Closer Challenges* in this book!

January 2

God's Hot Pursuit

Luke 10:38-42

What is God's hot pursuit? If that question was asked of a hundred Christ followers, it wouldn't be surprising to receive several different answers. But the most common answer would probably be living *for* God. Most would say, "As long as I'm upholding His law (being good) and living on mission for Him, that's what God desires most."

Martha would fit into this group of believers. She demonstrated this when she invited Jesus into her house. She was diligently preparing a meal *for* Jesus when she noticed her sister, Mary, was not helping. So she became irritated and spewed out her disgust. Instead of cracking the whip on Mary, Jesus calmly rebuked Martha and reminded her of the *one* thing He sought most. (Luke 10:42) The hot pursuit of God is that you engage and deepen your relationship with Him. God's hot pursuit is simply being *with* you! Everything you do *for* Him is a means toward that ultimate end of being *with* Him! It should be noted that you don't stop *doing* things for God, because being on mission is an important part of the gospel, but don't make it the core. The core of the gospel is communing with the Savior.

<u>Closer Challenge</u>: **Today**, seek being *with* Jesus. Take at least five minutes of your day (hopefully more) and get away from everything that's distracting. Let the Spirit of God speak into your life. Read Luke 10:38-42 again and pray for a communing spirit like Mary's. Today is the second step of a year-long journey of knowing Jesus better. Each *Closer Challenge* you accept and fulfill will draw you closer to Jesus, which is the ultimate goal of your faith. God is on hot pursuit to commune with you! Make it your hot pursuit to be close to Him.

January 3

More Rejoicing!

Luke 15:1-7

What strums the joy strings of God's heart more than anything else in this world? You might think it's when a righteous individual is being well-behaved and serving fervently, but that's not the case according to this parable. (Luke 15:1-7) God immensely rejoices when sinners repent or His wayward children return to Him. There is *more rejoicing* in the Kingdom of Heaven when just one sinner repents than over ninety-nine righteous people doing well. Maybe that's where your greatest joy should be, too?

Think about the concept of this parable in a different light. When a husband and wife have their first child, there is great rejoicing. However, at the birth of their second child, their joy focuses on this new child for a short amount of time because they are celebrating *new birth*. It doesn't mean they don't love the first child, but there is a call to rejoice because of a new birth. In the Kingdom of Heaven, when someone is *born again* or returns from rebellion, great rejoicing is focused upon that new birth or recommitment. God still tenaciously loves His other children, but the new birth or return to their Father calls for special celebration.

Closer Challenge: Do you want to pluck the heart strings of God and give Him more rejoicing than ninety-nine righteous men and women singing in church? If so, try this. **Today**, who is on your heart who either needs to be born again or return to God? (If there's no one, that's an indicator you need to intentionally engage in non-Christian relationships.) When you have that person in mind, set up a lunch appointment, a phone call, or something else to talk to that person about Jesus. Ask many questions about that person's spiritual life. Let that person do the talking, and at the right point, gently and respectfully (1 Peter 3:15), direct that person to Jesus. Bring joy to the heart of God by leading someone to commune with Jesus!

January 4

Who Is Your Musician?

―――――•―――――

Romans 6:13-14

At some point, everyone has probably attempted to play an instrument. For some, it was easily mastered. For others, it was a struggle, so it was dropped quickly to pursue something else. There's something interesting about an instrument. It's useless unless there is a musician to play it. Sure, it could be used as a decorative piece of furniture in a house, but that doesn't serve its main purpose. An instrument is created to make music.

Paul says we are instruments. We're created to play beautiful melodies *for* the Lord and *by* the Lord. As the Lord uses you for His purposes, you become an instrument of righteousness. However, when you sin, the musician switches, and you become an instrument of Satan, making you an instrument of wickedness. Whether you like it or not, by your actions you're either playing a sweet tune for the Lord or an off-pitch melody for Satan. Who is your musician?

Closer Challenge: Are you aware you are an instrument? Nothing you do is influenced without the force of good or evil. You're either influenced by God or Satan in everything. **Today**, keep your eyes open to ministry. The Lord has a specific God-glorifying opportunity for you in this day. But, you must be alert to His leading. It may be a small act of righteousness or a significant experience in the life of another. Either way, allow the sweet breath of God to blow through your life and play sweet melodies of praise to that person or situation. Stay away from sin, for you must not become Satan's instrument of wickedness. Be an instrument of righteousness to commune with the Great Musician!

January 5

I'm Only Trying to Help

Luke 17:3-4

Shortly after becoming a Christian, we quickly discover no one's walk with Jesus is flawless. Thus, since we haven't reached our glorified state, which we'll receive in heaven, sin still attempts to control us. Even mature Christians will struggle at times. For example, a man who loves his wife may have unintentionally shifted his priorities to his occupation. As a result, he needs a gentle rebuke to realign his life. Satan has a plan to distract and destroy. If he can get us to stop focusing on the most important issues in life, being first our *relationship* with God, he can slowly begin to destroy us.

Is there a believer you know who is not walking with the Lord in a particular area? It's possible this person knows right from wrong, but is choosing wrong at this time. Scripture teaches that we should gently correct each other, for it will ultimately help the one caught in sin. (Proverbs 28:23) This person may not like what you have to say, but if you do it, you can save that person from possible harm.

<u>Closer Challenge</u>: **Today**, go to someone in your circle of influence who is morally out of the will of God. In an attitude of kindness, attempt to turn that person back to God. (Proverbs 27:5) See this as a rescue attempt filled with love, not a court sentencing by a judge. Remember, this person may not change immediately, so leave room for the Holy Spirit to work. When this person chooses to be rescued, God will be honored and your friend will be delivered from the shackles of Satan. It should also be noted that if someone comes to *you* with a rebuke, you should accept this correction and learn from it, for you will gain knowledge and wisdom. (Proverbs 19:25)

January 6

Delayed Obedience Forfeits Favor

---

2 Samuel 20:4-5

King David had made Amasa the commander of his military. (2 Samuel 19:13) Amasa's charge was to round up the men and attack a troublemaker named Sheba. David had given Amasa *three* days to summon the men, but he missed his deadline. He was late. The task had to be completed, so David made Abishai the commander to replace Amasa and finish the task. (2 Samuel 20:6-7) Later, Amasa was killed by Joab. (2 Samuel 20:10)

Is your word important to you? When you make a vow to be somewhere or do something, do you keep it? Faltering on your word, such as being late, tarnishes your character. For when you choose to make a commitment, you become responsible to others. Most importantly, as you wear the label of Christ-follower, you reflect God, and God always keeps His word. It's not just a personality issue. It's a respect issue to people and God. As a result, if you're continually late in keeping your word, you'll slowly lose favor. You'll also bear the dreaded label of being unreliable. (Proverbs 25:19)

<u>Closer Challenge</u>: It's hard to believe anyone would want to be deemed as unreliable or untrustworthy, but the way you live will shape your reputation. More than likely you have recently given your word to someone or a cause. Take it seriously. Get to work on time, meet deadlines, leave on time, arrive at appointments when you say you will, keep your commitment with your spouse. With all your power, do your best to fulfill your word, for this honors your Master. **Today,** think about what or who you've given your word to in the past week. Whatever it is, be fervent to accomplish it as you said. Make this attitude a pattern in your life, so you'll be deemed as reliable.

January 7

Take It...It's Free!

Ephesians 2:8

When is the last time you've received a gift unexpectedly and undeservedly? Maybe it was a lucky win from a door prize drawing, a second chance on a big project at work after you've failed, or keys to a new car after you've wrecked yours. Regardless of what your scenario was, how did you respond to that *free* gift? Was it hard to accept?

God has given you the greatest free gift of all...eternal life. You didn't earn it or deserve it, but God gave it freely to you *if* you take it. Are you trying to achieve your salvation? Scripture teaches that salvation is a gift you merely need to accept thankfully, by faith. (Romans 3:24) As you continue to commune with God, it's good to be reminded of God's special gift for you. (2 Corinthians 9:15) Even though God instructs you to behave in many ways, it doesn't take away the *state* in which you find yourself... under grace. Paul's charge for you is to remember that though works are important to display your faith, your works are *not* the avenue of salvation. Only by grace have you been saved. (Ephesians 2:8)

<u>Closer Challenge</u>: If you constantly struggle with the assurance of your salvation because you feel you haven't done enough, you may need to try this exercise. Write on a piece of paper "eternal life," place it in a box, put some wrapping paper around it, address it to your home, and ship it to yourself. When you open it, remember that salvation is a gift much like this. All you need to do is accept it through faith. **Today**, stop trying so hard to earn salvation. Let the Spirit reshape your mind. When you serve God today in any capacity, do it out of an overflow of love from a heart of thankfulness, not obligation. Everything you do today for Christ, do it with the mind of a child who is unconditionally loved by his or her Daddy in heaven.

January 8

Grumble, Grumble

Exodus 15:22-27

Moses and the Hebrews were traveling in the Desert of Shur for three days, and they could not find any water. Then when they finally approached some water, it was bitter. At this, they complained and lost faith in God. Having no water in the desert sounds unfair; after all, were they not God's chosen people? Wasn't it a promise of God that He'd provide for them? It's important to note that just days earlier, God performed one of the greatest acts of nature of all time...the splitting of the Red Sea. (Exodus 15:22) With this context in mind, it may appear shocking that they had gone three days without fresh water! Where was God now?

As we mature in our faith, we understand more how God has a way of letting us come to the end of our rope before intervening. And in the optimal moment, He'll sweep in and rescue us in unusual ways. This may seem a bit unfair and cruel to keep us hanging like that, especially if our desire is truly a *need*. But God does this so that we'll stay completely dependent upon Him. Even when our suffering is at its peak, we need to continue to believe God will rescue us. That is *hope* in its truest sense. Through all this, we will discover *our need* is really God.

<u>Closer Challenge</u>: Have you been grumbling against God because you've been waiting for Him, but He has not provided as you have desired? You might even be waiting for a basic need, such as the Hebrews waiting for water. Don't give up on God! **Today**, explain your need to God, and then rest in Him. Share your need with someone close to you and pray together. Wait patiently. Even if it's a long time, continue making your request and drawing closer to Him, for that is ultimately where He wants you! Remember, *communing* with God through this struggle is His crown yearning.

January 9

Entrusting Your Faith

2 Timothy 2:2

Paul took great interest in Timothy. As Paul's apprentice, Timothy studied, watched, and copied his life. Paul was intentional about investing in young Timothy, because he was keenly aware of these two things: He couldn't spread the gospel alone, and he couldn't live forever on earth. As a result, Paul was compelled to pass on the baton of his faith to someone younger.

In 2 Timothy 2:2, two truths are conveyed in regard to discipling. First, the word must be *spoken*. Paul spoke truth into Timothy's life in the presence of many witnesses. It's also important to note that Timothy was around Paul, *listening* to his teachings. To be a disciple, you must hear truth. Secondly, once the spoken word is received, it must be *entrusted* to others. Never keep the gospel to yourself! In discipling, you must have *something* to say and *someone* to say it to. For Paul, the *something* was the gospel, and the *someone* was Timothy. There is no hoarding in regard to the gospel. Hear it and pass it on.

Closer Challenge: Are you being mentored in the faith? Are you mentoring? You should actively seek both as a believer. **Today**, begin the process of finding someone who can disciple you. You should seek someone full of wisdom and godliness. Spend time in prayer about it today. Once the Spirit impresses someone upon your heart, humbly ask that person to meet with you once a month. After you find someone who can mentor you, seek someone less developed in the faith for you to mentor. (See Appendix 1.) It's understandable that finding both individuals may not be a one-day event, but don't neglect this precious gift of being mentored and mentoring. You must continue to mature in your faith and entrust the gospel to others!

January 10

Rejoice in Suffering, Really?

Romans 5:3-5

It's quite certain there has been a time in your life when your heart has been shattered. Maybe you've lost a job, a loved one has died, a relationship has been severed, or your finances earned can't keep up with the demands of life. When something like this enters your story, it's hard to accept that this is the way life is supposed to be. The book you would have written for yourself would have been packed with dreams fulfilled and zero losses.

But fortunately, that's not the way it is. Yes, we are fortunate because of the things in our lives that have gone sour. Not that we seek out crises, but when they come, we have a wonderful opportunity for the Spirt to display and build godly character in us. And as godly character is witnessed by others, we're left with something more precious than anything we can earn in this world: likeness to Jesus.

<u>Closer Challenge</u>: Are you facing a trial of life inducing much suffering? If you're not now, reflect upon a hardship from your past. As you ponder this seemingly unfortunate turn of events, celebrate the godly character developed because of this challenge of life. Explore the positive results from your suffering and treat yourself kindly with a visit to a coffee shop, read a book, or simply get on your hands and knees and thank God for that experience. **Today**, share this perspective of hope through suffering with someone close to you. You may very well be able to encourage another with your story of suffering.

January 11

Grace Abusing

Romans 6:1-2

It's wonderful to rely on the grace of Jesus when we sin. His mercy is a never-ending flow of love. But some take advantage of His grace by making little or no effort to correct poor lifestyle behaviors. Even though we are under grace when we accept Jesus, our heart's joy should be to strive for holiness.

There are many Christians who live life arrogantly because they've trusted Jesus as their Savior, but they abuse that same grace. They take their salvation as a form of protection from hell, but they don't change their ways to reflect Jesus. As a result, they're being a *grace abuser*. A grace abuser knows the truth but refuses to live by it because God's mercy is taken for granted. This person lives as if there are no consequences to sin. However, it should be noted that even Christians will be judged by God for what they do, whether good or *bad*. (2 Corinthians 5:10) There is no escape from God's righteous judgment, so grace abusing is unwise for a believer.

<u>Closer Challenge</u>: Is there a habitual sin in your life where you have little desire to change? If so, you are grace abusing. It's time to repent. **Today**, first confess your sin to God and ask for His forgiveness. (1 John 1:9) Then, take extreme measures to rid *avenues* of sin out of your life so you can minimize the temptation. Find a mature Christian with whom you can confide your struggles. Ask this person to keep you accountable for the next month, with a simple phone call each week concerning your struggle. This will take humility, but God will lift you up when you humble yourself. (James. 4:10) Sin is destructive, and if you do not take extreme measures, it will continue to misguide you. Flee from being a grace abuser!

January 12

What Is Your Ministry?

---

2 Corinthians 5:18-21

At some point in your Christian walk, you've probably wondered what your ministry is. When answering this question, it's tempting to think of it *only* in terms of departmental service in a church setting, such as serving children, youth, ushering and more. Serving in these various ways is needed and should be commended, but your ministry goes beyond that.

Paul says a believer's ministry is reconciliation. Everywhere we go and everyone with whom we associate, we are to reconcile people to God and be reconciled to one another. We are the hands and feet of God to minister to people through reconciliation. As Paul says in 2 Corinthians 5:20, we are ambassadors of Christ. We represent *God* and *His will* on earth. Earth is not our home; our home is in heaven. Therefore, we are to represent our homeland on earth by fervently reconciling the world to God through Jesus.

<u>Closer Challenge</u>: Do you question your ministry? If so, start by adopting a ministry of reconciliation. Are you in a relationship that isn't on good terms? If you have a broken relationship with a co-worker, neighbor, classmate, or family member, seek reconciliation. ***Today***, make an intentional effort to show kindness to that individual. Regardless of your feelings, act objectively to show the love of Christ. With prayer, this act of kindness could open up a door to healthy conversation. Even if the other person refuses to cooperate, continue to seek reconciliation. Be patient with that person, just as Christ was patient with you. And keep in mind that as you seek a ministry of reconciliation, you'll be drawing closer to God!

January 13

Releasing Control

Numbers 27:12-23

Moses was at the end of his life and season of leadership. He had done some marvelous things, and he had made some mistakes. But regardless of his efforts, his life was coming to an end and someone had to replace him. Joshua became that person. The LORD instructed Moses to have Joshua stand before the priest, commission him publicly, and lay hands on him as a symbolic transfer of authority. After doing so, even though Moses was still the leader, he gave *some* of his authority to Joshua at that time to make the full transition easier at Moses' death.

There comes a time when we all must give away our authority to another person. An aging boss will turn the business over to a faithful worker. A teacher will allow a student to do a certain task for the first time. A parent will slowly release independence to their children. If we don't learn how to trust others by releasing our hold on things, we'll never be able to pass along what we know and have.

<u>Closer Challenge</u>: You may or may not be in a major leadership role, but even if you're not, there is probably someone you have kept under your wings to whom you need to transfer authority or independence. It's important that you realize God is at the helm. He is completely sovereign. Yet, He chooses not to control our every move. Could God fulfill His will on His own much better than using us? Yes, but He sees the value in letting us grow through our experiences. **Today**, give a small dose of independence or authority to the person who you know is ready for it. Your goal should always be to pass on what you know and continue to promote God's Kingdom. This is a small step, but in the long run, it is needed.

January 14

Changing Plans

———•———

Acts 3:1-10

Peter and John had a schedule to follow. At three o'clock, their time was set apart to commune with the Heavenly Father in prayer at the Temple. (Acts 3:1) But on their way to the Temple, they noticed a crippled man, and they stopped to heal him. The events that followed changed the course of their day, and as a result, they never made it to the Temple. As noble and right as it is to pray, the Spirit led them to change their plans and help someone in need. What if Peter and John saw this man and said, "Sorry, we don't have time to help you, for we are about to worship God in prayer"? They would have missed an amazing blessing.

It sounds silly for them to even think about missing this opportunity, but we're often guilty of this. How many times have you been on a mission to complete a task (even ministry-related), but you were unexpectedly interrupted by a needful situation? How often have you allowed that interruption to guide you the rest of your day? How often did you overlook it? Schedules are good, for it's important to be prepared for your day. But if you're led by the Spirit to change plans and help someone in need, do it! That's exactly what Peter and John did.

<u>Closer Challenge</u>: More than likely, you have plans today. Keep your schedule and follow through as best as you can because it is important for you to keep your word. However, **today**, as you follow through with your schedule, keep your eyes open for ministry opportunities. When you see an opportunity, take advantage of it. More than likely, God has an opportunity waiting for you if you just stop and take the time to help. Make proper contacts if you will miss your scheduled appointment, but don't get so wrapped up in the planned events that you omit room for God to move. He might have a miracle waiting for you if you just respond to His still small voice in your life. Be interruptible.

January 15

Releasing Grudges

───────•───────

Genesis 50:15-21

After the death of Jacob, Joseph's brothers thought he would hold a grudge against them for being cruel. So they sent word to Joseph that their father had instructed him to forgive them. Joseph wept because he had no ill will toward them. And to reaffirm his heart to them, he spoke these amazing words of forgiveness and love to his brothers in Genesis 50:20, "As for you, you meant evil against me, but God meant it for good, to bring it about that many people should be kept alive, as they are today."

What a great perspective when hurt by others! Instead of holding a grudge, Joseph not only chose forgiveness, he also fully reaffirmed his love to them and blessed them with provisions! (Genesis 50:21, 2 Corinthians 2:8) It would seem that Joseph would have every right to hold a grudge. He was teased, beaten, and sold into slavery by his brothers. Then, once in slavery, he faced many other trials. Yet he opted to forgive! This is an incredible example of how we should respond to our offenders.

Closer Challenge: Who has offended you? Are you holding a grudge against this person? More than likely, if you are, you're bringing grief upon *yourself*! **Today**, forgive that person and pray that blessings would overflow in your offender's life. True, you may not *feel* like extending forgiveness. But forgiveness isn't an emotion; it's a decision of the will. Furthermore, there is no gain in holding a grudge! It can further hurt you, your close loved ones, and your offender. Like Joseph, guard your heart with forgiveness. And when you do, you will draw closer to God and others.

January 16

Minus Me

John 3:30

In grade school, you can probably recall some teachers instructing you to trust in yourself. That may sound logical to the secular world, for who else do you know better than yourself? But as you mature in faith, you're quick to realize your own heart isn't worth trusting. (Jeremiah 17:9) As a result, it's important that you continually release more of self and trust more in God!

John the Baptist was considered the greatest man to walk this earth. (Matthew 11:11) As great as he was, he knew there was One greater than him. John acknowledged one thing for certain: he must decrease, and Jesus must increase in his life. It's a simple math equation: Jesus>Me. Unfortunately, practically speaking, our equations look more like this: Jesus<Me. Sure, your theology teaches you He is the King of Kings and all authority is given to Him, but much of your actions speak otherwise. If you live by John's formula, you may not gain all the selfish things you *want* in life, but you will gain the heavenly approval of our Lord.

<u>Closer Challenge:</u> Are you ready to increase Jesus in your life? **Today**, what's the one thing on your agenda you wanted to do for yourself? (Watch TV, golf, hunt, shop, surf the Internet, browse social media, etc.) Whatever time you have allotted for that one thing, give it up. Now, who do you see in your circle of influence who needs a touch from God? Whoever first pops in your mind, that's who you should touch! Meet a need for that person. It could be a card, email, phone call, Facebook message, text message, flowers, financial assistance, or merely a ride to the store for groceries. An indicator of Jesus being greater than you is *sacrifice*. Do this, and the thing you *wanted* to do for yourself will pale in comparison to the kind act you will display for another.

January 17

Loving Jesus
———•———

Matthew 25:35-36

Like most believers, you have a desire to display your love to Jesus. However, you might be confused by what it actually looks like. You might think your greatest act of love is attending worship services, teaching the children, or even becoming a leader in the church. Those are honorable ways to express your loyalty and service to the church, but if you want to speak the love language of Jesus, obey these words: Feed the hungry, quench the thirsty, host a stranger, clothe the naked, tend to the sick, and visit criminals. (Matthew 25:35-36)

The place where you find Jesus and express your love to Him is quite ironic. It seems more likely that you would find Him in a throne room filled with a wonderful aroma of spices and incense, singing praises to Him. Instead, you find Him on the streets with a stench of body odor and crime. If you are filled with blessings, such as a home, food, and clothes, it becomes difficult to explore beyond your comfort and touch a life less fortunate. But that is your calling. You're tasked to risk what you have to help someone in need. That's where you'll both find the Lord and express to Him your deepest affection. In addition, you'll be greatly blessed!

Closer Challenge: Do you want to love Jesus? If so, remove yourself from your place of comfort. **Today**, touch a life that needs help. If you don't know of someone in need, ask your church for guidance. Discover who you could visit in a hospital, rehabilitation center, or nursing home. For lunch today, go to the local homeless shelter instead of dining out. Speak to a criminal in a nearby prison. It may not seem like much, but even a simple conversation could radically change a life. Get out of your routine and lend a helping hand. Intentionally touch the life of a "least of these." That's how you can love Jesus today and commune with Him closely!

January 18

Removing Avenues of Sin

---

2 Kings 23:1-30

King Josiah gave us one of the greatest pictures of repentance in the Bible. When it was brought to his attention that he, along with all of Israel, was not following the Book of the Law, he called together all the elders, renewed the covenant, and began to clean house. (2 Kings 23:1-3) For the next twenty-four verses, he removed all the avenues of sin in the whole kingdom that had been causing disloyalty and disobedience to the Lord. He removed pagan priests, the Asherah pole, the quarters of male shrine prostitutes, the child sacrifice alters, mediums, spiritists, and many other *avenues* of sin. Josiah took action to change his life, and all those he influenced by removing those things that caused false worship.

When you truly understand how much your sin grieves the heart of God and how much it destroys your life, including all relationships, you'll be compelled to run from it. The magnitude of sin is intense, and it corrupts all things you touch. Josiah took swift and direct action to rid all *causes* of sin. Your response to sin should be no different, for it corrupts your closeness to God.

Closer Challenge: What is causing you to sin? Is there something you should remove from your life that will lessen the temptation and turn you toward God? You may need to walk away from a friendship, terminate a television subscription, set up boundaries for your online devices, cut up a credit card, or quit a job. **Today**, whatever that one, two or many things are that increases the temptation to sin, *remove* them! Do not allow Satan an opportunity to foster his plans in your life. Be like Josiah. Wholeheartedly and aggressively dispose of evil things so that you can leave room for God to work in and through you.

January 19

Trustworthy Tongue

Proverbs 11:13

Do people come to you with private, personal matters? If so, you have a reputation for having a trustworthy tongue. The simple fact that people confide in you intimate issues of the heart shows that you can be trusted.

Unfortunately, many people are gossips. Some want information just so they can have the inside scoop. Gossip can be shared in the subtlest ways. It can even be hidden in prayer requests or "ministry" discussions. As a wild animal becomes harder and harder to tame as it ages, the tongue becomes more and more difficult to control as we let it loose over the years. You must be proactive about stopping channels of gossip, or the tongue will become a source of untrustworthiness and sin. It will lead you down undesired paths.

Closer Challenge: Are you a gossip? Some are more prone to gossip than others, but we all have this temptation. **Today**, tame your tongue *and* ears. When the opportunity arises for you to gossip or listen to gossip, change the conversation or simply walk away from it. To take it a step further, when you hear gossip, stop and pray out loud for the person who is the target of gossip. Build your reputation as a safe harbor where people can come to you in confidence. Control your tongue, for it can be your best friend or your worst enemy.

January 20

Go Down

---

1 Peter 5:6

There is a simple formula from the Lord when gaining God's favor. You must *go down*. It's human instinct to believe that we should elevate ourselves at every opportunity so that we can gain attention and popularity. But God's favor is received in the completely opposite way.

God desires that you humble yourself at every opportunity so He will receive the glory, and you will be lifted up by Him in His time. Humility is a sign of submission to the Lord's mighty hand. It goes beyond putting others first; it's just *not* thinking of yourself! When you humble yourself, your character will be seen and admired by others and a place of honor will be reserved for you. Though Jesus was the Eternal King deserving royal treatment on earth, He humbled Himself by giving us the picture of a servant. He is our model to follow.

<u>Closer Challenge</u>: Do people view you as a humble person? Are you seeking your own glory or the glory of God? If your aim is to increase God's glory, your life should be radically different than the rest of the world. **Today**, as you see opportunities arise, practice putting others before yourself. Even simple things make a difference. Let others go before you in lines. Volunteer for less attractive roles. Do whatever you can to live a humble life. But be careful that you react with a heart that wants to glorify God, not your humble acts. There's a fine line between self-righteousness and really loving Jesus in your actions. So keep your focus on honoring Jesus.

January 21

Subtract, Then Add

---

2 Timothy 2:22

There is a simple principle in Scripture that we often overlook. That is, when you *subtract* sin in your life, you must *add* righteousness to fill that empty hole. Many people are courageous to remove a sinful habit for a period of time, only to fall back into that same sin. Often, it seems, the reason they fall back into that sin is because they didn't add righteousness to fill the void left by sin.

When you repent of sin, it's critical that you purposefully add something healthy and righteous. Paul is clear that when you *flee* sin, you are also to *pursue* righteousness. It's not wise to flee sin and then run aimlessly. Have a target to run toward. Similarly, Paul wrote in Romans 12:9 that we are to hate what is evil, cling to what is good. The Old Testament confirms this principle when Amos the prophet called us to hate evil, love good. (Amos 5:15) And Psalm 45:7 implores us to love righteousness, and hate wickedness. When you hate and flee the wickedness of this world, you must be proactive to fill those old desires with good by loving and pursuing righteousness.

<u>Closer Challenge</u>: Have you recently removed a sinful habit in your life? Have you then added a godly habit? If you haven't added righteousness, it's likely that you'll be tempted to fall back into that sinful pattern. **Today**, repent of a sinful habit, and in place of whatever you release, add a righteous habit. Help those in need, read a godly book, memorize Scripture, learn something new, but whatever you do, don't let that void go unnoticed. Actively pursue righteousness, for that is how your mind will refocus on good things and forget the old.

January 22

What Is Normal?

John 9:1-3

Often, you will encounter someone born with a disability that causes some limitations. Throughout the world, we see the blind, the lame, the deaf, the muscular deficient, the mentally challenged, and many other types of ailments. It's often asked, "Why are they like that?" as if there is someone or something to blame. But God doesn't make mistakes when it comes to creating life. And even in the case of human abuse or malpractice while a fetus is maturing, God still has a way to make *good* out of any situation.

What makes a person *normal*? We toss around the label *normal* as if there is a standard, a prototypical human being we must all model, and that will make us normal. That is a lie from the devil. It's true, we attempt to model Jesus in our character, but we cannot be perfect as He is. Each one of us has a uniqueness that is not duplicated in this world. God has created us all with a special touch so the work of God can be displayed in our lives! (John 9:3)

Closer Challenge: Do you have a tough time with favoritism? Do you look down upon people if they are not like you? Do you have a problem with looking in the mirror and only seeing *your* disabilities? **Today**, start looking at people and yourself in a different way. When people pass by you today, look to the heart of that person and believe the work of God is being displayed in their lives. Without showing favoritism, look to the potential in every person you encounter. Visualize the word, "potential," written on their foreheads. When you do, you will see them for who they really are and who they can be, not who you want or think they should be. Do the same for yourself. This can be a releasing activity if you truly practice it.

January 23

Border Control

Daniel 1:8

During the Babylonian Captivity, when the Hebrews were forced out of their homeland of Canaan, many young Hebrew men were selected to serve in King Nebuchadnezzar's palace. The training consisted of learning the language and literature of the Babylonian culture. Furthermore, they were fed royal food from the king's table. However, the royal food was considered contaminated by Daniel, because the first portion of it was offered to idols. Due to his strong conviction only to serve the LORD, Daniel convinced the king's official to allow him and the other Hebrews to eat only vegetables and water, that which was *not* dedicated to idols. For ten days, they ate vegetables and water, and they were better nourished than the rest. Their firm conviction regarding their boundaries found favor with both the king's official and the LORD.

Do you have strong commitment to boundaries in your life? If you haven't already set boundaries for yourself, there's a good chance you're setting yourself up for a fall. Boundaries have been given a bad name over the years because they appear to limit freedom. But that's a faulty perspective. Boundaries protect us, not hinder us. A firm boundary will save a marriage from adultery and a family split. A firm boundary will deflect the influence of substance abuse. A firm boundary will keep us from cheating at work or school. Boundaries are needed to keep our lives pure!

Closer Challenge: Are there boundaries in *every* area where you could be vulnerable to sin? If not, you need to set some. **Today**, make a list of actual or potential struggle areas in your life. Set some firm boundaries and discuss them with a close friend. Stay true to your boundaries, so you will be better protected from the damaging results of sin!

January 24

Simple Faith

———•———

Matthew 18:1-4

There is something about children that makes them so fascinating when it comes to understanding of the Christian faith. It's the simplicity of their belief system. Something tragic happens when we become adults. We lose some of our imagination and trust. A child will simply acknowledge that Jesus walked on water, while a reason-filled adult will look at that miracle through lenses of doubt. A child will be amazed that Jesus healed a blind man, but an adult will question the possibility of the experience. Why are children the greatest in the kingdom of heaven? It's because they simply trust and obey the Lord in faith. Their hearts are receptive to His wonder, and their minds are moldable to believe the impossible.

God loves children because He is to them what He wants us to believe He is. Children see God as a daddy who will protect them, the mother who will provide for them, the big brother they will model, and the sister who will be close to them. Children know God will meet their every need without doubt. It truly is a beautiful sight to behold a child loving the Lord. It may seem odd, but children are the greatest in heaven due to their complete dependence upon God.

Closer Challenge: What is your faith like? Are you a skeptic or do you simply trust God like a child? **Today**, in what way has your trust in God slipped? Whatever that one thing is, stop doubting and start trusting God like a child. Take action to begin moving in that direction. Put on the lenses of a simple faith, and allow God to be the caring Father He is. When you do, you will experience what children know about the Lord.

January 25

Doing Your Part

Numbers 4:24-26

When God presented instructions for the Israelites to care for and maintain the Tabernacle, He assigned the Gershonites the duty of carrying the curtains of the Tent of Meeting. The Merarites had a similar duty, for their role was to carry the frames, crossbars, posts, bases and all other equipment relating to the Tabernacle. (Numbers 4:29-33)

The Gershonites and the Mererites did the grunt work. They were the behind-the-scenes workers who served the entire community. At first look, these duties don't seem to be very glamorous. But if these roles were not assigned and fulfilled, the Tent of Meeting would be left at the last campsite. These roles were very important for the good of the *whole* community! So these men had to serve with the *whole* in mind.

Closer Challenge: Do you have a role in your church? If not, it would be wise to accept one because people are depending on you! Are you serving in a role that is less glamorous? If so, you can relate to the Gershonites and Merarites. Don't give up, because you are serving the *whole* and honoring God. You are just as important as God's mouthpiece on Sunday morning. ***Today***, whatever you do in your church or community, rev up your passion and serve with the fervency of the Lord. Find ways to elevate your role and make it more God-glorifying than ever before! As you do this, you will honor God and draw closer to Him. If you don't have a service in your faith community, commit to one soon. They need you!

January 26

Speaking Jesus

John 18:15-18; 25-27

Peter was Jesus' close companion. He was also the vocal leader of the twelve disciples. On one occasion, he made a great claim that Jesus was the Christ, the Son of the Living God. (Matthew 16:16) Yet, Peter is the same disciple who rejected any sort of relationship with Him during Jesus' trial. (John 18:15-18; 25-27) It appears that fear and insecurity overwhelmed Peter, so he pulled away from that bold claim by denying Him. It was a low moment for Peter.

When the opportunity arises for you to voice your loyalty for Jesus, are you able to speak up? If you aim to follow Jesus and make the claim that He is "the Christ, the Son of the Living God," it's not a question of *if* you will be ridiculed but *when*. When those opportunities come, will you have the courage to speak truthfully of your faith and commitment to Him? Peter failed when it mattered most. What will you say when it's your turn to speak up?

Closer Challenge: In what context have you failed to speak up in regard to your faith? **Today**, talk about your faith to someone who doesn't want to hear it. This person could be a neighbor, a friend, an ex-friend, a co-worker, or even a family member. Most Christians know individuals who challenge them to keep silent about their relationship with Jesus. In spite of this opposition, pray for an opportunity to talk about Jesus with at least one person who is resistant. When that opportunity comes, don't clam up like Peter; speak up! You may get ridiculed, but you will have the peace of mind knowing you shared with this person the most important relationship in life. Furthermore, you might discover that person isn't as resistant to the gospel as you once thought. Boldly speak up!

January 27

The Turning Point

John 6:66

Jesus is at the pinnacle of His ministry. He had just performed two of His greatest miracles, the feeding of the 5,000 and walking on water. At no other time in His ministry did He have more people following Him. After these miracles, He taught a hard lesson about Him being the Bread of Life. (John 6:53-60) At this very point, many of His followers refused to believe in Him. John 6:66 is one of the saddest verses in the Bible because many seekers turned their backs on Him and no longer pursued Him.

There comes a point in your life where you must decide to follow Jesus or to turn your back on Him. As you increase in knowledge of Jesus, both His teachings and actions become more difficult to accept through reason because no one can say or do the things He says and does. Following Him takes faith. Like the disciples, there will be a point where there is no turning back. And like Peter when Jesus asked the twelve, "Do you want to go away as well?" boldly proclaim, "Lord, to whom shall we go? You have the words of eternal life, and we have believed, and have come to know, that you are the Holy One of God." (John 6:68-69)

Closer Challenge: When tough questions are raised about Jesus, how will you respond? Will you turn your back on Him or hold fast to your belief in Him? **Today**, simply make a conscious decision to *believe*. If you are not a Christian, do as the Bible teaches, confess He is Lord and believe in your heart He was raised from the dead. (Romans 10:9-10) Make your decision public by sharing this with a church leader. If you are a Christian, but you've doubted, firmly make your decision to follow Jesus wholeheartedly. There's no middle ground. You are either for Him or against Him. Make today the turning point in your life to stay close to Jesus.

January 28

Family Care

---

1 Timothy 5:8

God gives you a litmus test to discover if your faith is genuine. Do you love your family? Your heart is quickly evaluated by the way you care for your God-given family. Some talk a big game about their faith but treat their families like strangers. Specifically, if you want to please God, then you must repay your parents and grandparents with the care they granted you when you were dependent upon them. (1 Timothy 5:4)

In a culture where we like to delegate care responsibilities to institutional medical facilities, we're missing our God-given role to nurture and care for our aging relatives. Sure, medical institutions may be needed for physical health issues, but emotional and spiritual support should *never* be absent from your family! Many Americans have lost this ancient truth by allowing busyness to take the front seat. There is no excuse for omitting care to your family. For when you lose family care, you have denied the faith and are worse than an unbeliever. (1 Timothy 5:8)

<u>Closer Challenge</u>: Are you caring for your family or are you leaving it for someone else? **Today**, rethink the way you care for your family and make some significant changes if you're neglecting this calling. Instead of limiting responsibility, assume it. At the very least, kindly reach out to a family member who may not expect it. Regardless of the way you were treated as a child or how you are treated now, it doesn't cancel your responsibility to care for your parents and grandparents. Remember, your heart is to please God the Father, and caring for your family is what He desires.

January 29

Yes, Lord

———————•:———————

Genesis 6:22

Scripture teaches that Noah was a righteous and blameless man who walked with the Lord. (Genesis 6:9) Expectedly, someone who carries these qualities will be a man of obedience. When God spoke to him concerning a great flood, he didn't question God; he simply began to build this monstrous ship. Noah was a "Yes, Lord," man of God.

God wants to draw closer to you, but you must walk by faith to experience closeness. (Hebrews 11:6) Each day, you are given situations that will stretch your devotion. He does this to test if you'll come to Him by faith. He desires that you take the first step; and when you do, you'll see Him on the other side of it. Many people want to grow in their faith but they're unwilling to take God-ordained risks. If Noah didn't execute God's request, he would've missed out on experiencing the power of God through him. When God calls, you have one response, "Yes, Lord."

Closer Challenge: When God calls you to do an unlikely task, do you follow through in obedience or do you look for an escape? Keep in mind that delayed obedience is disobedience, and disobedience is sin. Don't create sins of omission in your life! **Today**, listen to the voice of God. What is He telling you? Has He been speaking to you about a certain calling, but you have refused it? Has He just now started burdening you about a particular way to bring Him glory? Whatever it is, do not delay your obedience. Be a "Yes, Lord," servant, and you'll be communing with God in a fresh way.

January 30

Thorny life

———◆———

2 Corinthians 12:7-10

We all have our struggles. If you don't believe it, watch out! The Apostle Paul was deemed as a man of many strengths, but he also had his weaknesses. For Paul not to become conceited with his wealth of knowledge and incredible leadership abilities, he was given a thorn in his flesh – a messenger of Satan. No one really knows what Paul's *thorn* was. But it's probably better that we don't know, so that we don't become fixated on *his* actual struggle. But instead, we identify with Paul because of our own weaknesses.

Many people quickly connect their thorn to a specific sin temptation. Though a sin temptation might be your thorn, more often than not, it's something out of your control. A limitation, a significant loss, or some sort of deep grief could be your thorn. Whatever it is that creates pain either physically or emotionally and won't go away, that's your thorn. So, what's the purpose of a thorn? Jesus makes it clear to Paul when He said, "My grace is sufficient for you, for my power is made perfect in weakness." (2 Corinthians 12:9) It's a paradox, but in your weakness is where God can be closest to you and use you the greatest!

Closer Challenge: Can you identify the thorn in *your* flesh? Be honest, what is the struggle or pain in your life that you wish wasn't there? Whatever it is, God wants to be your strength in that weakness! **Today**, find a way to use your weakness to help another. Stop focusing on the pain it brings you and start using it as a tool for God's kingdom! Seek peace in your thorn because it can draw you closer to God, lead you to maturity, and glorify Him. Your thorn makes you dependent upon God, and that's exactly what He wants as He communes with you!

January 31

Honoring God's Leader

Numbers 12:1-16

This story teaches us much about the respect that should be given to God's anointed leaders. Do you look at your church leader with contempt? Have you ever said or thought, as Miriam did, "Has he not spoken through us also?" (Numbers 12:2) It's true, God has probably spoken to you, but it doesn't take away the God-ordained role of your leaders. When you start to gain knowledge and experience in spiritual matters, the temptation is to think you should be the leader. Power struggles can divide the whole when unrestrained. Miriam and Aaron became power-hungry and doubted Moses' leadership. Seeds of dissention were sowed in their hearts and the Lord rebuked them for it.

God ordains leaders to lead. This isn't to say church leaders never fail or cause problems. But when God calls out an individual to lead, and it is confirmed by the whole, unless sin entangles the leader or God calls him away from the role, the followers are to submit to the appointed leader's direction. The ultimate response from the followers is obedience. (Hebrews 13:17)

Closer Challenge: Are you publicly or privately disrespectful to your leader? Do you sow seeds of dissention or possibly aspire to take that role? If so, repent. God has ordained your leader to lead, and your role is to follow with passion. **Today**, help your leader(s) see your support. Write a letter, send a gift, or give a word of encouragement to your pastor and other significant leaders. And most importantly, if God has birthed a vision in that leader's heart, find ways to support it to see the vision materialize. Make your leader's work a joy, not a burden. (Hebrews 13:17) This will keep peace in the church and honor God.

February 1

I Want That!

―――――•―――――

James 4:1-2

Often, when someone close to you attains what you want, it stirs up deep cravings from within you. Inside, you long for what that person has. The Bible calls this *coveting*. Coveting is hard to recognize because it's inward. As James says, it's a battle within that we cannot see, which eventually manifests itself into fights and quarrels. We typically address the symptoms (fighting and quarreling), but overlook the root problem of coveting.

Of all the Ten Commandments, coveting is the one that may seem out of place at first glance, but when you actually investigate the ramifications of it, you'll see why God included it. Coveting can spark jealousy, arguments, bad thoughts, and fights. All of which can destroy relationships. In your own life, it will create bitterness, anger, and most tragically, it hinders your closeness with God. There is great reason why "do not covet" is the tenth commandment.

<u>Closer Challenge</u>: Are you coveting what someone else has? Is there a material, spiritual, or relational aspect of another's life that is creating an unhealthy desire in your soul? **Today**, examine your life closely. Investigate if there is something in someone else's life that you want. Confess your sin and replace it with contentment. (Hebrews 13:5) Here's food for thought: it's highly possible God has allowed that person to gain something you want to test you. So instead of coveting, be thankful for that person's blessings and intercede for more in his or her life. As you do, the bitter root of coveting will begin to fade.

February 2

Entertaining Others

———•———

Hebrews 13:2; 1 Peter 4:9

Throughout Scripture, we see that God has ordained us to practice hospitality. (Romans 12:13) Hospitality has somewhat become a lost art in our culture because of busy lives, the accessibility of good restaurants, and a fear in some to engage in an intimate setting. But there is something special about opening up your home and preparing a meal to treat someone with utmost honor and respect.

Hosting takes more effort than going to a restaurant and paying someone else to do the work, but it will bring more intimacy to the relationship. Not that restaurants are bad, but there's great value when you invite people into your home, especially strangers. (3 John 5-8) When you host, guests are able to see you in your home for who you really are, and you are able to make a better connection with your guests. Ultimately, your hosting might be the very thing that helps someone experience the love of God and turn to Him.

<u>Closer Challenge</u>: It's time to be a godly host. **Today**, pray for clarity concerning who you could invite into your home, and schedule a gathering with that person(s) over the next couple of weeks. Seek someone who is not close to you. Stretch outside your comfort zone and invite someone or a family who needs a touch from the Lord. Pray for that person at some point during the event. And as you do all this, your genuine concern could be the catalyst to help pull that person through a rough patch of life. Furthermore, it's possible that you could entertain an angel without even knowing it! (Hebrews 13:2) Practice hospitality.

February 3

Home Building

———————•———————

Psalm 127:1

The home is the most sacred of all institutions. Not even the church has more history than the home shared by a husband and a wife. God instituted the home in the Garden of Eden when He declared to Adam and Eve that the two of them shall become one flesh. The bond created in marriage is truly a sweet picture of love, respect and unwavering loyalty. However, the ultimate loyalty of a couple is to the Lord. The greatest thing one spouse can do for the other is to commune with God passionately. It will guide their marriage to a deeper and stronger relationship together. God is the foundation, builder and sustainer of the home!

Foolishly, many people enter marriage under the shadow of their own philosophical biases. Paul warns that marriage will carry with it many troubles (1 Corinthians 7:28), so to add secular teachings and ungrounded opinions will only increase the trouble. To avoid additional burdens, honoring God must be placed in the center of all affairs. He is the filter through which all decisions are made. Cherishing the home by cherishing the Lord is your most treasured task.

Closer Challenge: Are you married or do you aspire to be married? Either way, this simple truth must be etched on the heart. The Lord must be the builder of your home. **Today**, if you are married, talk about this entry with your spouse. It could serve as a reminder to have or begin an open-hearted discussion. Discuss new ways to make God the builder of your home. Pray together, read scripture together, and learn how you could serve the Lord together. If your spouse is not willing to cooperate, do your part to present a godly marriage and pray for your spouse. (1 Peter 3:1) If you are not married, be content with your singleness. (1 Corinthians 7:8) And as God leads, be selective in choosing your spouse. Wisely court those who not only speak about God being the builder but practice this truth prior to marriage. Begin now to pray for your future spouse. Marriage is a true blessing from the Lord, but be sure to do it His way.

February 4

Where's Jesus?

John 6:16-21

Have you ever been in a challenging situation and wondered, "Where's Jesus?" The disciples can identify with you. During one particular evening, the disciples set out across the Sea of Galilee to Capernaum. A couple things were against them. First, it was dark. But, most significantly, they went without Jesus! The force of the wind and waves caused them to lose control of the boat. And after they had been rowing for over three miles, Jesus finally appeared to them, casually walking across the sea. When He climbed aboard the boat, immediately they reached the shore.

Are you in a pinch right now? Do the waters of life seem to be crashing in all around you? If so, ask yourself this important question: have I left Jesus on the shore? In this story, the disciples left Jesus behind. It's possible that they grew impatient while Jesus was in solitude, or they thought they could make it across the sea on their own. Regardless, they quickly discovered they needed the *Light* to steer them through the darkness and carry them to the shore safely.

<u>Closer Challenge</u>: Where is Jesus in your life? Have you forgotten Him or is He immersed in all your affairs through prayer and His Word? **Today**, evaluate your struggles. Is Jesus in the boat with you or have you taken off without Him? If you've left Him on the shore, stop what you're doing, and refocus your thoughts and affections upon Him. If possible, attend a Bible study or Christian gathering of some sort this week to help regain focus. All the power in the universe rests in Jesus, so don't leave Him on the shore. Depend on the *Light* to show you the way through your struggle, and as you do, you'll experience His closeness!

February 5

Can You Give It Up?

Mark 10:17-25

A rich young man came to Jesus and asked what he *needed* to do to have eternal life. He was a *good* man because he followed the law, so Jesus asked him to sell all he had and give it to the poor. As a result, he became sad and walked away. Jesus then added, "It is easier for a camel to go through the eye of a needle than for a rich person to enter the kingdom of God." How can this be?

One of the first things to learn about eternal life is that it's an all-or-nothing decision. Surrendering to Christ includes every part of your life! If there is even one small corner of your life that you're unwilling to relinquish, you're not ready to follow Him. The rich man honored God in many ways, but he was unwilling to submit to God with his finances. He wasn't willing to give it *all*. At first glance, it's tempting to think this story only pertains to the rich. Not so. The core message of this story focuses on surrendering control. The rich man, like many of us, had a *control issue* not a money issue. Hanging on to money was just the manifestation of his failed attempt to surrender to God. Giving over money may not be your struggle, but if there is anything you can't let God control, that's your struggle. Until you're able to trust Him in full surrender, you can identify with the rich man.

<u>Closer Challenge</u>: Does Jesus have *all* of you? If Jesus asked you to give up something of this world that is extremely valuable to you, how would you respond? *Today*, if there is something that you couldn't give up, be *willing* to turn it over to Him. It could be something besides money. It might be a habit, a material possession, or even a career. Release control now! If you're not willing to give it up, Jesus doesn't have all of you. It's harder for a rich man to enter heaven because he has more to give up. But even if you're not rich, you must treasure Jesus over all you have. When this happens, you'll find He has something greater waiting for you on the other side of obedience.

February 6

Blessed Be Your Name

---◆---

Job 1:20-21; 2:10

Few people have faced the testing that Job did. For the first test, Job lost his children, servants, and livestock. Then, in a second testing, he was afflicted with painful sores and a doubting wife. The temptation for Job was to walk away from God, yet he remained faithful. Similar to Job, your commitment to God will be tested. And when that happens, will you cling to Him or walk away?

When things are good, we have an easier time praising the Lord. We lift our hands and wear a smile because the world is at peace in our lives. But what happens when things turn for the worse? Are you still able to lift your hands and praise the Lord? Job taught us a timeless lesson. Through the good *and* the bad, worship God! Our circumstances should never hinder the way we view God. God is good even when the world is bad. Your test may be painful right now, but when you bless the Lord, you can attain peace.

Closer Challenge: Whether things are good or bad, do you praise the Lord? Do you praise Him when things are routine? Whatever season of life you are in, worship the Lord! **Today**, commune with your God! Carve out at least fifteen minutes of your day to spend some extra time praising God for what He has done in your life, whether good, bad, or routine. Listen to some worship music, read a few of the Psalms, or spend time in prayer, saying as many names of God as you can. Be thankful for your salvation, because when all else fails, you can be sure of that!

February 7

Owner Verses Manager

Psalm 24:1

Make sure you read Psalm 24:1 before you begin reading this entry. After reading, answer these questions honestly: Do you own clothes? (If yes, read Psalm 24:1 again.) Do you own a computer? (If yes, read Psalm 24:1 again.) Do you own a car? (If yes, read Psalm 24:1 again.) Do you own a phone? (If yes, read Psalm 24:1 again.) Are you getting the picture? According to Psalm 24:1, you really don't *own* anything! You might say you own these things and more, but in the truest sense, *everything* on earth is the Lord's! If you really grasp this truth, the way you view *your* possessions should change. You are really a *manager* of the Lord's stuff. And when you're a manager, you supervise someone else's things with care because the owner is also caring for you in the process.

It's a great responsibility and privilege to manage the Lord's stuff. But you might ask, "Why has God entrusted me with *His* stuff to manage? Why can't He manage it Himself?" Well, He could, but He desires to involve you in the great blessing of distributing His wealth to those with needs. You are to use the resources He's given you to show others His love. God grants you the honor of joining Him in the fulfilling work of bringing glory to His name.

<u>Closer Challenge</u>: Think about the things you've been entrusted with. Have you settled it in your heart that it's *all* God's? If not, reread Psalm 24:1 and read 1 Chronicles 29:11. Hopefully, you're in agreement with Scripture now. To test your faith, **today**, think of a creative way to manage the Lord's resources in your care. You can use *His* house, *His* money, *His* car, *His* boat, *His* tools, *His* clothes, etc., to point people to Jesus. Meet at least one need using one or more of these resources. Make this a healthy habit in your life. Naked you entered this world and naked you will return, so honor God with the things He has entrusted to you. (Job 1:21) And as you do, you'll experience closeness to Him.

February 8

Experiencing Jesus' Teachings

Luke 5:1-7

One day, as Jesus was at the water's edge, He taught the crowd from a boat. No one knows what He taught that day because Scripture doesn't say. But one thing is certain: whatever He taught, He wanted the disciples to put their trust in His words. So He took them out to the deep water to catch fish immediately after the lesson. According to Peter, the fish weren't biting. But Jesus insisted, and when they dropped the nets, they caught more fish than they could hold in one boat! Jesus gained faithful followers that day, not only by what He taught, but by what they had *experienced*.

You might be like these first disciples. Sure, you've listened to His amazing teachings, but have you actually put those teachings into practice? The Christian life is about *experiencing* God, not just *knowing* about Him. You've probably recently heard a marvelous teaching from His Word, but have you put it into practice? Have you experienced God in that area of your life? It's not enough just to *know* His Word, you must *live* it. Otherwise, your faith will become stale.

Closer Challenge: What have you learned *new* from God's Word? It could be something from a sermon, a personal Bible study, a small group lesson, this book, etc. **Today**, identify that truth and don't delay in putting it into practice. A dreadful thing you could do is learn a marvelous truth and not apply it to your life. If you want your life to catch on fire for Christ, take the things you've already learned and practice them. God might not give you anything new until you apply what you already know but aren't living. So, put what you know to be true into practice and experience Jesus today!

February 9

Praying for Others

———◆———

1 Timothy 2:1-4

Rarely will you find someone who will refuse prayer. Even an unreligious person will typically receive your prayers as a kind gesture. They will accept it because praying demonstrates a deep care. When you pray for others, it reaches into their soul, producing a closer bond in the relationship with you and God. So, why don't we pray more for others? If it's so *good*, why have many Christ followers relegated prayer to times of desperation? Why is it not a predetermined way of life in all Christians? Though reasons vary, a primary barrier to praying more for others is that we fail to establish the disciplined time and work needed to make it effective.

Prayer is not conducive to our fast-paced world. A deep, effective prayer life slows down and waits patiently on God. That's something this generation isn't used to doing! However, if we would discipline ourselves to set aside time for prayer as Jesus modeled, heaven would be shaken and lives would be changed! Paul urges us to pray for each other as a matter of first importance in our worship (1 Timothy 2:1), for it pleases God and leads people to salvation. If that weren't enough, it also initiates the ultimate end goal of communing *with* God. How can we *not* pray more?

<u>*Closer Challenge*</u>: It's time to make a difference though your prayer life. ***Today***, your challenge is to go deeper in prayer by setting aside *undistracted* time in prayer. Begin a new journey in your prayer life by writing a list of people you want to see accept Jesus. Spend time on your knees in prayer, pleading for their salvation. Pray at least ten minutes for these individuals each day for the next week. Hopefully, it will become a pattern. Ask God to open up their hearts to salvation. Be persistent and patient, and allow God the time to do His work. And as you stay faithful to this commitment of prayer, you'll see change.

February 10

Never Growing Up

Mark 10:13-16

In the sanctification process, after we become Christians we are to mature spiritually in every area of our lives. We are to grow in prayer, love, patience, kindness, grace, knowledge, forgiveness, and so on. But there is one area in our Christian walk where we should never grow up. It's the way we accept Jesus...like a child. Jesus rebuked the disciples for attempting to usher away the little children from Him, because He wants all adults to imitate a child's simple faith. We have much to learn from children.

Even though our faith and character will mature through knowledge, circumstances, and other experiences, the way we approach Jesus and accept Him should never change. As a child trusts and fearlessly approaches a father for protection, provision, and love, we should do the same with our heavenly Father. It's a shame that as we grow older, we move away from this simple faith by choosing reason over trust in God's care. Come to Jesus like a child, for that's how He accepts and sustains you.

<u>Closer Challenge</u>: Have you lost your sense of being like a child before God? Are you *too big* to run to your Father like a child? **Today,** come to the Father like a child. If you need a question answered, a provision, protection, correction, or comfort, turn to Him right now and talk to the Lord like a child. Then in simple faith, believe the Lord will deliver. Dads are often seen as superheroes to their children because they think their dad can do anything. Believe in God the Father like that, because after all, nothing is impossible for God. (Luke 1:37)

February 11

Being Grateful

Luke 16:19-31

There are days when you may feel as though the world is against you. When those days come, it's easy to become consumed in your unwelcomed situation and forget about the good things the Lord has done for you. When this happens to you, think of this story in Luke 16. The rich man failed to believe in and follow Jesus; and when he died, he was cast into hell. Hell is a dreadful place: it's hot; it's full of torment and pain; it's separation from God and love. Maybe most dreadful is that it's final. Nothing about hell is appealing, but it is a reality for many. (Luke 13:24)

People don't like to talk about hell, but if you're a Christ-follower, you have nothing to fear. When hell is mentioned, your response should be joy in knowing you're not going there! Even in a nightmare situation, as a believer, you can rejoice that hell is not a reality for you. Due to your deliverance from hell, gratitude should fill your heart and lessen the pain you're currently facing. Pain will not completely go away while on earth, but nothing on earth should be able to steal your eternal joy secured in heaven.

<u>*Closer Challenge*</u>: Have you been consumed with a present or past hardship? When is the last time you thought about your salvation? **Today**, throughout the day, remember these sad truths mentioned above concerning hell. When you do, you will be reminded of what you're saved from in Jesus. Find peace in knowing you'll be with Jesus in heaven, and not with the rich man in hell. Share this story with someone today. It will either help a Christian be grateful or possibly help an unbeliever turn to Jesus. Hell is real, so be grateful you're not going there; but also be urgent to tell those who are not secured in heaven about hell.

February 12

A New Adventure

Joshua 3:1-5

After the Hebrews had been wandering in the desert for a whole generation, it was time for a new season of life; it was time for them to march into the Promised Land. They were not sure of the direction, or the conflicts they would face, but it didn't stop them from going. Since they were venturing into a land where they had never been, it was essential that they followed *God's* lead. (Joshua 3:4) They didn't know all the details, but they trusted in the general direction.

There are times in your life when God will set you in a new direction. Life is a series of seasons. Not all seasons of life are pleasant, but they will bring Christian maturity if you have the right perspective. Some seasons of life last for a long time, while others are very short in duration. Regardless of the length, there will be a time when God will call you to move from your place of current familiarity. When this happens, will you be able to let go of your present situation to take off on a new adventure? This faith step will allow you to see God in a fresh, new way.

<u>Closer Challenge</u>: Have you been in the same season of life for a long time? Or have you just entered a new season of life but feel lost and overwhelmed? Either way, it's time to embrace the new adventure with God leading! **Today**, identify your current season of life. It could be parenting small children, retirement (from a career, never ministry!), singleness, mourning, a ministry, a job, etc. Is God keeping you in that season or is He leading you to another? Spend some time alone today, reflecting on and considering all possibilities. It's not wise to be rash; but if this new opportunity is not contrary to God's Word and He is leading, go in faith! Talk about it with a godly friend to receive advice. (And if married, definitely converse with your spouse.) A new adventure could be waiting for you.

February 13

Two by Two

Luke 10:1-4

Though sharing the gospel strikes fear in the average Christian, it's still a mandate of Jesus. (Matthew 28:19-20) If we omit this command, we've disobeyed God, and most importantly, we've neglected a portion of our purpose. Sharing your faith could be argued as your greatest act of worship. The other forms of worship are honoring to God, but only leading people to Jesus will enrich the Kingdom with more worshipers, pleasing God, who desires to be close to all. Since God desires that all commune with Him, there should be a burning passion in us to introduce people to the Savior.

Often overlooked in this passage is the instruction to go out among the lost in pairs. (Luke 10:1) Jesus didn't call these believers to be soloists. He sent them out two by two so that they would have accountability, encouragement, confidence, and more knowledge of His Word. When one grows weak, the other stands strong. We should apply this partnership model when we're sharing our faith.

<u>Closer Challenge</u>: Are you fearful of sharing your faith? Have you tried sharing with a partner? **Today**, find yourself a partner. (Hopefully, this is a person who is also working through this discipleship tool.) Agree on a time when you can both visit with someone who is not a Christian. Maybe this unbeliever is a common friend, a church visitor, neighbor, or a stranger. Be creative in your bridge building, but don't make sharing your faith harder than it is. At the right moment, simply tell your story and talk about the change Jesus has made in your life. Then, call that person to trust in Jesus. If this person doesn't, don't become discouraged. You're just the messenger. Pray the gospel seed will grow in due time. Remember, God can use a shaky voice better than a silent one. Be on a mission to add worshipers to the Kingdom for God's glory!

February 14

Love Much

―――――•―――――

Luke 7:36-50

It's often asked, "What does true love look like?" It's like this: A woman, known in the community for her unholy living, came to a house where Jesus was dining with the Pharisees. Immediately, she fell at Jesus' feet and wept, wiping His feet with her tears and hair, kissing His feet, and pouring expensive perfume on Him. It was a worthy display of respect. A Pharisee was appalled by her actions, for his prideful heart couldn't comprehend this kind of love. So Jesus shared a parable about love, reminding us all that until we've been forgiven much, we can't love much.

What made her love so special was that she didn't have to work at it. It was a natural response from an overflowing heart of gratitude due to forgiveness. And as a result of being forgiven, she was compelled to love Jesus outwardly through humble service (7:44), sincere affection (7:45), and sacrificial giving (7:46). Her *inward* gratitude resulted in an *outward* display, providing us with a true model of love.

Closer Challenge: Do you think you love Jesus as much as she does? If not, think about the forgiveness Jesus has granted you. **Today**, from a motivation of being forgiven, find a way to *outwardly* love Jesus by expressing humble service, sincere affection, and sacrificial giving to someone in need. The way you treat others is the way you show your love to God. (Matthew 25:35-40) Be creative and go out of your way to express this kind of love displayed by the sinful woman. After all, Jesus first loved you by accepting the penalty of the death you deserved. Your motivation to love originates at the cross.

February 15

Slow Down

Matthew 11:28-30

Our lives are busy. From children to adults, we are all saturated with activities and responsibilities that consume our time. We have jobs, children, school activities, athletic practices, shopping, appointments, musical performances, volunteer work, entertainment, and oh yeah, church activities. Before we know it, a day can become so full of busyness that we leave out the most important chunk of time—time to commune with God.

Jesus gives us a gentle command in these verses. (Matthew 11:28-30) When we are weary, we're to come to Him, and He promises to bring us rest. Yet, our problem is that we won't permit our schedule enough time to slow down to experience this promise! Our souls can become easily overwhelmed with the stresses and burdens of life. So when we refuse to rest in Jesus on a regular basis, we add to the chaos in our lives. Maybe it's time for you to slow down and turn to the caring, peaceful arms of Jesus.

<u>Closer Challenge</u>: Assuming that you're like most people, you're probably busy. **Today**, within the next seven days, schedule a day when you can slow down to rest in Jesus. Even if you can't plan a full day off to rest, take off a portion of the day to simply commune with Him. Make this appointment as important as any other planned event for the week. Get away and read the Bible or a book that will help you abide in Christ. Turn off your cell phones, stay off the Internet, and relax in a place that is free from distractions. Odds are, you need this day more than you know. God is in hot pursuit to commune with you. Don't miss out on time with Him.

February 16

Calling

Micah 3:8

Micah had a direct calling from God. He was to speak truth to Israel, his people, about their sin, and convince them to return to God as it is written in His law. What a challenging task! If Micah wasn't careful, he could've become overwhelmed by the enormity of the task and shrunk back. But fortunately, he trusted God by relying on the Lord's Spirit, power, justice, and might.

Micah was given a specific calling by God. It certainly was not his idea, for who would've volunteered to take on such a task, knowing his own people could reject him? Regardless if Micah *wanted* to do the will of God, he *obeyed* the calling and served his purpose. God has a calling for *each* of His children, not just prophets, pastors, and missionaries. Whether it's a small or large calling in the eyes of man, each role is extremely important as we all further God's Kingdom on earth. We all have a God-given, unique calling to allow Him to shine in our specific sphere of influence. As a result, it's essential to discover what His calling for your life is and commit to it.

<u>Closer Challenge</u>: Are you living out your calling? It's not a question of *if* God is calling you, but whether you know it and are executing it. **Today**, spend some time evaluating God's unique calling for you. As Micah wrote a "one verse purpose statement," create a personal purpose statement for your life. Make it specific and brief. Use your purpose statement to guide your life. When you have a question about determining God's will, always filter your decision through this statement. It will help you stay on track and complete God's will through you.

February 17

Surround Yourself with Believers

Hebrews 10:23-25

Some Christians believe they can journey through their spiritual life alone. They believe that as long as they have God and the Bible, they're ready to take on the world. Certainly, you can accomplish much with God and His Word, but you would be foolish to not link arms and spirit with other Christ-followers. The author of Hebrews knows we need each other for love, good deeds, and encouragement. We must rely on each other. For as we draw closer to the dreadful final days, the support of other believers will help us endure to the end.

The church was established by God to promote His work on earth through people who have turned their lives to Jesus. Whether it's a mega church or a rural, small family church, *you* need that constant fellowship, and they need it from *you*. If you start to believe you're mature enough to grow spiritually on your own, you've begun a slow and steady drift away from God. The church was not only established to accomplish God's mission in the world but His sanctifying work in you.

Closer Challenge: Do you regularly meet and serve in a local church, or do you casually attend? **Today**, if you are not fully engaged in your church's vision and strategy, it's time for you to step up your commitment. Find ways to become more plugged in at your local church. If you're already serving and participating extensively, help direct someone else toward deeper connection. Gently steer this person to be more involved for his own sake and the sake of the church. Odds are, this person is waiting for someone to invite him toward greater participation. Take full advantage of God's church. It's His plan to further His ways and mature your faith.

February 18

A Time to Fast

Acts 14:21-23

Fasting is a spiritual discipline typically omitted from our daily lives because we often do not know when it's appropriate. In this passage, Paul and Barnabas gave us an example of when to fast. They prayed and fasted for the elders they appointed and commissioned to lead several churches. Paul and Barnabas knew these leaders would come under attack, so they took seriously the role of praying and fasting for these new leaders.

Church leaders have a special calling to sense God's vision and lead the church in that direction. But Satan has a plan, too. He typically attacks the church leaders, because if he can strike them down, the church will fall into disarray and not fulfill God's purposes. That is why it is especially important that you pray and fast for the *sent* ones, for they might be under attack this very moment.

Closer Challenge: Do you fast for your church leaders? When is the last time you spent a significant amount of time in concentrated prayer for your leaders? **Today**, if you are physically and medically able, choose at least one meal you can fast from and use that time to pray for your church leaders, especially newly appointed leaders. If you can fast the whole day, do it. When you fast, drink lots of fluids, but do not eat anything solid. Every time you hear and feel your stomach growl for food, let it be a reminder for you to pray for your leaders. They need your prayers to hear the voice of God and resist the devil.

February 19

Telling the Truth

———•———

Acts 5:1-11

After reading this story, it's hard to comprehend why God would bring such harsh judgment to Ananias and Sapphira. After all, didn't they give *most* of their financial gain to God? It's not like they kept all the profits for themselves. They still placed much of the money they earned at the feet of the apostles. Why would God bring such a swift, merciless punishment on them? Well, in the eyes of God, all sin is serious, even the ones we might consider lesser. This story is an example of what can happen when we deliberately choose to disobey God in any manner contrary to holiness. Fortunately, God's mercy keeps this kind of punishment from happening more often, but this story is a great reminder that even false testimony grieves the heart of God!

There are few stories that strike more fear in the hearts of Christians than Ananias and Sapphira. The fear comes from the fact that we all can identify with them. Their sin was not a murder, a rape or something else extremely gross or taboo, but a simple lie. They made it appear by their words that they were giving it all, but the truth was far from it. We cannot mock God, for He sees our every thought and action. (Psalm 139:1-12)

Closer Challenge: Do your words match your actions? Do you make yourself appear better than you are? **Today**, think about how you present yourself. If your words are not matching your actions, it's time to change. Make sure everything you say is exactly the truth. Even the smallest stretch of the truth is not the truth. Whether you are speaking to a friend, a family member, or a co-worker, don't fabricate or even exaggerate truth. This does not mean to be untactful, but let *all* your words be integrity-filled, and you'll honor God in the process.

February 20

Enjoy Life!

John 10:10

There is a misconception that once you become a Christian, life becomes boring. Many believers view the Christian faith as a list of do's and don'ts. In the process, these Christians live a meager life of no fun. That is a lie straight from the enemy. He has come to steal, kill and destroy your life, and one way he does that is by swaying you to remove the fun. However, Jesus has come to give life, and let you live it to the full! (John 10:10)

There are so many fun things you can do in the Christian life while staying within the boundaries of godly principles. The Bible was given as a guide to salvation and a map to pursue closeness with God. But it was not written to take away your enjoyment in life. It's a bit subtle, but some of the major figures of the Bible had fun. David enjoyed to play the harp and write, and Paul seemed to have at least an appreciation for sports. (2 Samuel 6:5; 1 Corinthians 9:24-25) These men knew how to have fun and still seek to honor God.

Closer Challenge: When was the last time you had real fun? Have you stopped worrying about life enough to enjoy it? **Today**, plan a fun activity for you and your friends or family. Whatever you enjoy, do it! Plan a trip, go to an event, play a game, relax with a book, etc. As always, stay in the boundaries of Scripture, but cut loose from all your heartaches and enjoy life. If you don't enjoy life, you run the risk of letting life pass by without living it to the full. So take today to enjoy the things God has given you!

February 21

Worship with Your Gifts

Romans 12:1-8

Romans 12:1-2 are popular verses concerning worship, but if you stop at verse 2, you dismiss the function of *how* to worship. Paul begins a discourse about using spiritual gifts to worship the Lord. Once you determine that you should not view yourself too highly (Romans 12:3), then you start to look outside your personal bubble space and help others by using the gifts God has given you.

We are all members of one body, a body with many different gifts. If you refuse to use your gift(s), you encumber others parts of the body. Your spiritual gifts could be one or two of several different kinds. It's important for you to discover what your gift(s) is and then immediately use it to help the body of Christ. When you do so, you will offer yourself as a *living* sacrifice, holy and pleasing to God. That is the worship God desires.

<u>Closer Challenge</u>: Do you know your spiritual gift? If not, have you even attempted to determine what it is? **Today**, first, determine what your top two gifts are. You may need some assistance by taking a spiritual gifts test. Many books can point you in the right direction, and quality tests online can help guide you. Talk to your pastor if you need help finding a good tool to use. Once you discover your spiritual gift, immediately find an area in the church to exercise it. There are people in the church waiting for your assistance. Worship the Lord through the gifts He has uniquely given to you!

February 22

Pure in an Impure World

―――――•:―――――

1 Peter 1:22

As you are well aware, this culture will cast any and every impure thought and action it can straight into your life. The prince of the world, Satan, wants to destroy you at any given moment. (John 10:10) He is persistent, taking every opportunity he can to lure you into corrupt thinking and wrongful actions. So, you must seek purity in all ways. Yet, how do we do this?

Purity comes from one source, God. We cannot remain pure if we do not commune with God daily and immerse ourselves in His truth. Peter wrote that we are purified by obeying truth. (1 Peter 1:22) There are two assumptions here. One is that *you know what truth is* and the other assumes *you are obeying it*. If you want to remain pure, you must <u>know</u> God's truth and <u>obey</u> it. So as you strive to remain pure in an impure world, filter every decision through God's truth and obey what He commands. It is for your good and God's glory.

<u>Closer Challenge</u>: Are you feeling pulled away from God by the world's influences? Are you immersing yourself in God's word? **Today**, make a list of two or three weighty decisions you must make. Spend ample time in God's Word to filter those decisions. Before you can make a decision, you must make sure it is morally supported by God's truth. Many times, the decisions are already made, but you just have to go to His Word. As always, be sure to filter all your decision through God's truth, for it will keep you pure and bring peace to your life.

February 23

Identity Crisis

———•———

1 Peter 2:1-12

The Church is in an identity crisis. Many Christ-followers have become confused about who they are, their reason for life, their alignment of priorities, and even their sexual origins. What have we done to arrive at this crisis? Have many listened too closely to the voice of the flesh and neglected the voice of God as found in His Word? Unfortunately, yes. The Church must rediscover who we are according to our Creator so we can rightly worship Him and accurately portray our created purpose.

In 1 Peter 2, Peter outlines a biblical picture of your identity. As a forgiven Christian, you are a newborn (2:2), dependent upon your Father at all times. You are a living stone (2:4-5), a part of the larger community of God to help build His Kingdom on earth. You are a holy and royal priest (2:5, 9), offering sacrifices of *praise* to God and loving *service* to people. You are a chosen people (2:5), owned by God as a slave to righteousness to reflect the character of God. You are part of a holy nation (2:9-10), together (not just as one voice) declaring and modeling the character of God. You are an alien and stranger in this world (2:10-11), knowing heaven is your real home. You're only visiting this world for a while, doing the work of God until Jesus calls you home or meets you in the sky! That is who you are, and that is your purpose. Live and think differently!

Closer Challenge: Do you know who you are? Does it line up with God's Word in 1 Peter 2? **Today**, write down all the confusing thoughts that have influenced *who you are* over the years. It could be an appearance issue, a priority issue, a character issue, a handicap, an addiction, or any other perceived shortcoming or failure. Now, quit seeing the core of who you are in that light. Accept that your real identity and significance are safe and secure in Christ Jesus. Live differently, knowing who you are!

February 24

Underserved Blessings

Genesis 45:17-18

In this familiar story of betrayal, love, and forgiveness, we see what it looks like to receive blessings undeservedly. Joseph's brothers were jealous of him, so they tossed him in a pit, and he was eventually sold into slavery and taken to Egypt. (Genesis 37:28) Joseph faced many hardships over the years, but due to his closeness to God, unwavering integrity, and sincere humility, God had exalted him to second in charge over all of Egypt. (Genesis 41:40) Eventually, a famine came to the land, and Joseph's brothers came to Egypt for help. After a series of events, Joseph revealed to them who he was, and under the blessings of Pharaoh, the brothers and their families were offered the fat of the land. (Genesis 45:18) Even though the brothers were wrong for their actions, they experienced grace by receiving the best of Egypt!

If you've ever been completely wrong but received a blessing anyway, how did that make you feel? Were you grateful to the person extending the blessing? Did it make you want to give back? In a similar way, we deserve life apart from God in hell. But God, in His mercy, extends to us ALL the blessings of heaven if we trust in Him. We receive the *fat* of heaven. As a result, when you accept His blessings of forgiveness and eternal life, it ought to make you want to share His goodness with others.

<u>Closer Challenge</u>: Assuming you have believed in Jesus, you have experienced the greatest act of forgiveness and blessing by receiving heaven. Since you know what it feels like to receive an undeserved blessing, do the same for others. **Today**, go to someone you know who has failed you or someone else miserably. Extend grace to that person like God gave you. Go the extra mile so that person can see the love of God and turn to Him. Be creative in the way you bless him to move him toward Jesus. As you do, watch how God will touch both you and the person you're blessing.

February 25

Are You Willing?

Matthew 8:1-3

Have you ever faced a seemingly helpless situation? If so, you can identify with this man afflicted with leprosy. Slowly but surely, his body was falling apart due to this degenerative disease. There was no cure, no medication, and no way out. Furthermore, he was not able to worship with others, for he was ceremonially unclean. Not only was he falling apart physically, but probably he was dying spiritually, too. Out of desperation, he turned to a man who was said to be healing people with power from above. So he ran to the feet of Jesus, knelt down, and said, "Lord, if you will, you can make me clean." Jesus replied in a simple and meaningful way, "I will; be clean."

This man with leprosy is not the only person with a problem in life. We all have our issues. Some seem to have greater challenges than others, but we all need a touch from God. However, in the simplest way, many of us are not willing to turn to Jesus like the man with leprosy. Jesus is quite willing to help you, but are you willing to *receive* His help? Countless times, there are people with problems, but they're not willing to reach out to the Healer.

<u>*Closer Challenge*</u>: Are you going through a tough time? Maybe you're facing an issue that has been lingering for quite a while. **Today**, ask yourself a simple and honest question, "Am I *willing* to have Jesus help me?" It could be a sin issue, a health issue, or a relational issue, but whatever it is, know that He is willing. However, the help He offers doesn't have to be the result of a mindboggling miracle; for Jesus may have already provided help, but you are too stubborn to take it. Either way, it is God's provision, so be willing. If you're not released from your trial, even if you are willing, be patient and rest in God's present care. God's ways are not ours.

February 26

Representing Your Homeland

2 Corinthians 5:20

Each nation typically has ambassadors in other nations. The ambassador lives and carries on with life in a foreign land while representing his homeland. An ambassador takes care of affairs concerning his home nation while living in a foreign land. In addition, ambassadors carry on the role of being the voice and reflection of their homeland.

For Christians, having the title of ambassador carries some interesting implications. First, we understand we are not in our homeland. Heaven is our home, but we are stationed on earth until our work here is done. Secondly, it's our duty to take care of the affairs of our homeland. According to this passage, our main primary duty is to reconcile all people to God. Finally, it's important to understand our role as an ambassador will end. When this happens, we will be taken home. As a result, we should have a sense of urgency to make the most of the time we have to represent our *true* nation well.

<u>Closer Challenge</u>: How are you representing heaven, your homeland? Are you reconciling people to God? **Today**, do the work of an ambassador as a minister of reconciliation. Whether it is a friend or a stranger, find someone who you know is living far from God. If this person is a friend, take that person out for coffee or lunch and encourage this person in the ways of heaven. If this person is a stranger, look for an opportunity to shine the light of your homeland in this person's life. Hopefully, you will be able to reconcile this person to God. Do your work as an ambassador until you are called home!

February 27

Risky Business

Matthew 10:16

In the wild, sheep do not belong with wolves. If a sheep encounters a wolf in the wild, the wolf will make it dinner. Wolves do what is natural for them. When they see a helpless sheep, they kill the sheep for food. It's hard to blame the wolf because its worldview is simple: Kill to eat.

Why would Jesus use this imagery to explain what it's like for the disciples to carry the message of the gospel to foreign towns and villages? Well, He uses it to remind us that spreading the gospel is risky work. The enemy has warped the minds of people all over the world. It's no secret that people are resistant to the gospel. So when the message is presented, it disrupts their worldview. The proclaimed gospel causes the messenger to become like a helpless sheep, enticing a wild wolf to attack. Gospel sharing is dangerous work, but it's our calling. This doesn't mean we should be unwise in our sharing, for Jesus calls us to be shrewd like a snake. In the process, though, we should keep our innocence (like a dove), so we'll be able to win them over.

<u>Closer Challenge</u>: Do you grasp the potential risk for sharing the gospel? **Today** (or very soon), watch (or read about) the movie *End of the Spear*. This is the story of five missionaries who traveled to an unreached area of the Amazon. Let the story inspire you to action. Jesus did not sugar-coat the task of sharing the gospel. You will face opposition when you share His truth. It's possible that God might be calling you to commit to foreign missions like these families; but if not, He *is* calling you to be a local missionary! Whether it's foreign or local soil, do the work of a missionary. It's risky, but the rewards outweigh the risk!

February 28

Farming for Jesus

James 5:7-9

Farmers are some of the most patient people. Each year carries difficulties as they seek to yield a valuable crop. Some years are full of rain, in fact too much rain, which can kill the crop. Then there are years of drought, so they must irrigate their crop. There are also years when the weather has been perfect, but animals and pests damage the field. It's hard, *physical* work being a farmer, but it's also a *mental* challenge, waiting for the crop to arrive in spite of the elements.

We can learn much from farmers, and that's why James discusses the life of a farmer in his letter. Farmers face suffering as they toil in their fields to yield a good crop. Likewise, as we minister to people, we might also have letdowns due to circumstances. The hard work you invest in people sometimes challenges your faith, because their circumstances make it difficult for them to change. Instead of pouting, causing more conflict, or giving up, be patient like a farmer. The person you're investing in needs your dedication and drive just as an unyielding crop needs it from a farmer.

Closer Challenge: Who have you attempted to minister to, but circumstances have made it difficult? **Today**, be like a patient farmer who waits for his crop. Instead of lashing out in frustration or even giving up, seek ways to work with the situation handed you and continue your faith work. The farmer doesn't ignore his difficulties; he adjusts to his environment and does what he must to bear a valuable crop. Think about that one person who challenges your patience. You might need to alter your methods to make good of the situation. And as always, continue to wait on God, for that's the job of a farmer.

February 29

Take Your Spiritual Jubilee

Leviticus 25:8-13

Every fifty years, the Hebrew people would celebrate jubilee. The Year of Jubilee is observed as a holy year, set apart to remind the people that God is sovereign over the land and their hearts. This event began after the Day of Atonement, symbolizing that guilt and sin had been exonerated. Even servants were released, because all of Israel belonged to God. The Year of Jubilee is a symbol of freedom from debts and rest from all work over the past forty-nine years.

Spiritually speaking, we all need a Year of Jubilee. Fortunately for Christ-followers, every day falls in a Year of Jubilee! Christ has redeemed us and given us a new start each and every day. Life is not to be seen as a drag, for we have the privilege of being cleansed with the blood of Jesus. There is no need to be bogged down in a sea of guilt, for you are in a never-ceasing Year of Jubilee!

Closer Challenge: Have you been sinking into a swamp of guilt due to past sins? Do you need a fresh start on life? Good news! Jesus can give you a new beginning that you desire! **Today**, jot down on a piece of paper all the past sins that have been haunting your soul and keeping you from freedom. Release those sins to Jesus by tearing them up and throwing away the pieces of paper. Celebrate your constant spiritual state of the Year of Jubilee by treating yourself to something special. Through it all, be mindful of the amazing grace and unconditional love of your great God!

March 1

Jump at the Opportunity

Ephesians 5:15-16

Paul was aggressive about making things happen for Christ when the opportunity arose. Even if there was the potential he would be harmed, Paul leaped at new opportunities. In Acts 14 alone there are multiple opportunities that he took advantage of: he preached the gospel in synagogues (14:1); he healed the crippled (14:8-10); he preached the gospel in the streets (14:14-18); he strengthened disciples (14:22); he trained and appointed leaders (14:23). Even a stoning would not stop Paul from making the most of an opportunity! (14:19-20) At every chance, whether Jew, Gentile, believer or non-believer, Paul did whatever he could in the power of the Spirit to shake up his environment for the gospel.

Scripture teaches that you are wise when you readily take action in a God-ordained opportunity. (1 Peter 3:15) *Each day* God offers opportunities for you to connect with others and point them to Jesus. Whether your opportunity is for a member of God's family (Galatians 6:10) or an outsider to the faith (Colossians 4:5-6), you ought to have your heart and mind ready to take action and touch someone for Christ.

Closer Challenge: Do you open your eyes to the opportunities that God has for you each day? ***Today***, be alert to make at least one move in faith to help another. Your opportunity could be at home, at work, or somewhere public. Go above and beyond to reveal God's love in that situation. Be creative and sensitive to the needs at hand. God has an opportunity waiting for you, so open the eyes of your heart and make the most of it. And as a result, you'll also draw closer to God.

March 2

Hearing God

---

1 Samuel 3:1-10

Samuel was a young boy when God began to speak to him. One night, God came to Samuel with a mysterious voice. Since the audible voice of God was rare (3:1), Samuel didn't recognize God was calling for him. Instead, he thought it was Eli, his mentor and the priest over Israel. Three times Samuel ran to Eli, asking what he needed. Finally, Eli realized it was the Lord talking to Samuel, and he instructed Samuel to say, "Speak, for your servant hears." At the fourth calling, Samuel did as Eli asked, and God spoke a vision to him.

When was the last time you heard God speak to you? More than likely you didn't hear His audible voice, for unlike biblical times, we now have His written Word to speak directly to us. But when was the last time you read something in His Word, or through a reoccurring situation, you realized the Spirit's quiet voice speaking to your soul to act in a particular way? Like Samuel, God may have been speaking to you clearly, but you haven't recognized His voice. Maybe it is time for you to say, as Samuel did, "Speak, for your servant hears."

Closer Challenge: Has there been something that continues to disrupt your life, but you have ignored it or misinterpreted it? ***Today***, be attentive to God. He might have been speaking to you concerning a vision for quite some time now, but you haven't been aware it's Him. Search God's Word, be aware of your surroundings, and listen to the Holy Spirit, for God might be sending you a fresh revelation. The way you will move from one level of faith to the next is through obedience to God's voice. Listen to God and obey.

March 3

Facing Death

Genesis 49:33-50:14

Death is never easy to face. In fact, death is typically the hardest reality of life to embrace. We constantly try to avoid death with medicine, vaccines, and other aides to extend our lives. But even in our greatest attempts to fool death, it's unavoidable. So how do we face death biblically? Joseph gives us an example of care by displaying valuable principles for mourning when a loved one dies. Here are those principles: give grieving time (50:3); honor the request of the deceased (50:5-7); mourn *with* others (50:9); weep loudly if necessary (50:10); and understand the time of mourning will expire (50:14).

Each of us will face death on a regular basis. So it's important to know how to care for someone who has lost a loved one *and* how to respond when you lose a loved one. There are no paths to maneuver around death, but as we see in Joseph's case with the death of his father, a proper time of mourning will help ease the pain.

Closer Challenge: Have you recently faced the death of a loved one? Do you have a friend who has lost a loved one? **Today**, think of someone who has recently experienced a death. Become a caretaker to that person. As the Egyptians mourned with Joseph, mourn with your friend or family member. Notice that not many words were spoken; it was mainly weeping and reflection. If you are the one facing death, apply these principles to your life. It will help you cope with your loss and continue to glorify God with the remaining life you have. Ultimately, remember that there is life after death, both for the one who is deceased and those remaining on earth. As a result, be prepared for the next life by trusting in Jesus, and make the most of what you have left on this side of eternity.

March 4

Faith over Doubt

John 20:24-31

Thomas, like most logic-minded individuals, had a difficult time believing Jesus had actually risen from the dead. Along with all the other disciples, he experienced the gruesome death Jesus faced. How in the power of heaven could Jesus return to life after what he witnessed? So when Thomas heard the news that Jesus had appeared to the other disciples, he refused to accept this as truth until he saw and touched Jesus for himself.

Have you ever felt like Thomas? More than likely you have. Life has a way of bringing us face to face with impossible situations. Yet, if we believe God at His Word, we know nothing is impossible for Him. (Jeremiah 32:17) Jesus desires that we come to Him in faith because it is our invisible faith that brings light into dark situations. Child-like, pure faith brings hope, while doubt brings discouragement. Scripture even teaches that you are blessed when you believe in Jesus without seeing Him. (John 20:29) So, will you choose faith or doubt?

Closer Challenge: Is doubt invading your life concerning a particular area? Do you struggle to *see* God's hand working through that difficulty? **Today**, recall a circumstance in your life where there is doubt. If you have doubt in a relationship, in a health matter, a financial predicament, or anything else, find rest in God's all-encompassing power. Stop *looking* with your eyes and start *believing* in your heart that God is able. Walk forward in confidence that God has your best interest in mind for *His* glory. Even if the situation grows dimmer or does not turn out the way you desire, believe that God has a way of working all things for the final good for those who love Him. (Romans 8:28) Stop doubting God; start believing!

March 5

What Really Matters?

───────•:•───────

Ecclesiastes 1:2

In this life we have many ways in which we can spend our time. This world is full of hobbies to enjoy, jobs to choose, adventures to discover, lands to visit, things to buy, books to read, sports to play, people to meet, lessons to learn, and so on. We have a buffet of options to make our time in life interesting and full. But what really matters?

Solomon wrote that everything is meaningless. Does he mean we live a purposeless life? No. But he does mean that everything we do without the Lord in mind is meaningless. Frivolous things will pass away like the wind. Sure, some of those things are not inherently bad, but when it is all said and done, only those things that have eternal impact will remain with you when you die. And as a result, everything else is meaningless.

<u>Closer Challenge</u>: What is your greatest endeavor? Where do you spend most of your time? Does it have eternal impact? **Today**, purposely aim to do something that has an eternal impact. If needed, replace something of personal interest with God's interest. Seek to do that one thing above everything else today. Don't be misled; God wants us to enjoy life, but be careful not to confuse fun with what's most important. Strive to allow the things of God to rise to the top in your daily agenda and make this a pattern in your life. If you set your mind on eternal matters, you'll find that life isn't meaningless but full of purpose.

March 6

Every Nation, Every Language

Acts 10:34

After Peter received a dream and was led to a foreigner's home (Acts 10:1-33), he was convinced that the gospel was not only for the Jews. He was fully persuaded that God accepts all people from every nation who fear Him and do what is right. God does not show favoritism according to skin color or language spoken, for He desires that all men and women should be saved! (1 Timothy 2:4)

In America, reaching the nations for the gospel has become easier. With the advancements of travel and technology, the world has come to us. There is still great need for foreign missions in places where there are people who will never set foot in America. But in many regards, you can be a missionary in your own community. All you have to do is open your eyes. Everywhere you turn, there are different nationalities in your sphere of influence with whom to share the gospel. You just have to eliminate your excuses and go!

Closer Challenge: Do you know of a foreigner in your community who doesn't know the gospel? If not, it shouldn't be too hard for you to find one. **Today**, seek to build a relationship with someone in your community who was not born and raised in America. *Bring* (not just invite) that person (maybe even the whole family!) to church with you. But don't stop with church attendance. At the appropriate time, share the gospel with him. Just like the Roman Cornelius needed a human messenger of the gospel, so do the foreigners in *your* community. Who is *your* Cornelius to touch for the gospel? And remember, as you share, you'll be communing with Jesus.

March 7

Release the Legalism

―――――――•:•―――――――

Luke 13:10-17

In the first century, the law had been grossly abused. Religious leaders forced strict obedience to godly commands that were perverted. For example, the Sabbath had always been deemed as a day of rest. But religious leaders had distorted it so much that they would refuse help to people in need. On one particular Sabbath, Jesus encountered a woman who had been crippled for eighteen years. Seeing her need, He healed her. The synagogue ruler became upset and attempted to rebuke Jesus for disobedience to the law. In response, Jesus sternly corrected him and other religious leaders because the law was never intended to remove our zeal for care.

Likewise, you can become a hypocrite like these religious leaders if you're not careful. Legalism can sneak in even with the greatest intentions and disrupt joy, unity, and service. Instead of following true New Testament precepts, manmade rituals can subtly guide you. It's always important to obey biblical truth, but make sure you're actually following real New Testament teachings and not church tradition. Don't let traditions lead you down the path of legalism and forfeit ministry.

Closer Challenge: Are you aware of any kind of legalism forming in your practices? Are you misinterpreting a teaching of Jesus because you've been misled by church tradition? And as a result, is this practice causing a rift in your personal life and ministry? ***Today***, let God reveal to your heart any form of legalism. It's often hard to see it on your own, so ask a mature believer to be honest with you. If this person reveals a form of legalism seen in you, humbly receive this correction and take immediate action to remove it. It will help set you free to enjoy the love of Christ and expand your ministry potential!

March 8

Confession Before Capture

2 Corinthians 7:10

It's a fact. We all sin. We all stumble spiritually and do things that dishonor God. Since we can agree that sin exists in our lives, why is it that we fail to come clean? Why do we tend to keep our failures secret? Maybe it's because we're fearful of what others will think; and honestly, we might believe we won't get caught. But as Scripture teaches, sin will eventually be exposed. (Numbers 32:23; 1 Corinthians 4:5) You cannot run from your sin. So it's better to confess now than wait to be exposed and face greater humiliation and repercussions when caught.

Paul speaks of two ways you can deal with the sorrow of sin. There is godly sorrow and worldly sorrow. Godly sorrow deals with a spiritual brokenness from deep within because you know you have dishonored God as a disobedient child. This kind of sorrow leads to true repentance. (2 Corinthians 7:11) Worldly sorrow results when you are caught; and then, you are sorrowful because you have to face the consequences of your sin. This kind of sorrow has little to do with the pain you feel over disappointing God. It proves you are self-centered, not God-centered. We must strive for godly sorrow when dealing with sin.

<u>Closer Challenge</u>: Are you holding on to a secret sin? Have you maneuvered your life in such a way to keep from being caught? It's time to come clean. **Today**, confess your sin to God with a heart that understands you have broken *His* heart. (Psalm 51) Don't wait to get caught by mankind. After you have confessed your shortcoming to God, speak about that sin to a close, godly friend who will love you unconditionally and keep you accountable. (Hopefully, your friend is walking with you through this book.) You may also need to confess this sin to the person(s) you've offended. It will be tough, but when you do this, you will release the burden of guilt in your life and experience God's healing power of forgiveness. Expose your sin before you become exposed!

March 9

The Cost of Leadership

---

1 Kings 11:1-6

In all of Solomon's splendor and wisdom, he made a couple of major personal mistakes that affected him as a leader. First, he married multiple wives. (1 Kings 11:1; Deuteronomy 17:17) Secondly, to make matters worse, he married wives who served other gods. These failures initiated the downfall of his reign in Israel and disrupted his closeness with God. Solomon began to worship other gods, and as a result, God withdrew his favor over the *whole* nation of Israel. (1 Kings 11:11-12)

It's a wonderful blessing to gain the responsibility of a leader in God's service. For a spiritual leader has the role of discovering God's heart and urging people to go in that direction. As you lead according to God's will and desire, you gain God's favor for all who follow. But, if you lead poorly, you influence people to follow your example, resulting in a loss of God's favor. Solomon turned from God to serve idols. And as a result, God released His protection and provision over *all* of Israel. His poor leadership caused suffering to all people, which began the downward spiral of God's *holy* nation.

Closer Challenge: Do you aspire to lead? In what ways are you already leading any sort of group? **Today**, count the cost of leadership by ridding anything in your life that is causing you to misdirect others. To make sure you don't have blind spots in your leadership, ask at least one person whom you influence if they see flaws in your leadership. If so, don't lash out at that person. Instead, humbly receive the correction, for it may preserve and even increase your leadership influence. Above all else, stay close to God in daily communion. He is the heartbeat of your leadership. Without Him, your influence dies!

March 10

Your Testimony in the Eyes of Others

John 5:31-33

The greatest way to validate your testimony is through the eyes of others. Make no mistake, Jesus understood who He was. But for others to believe His testimony, both God the Father (John 5:32) and John the Baptist (John 5:33) gave witness to His identity. He didn't *need* human testimony to confirm who He was (John 5:34), but He embraced John's testimony to strengthen our faith in His words and actions.

When being hired for a job, a potential employer often seeks a reference from former employers because their testimony of you is more powerful than your own. Likewise, your testimony of a Christ-follower is more authentic when told by others. With that in mind, what do others see in you? Do they speak favorably of your faith? From a deep relationship to a simple acquaintance, would those who know you be able to testify that you are a true believer? Your testimony is most powerful when others can speak of your closeness to God.

Closer Challenge: What does your life reflect in the eyes of others? Would their description of your life match your own description? **Today,** allow others to evaluate the appearance of your faith. Ask three people this simple question and listen to their responses: *How would you describe my walk with Christ?* Direct them to be honest, and let them know you will maturely accept whatever they say. This is healthy for you! The testimony of another is powerful because it provides a valid measure of evaluating and sharpening your faith.

March 11

Fresh Perspective

———•———

John 9:1-7

When the blind man was healed by Jesus, imagine the new world he encountered! This was not a man who lost his sight early in life, which would have allowed him somewhat of a perspective of the visual world. But this man was born completely blind. He had no perception of reality concerning the visual world. So when Jesus rubbed the moist clay on his eyes, and then he washed it off, he gained a totally new perspective with this simple cleansing!

Spiritually speaking, we are exactly like this man! When you became a Christ-follower, you were granted new vision. Before you were cleansed, you had no perception of reality in regard to the spiritual world. You were completely blinded to it. But when the Holy Spirit entered your life at salvation, the scales blocking the spiritual world fell off and things became clearer. And as you know God more each day, you gain a greater understanding of your life and purpose in this world. Yet, so many Christians are living blind because they refuse to view life with their new sight. It's like you have been given a pair of glasses to correct vision, but you refuse to wear them. As children of God, we must view life from our new perspective!

<u>Closer Challenge</u>: What lenses are you using to view the world? Is it a secular perspective or a sacred perspective? **Today**, put on the lenses of the gospel as you go throughout the day. In *each* conversation and in *every* encounter you have with people and circumstances, pause briefly in your thoughts to imagine the world as Jesus sees it. This will take a conscious effort on your part, so you'll have to be attentive throughout the day. But if you do this, it will create opportunities to glorify God, and help you discover meaning in that day.

March 12

Obey Now

Isaiah 55:6

When the Lord provides a clear mission, the time to act is *now*. When the Spirit of God urges, you cannot delay His work, or you might miss out in the privilege of serving Him and worshiping Him in that moment. If you hear His voice but do not respond immediately, it's quite possible that God could turn to someone else to fulfill His desire in that particular area. God's work will get done whether it's through you or another. As a result, even if God's mission may seem strange to you, trust that God knows best and obey *now*. (Isaiah 55:8)

Each day is filled with multiple, seemingly minor God appointments. These engagements may not always produce a large amount of spiritual excitement, but they are opportunities that demand your faithful obedience. As small as it may seem to you, God could be planting a seed of His glory in someone's life if you just obey. Furthermore, that one act of obedience could be the blessing in your day that broadens your understanding of God. If God has been calling you to meet a spiritual, emotional, or physical need of someone in your sphere of influence, *now* is the time to act.

<u>Closer Challenge</u>: From the past week, who is the first person who comes to mind who needs a touch from God? ***Today***, find a way to meet a need in that person's life. You might give that person a word of encouragement, provide a meal, play a board game together, provoke laughter, pray with that person, just be physically present, or something else. Do whatever is necessary to give that person a clear vision of God's love. Don't delay. For not only will you touch that person's life, but you'll draw closer to God!

March 13

Promoting Harmony: Be Sympathetic

1 Peter 3:8

In 1 Peter 3:8, Peter explains how to live in harmony with others. He begins by telling us to be sympathetic. Being sympathetic means we have a readiness to enter in and share with others in both their joys and sorrows. When you are willing to merge with someone emotionally, harmony is established between the two of you because you create a deep bond of emotional connection. Furthermore, it can lead to a spiritual encounter.

Not everyone desires to be sympathetic, because you must be willing to hurt with someone. You have to be vulnerable to pain. But you *also* must be willing to rejoice with others when they gain success or victory in life. If you have a heart of envy or jealousy, this can be difficult. To establish harmony in all relationships, a Christ-follower must learn to rejoice with those who rejoice and mourn with those who mourn. (Romans 12:15) When this happens, harmony will exist in your relationships.

Closer Challenge: Do you know of someone who is emotionally distraught? Or can you think of someone who has gained great victory in life? ***Today***, practice sympathy with that person. Give that person a phone call or write a message of some sort as a word of encouragement. If the struggle or victory is rather large and significant, take that person to lunch and simply listen. Open up your heart and unite with this person emotionally. By doing so, you will display sympathy and promote harmony.

March 14

Promoting Harmony: Love as a Brother

1 Peter 3:8

The Greeks had many ways to define the word *love*. In this particular verse, the word is *philadelphos*, meaning *brotherly love*. This is not a romantic love, it's an unconditional family love that exists between people who dearly support and care for each other. In this context, it is most directly pointed toward the family of believers, the Christian community. (1 Peter 3:8-9)

Jesus is clear that the way outsiders will know you are one of His disciples is by the way you love others in the Christian community. (John 13:34-35) Therefore, it is your charge to support, care, nurture, encourage, forgive, and even bless those in the church. As you do, you show the world what true love is, and they will be more inclined to be drawn to faith in Christ. In a world that is riddled with disharmonies, it is vitally important that the church displays a place of unconditional love for one another.

Closer Challenge: Are you intentional in demonstrating love to the family of believers? **Today**, determine what you can do to provide a touch of love in your church. You could visit someone who is ill in the hospital, or an elderly person in a care facility. You can provide a much-needed gift to a single parent, or have lunch with a child who does not have a father or mother. You could prepare a meal for a family in crisis. You could labor in the yard of someone who is physically challenged to do such work. You could just *be* with someone in need of emotional support. Think creatively, and then act faithfully to touch your church with the love of Christ. When you love like this, you will promote a harmony that is irresistible to an outside world.

March 15

Promoting Harmony: Be Compassionate

1 Peter 3:8

The word *compassion* conveys a beautiful meaning. By splitting the word apart, we can better understand its true meaning: *passion* means *suffering* and *com* means *with*. As a result, being compassionate means that you **suffer with** someone. This is not just a simple I-am-sorry that-you-are-hurting statement. It goes well beyond that. When you *suffer with* someone, you enter in and share the burden of that person's pain.

Someone who is compassionate can look beneath the surface and behind the fake smiles to identify with the hurt of others. Being compassionate can be difficult. It means you must expose your heart to the pain of others and experience their agony. Most of us like to avoid pain at all costs, but if you seek to be a compassionate person and promote harmony, you must allow yourself to become vulnerable to the burdens and hurts of others.

Closer Challenge: Who do you know who is suffering? **Today**, go to that person and share in the pain. If no one comes to mind, as you go throughout your day, be alert to those around you who are hurting. When the opportunity arises, open up yourself and share in that person's pain. Listen more than talk. Act wisely and accordingly. When you do this, you will find a deeper connection with that person and create harmony between the two of you. Above all, remember Jesus was compassionate toward you, so honor Him by doing the same for others.

March 16

Promoting Harmony: Be Humble

1 Peter 3:8

Humility is the foundation for harmonious living. It's understood as not only thinking lowly of yourself, but not thinking of yourself because you're primarily thinking of others. (Philippians 2:3) It involves viewing yourself as a voluntary servant to people for the sake of Christ. In fact, the greatest example of humility and service comes from Paul's description of Jesus. (Philippians 2:5-11) Though Jesus was greater than all as He walked this earth, He displayed a life of humility by placing the needs of others before Himself.

This world needs a good dose of humility. With all the disharmonies causing wars and conflicts around the globe, humble living could turn many of these selfish battles into harmony. If we could *all* live in humility, conflicts would be minimized, wars would end, divorces would decrease, and our lives would be different! As Christ-followers, our aim is to live humbly so that the world will have a good picture of what it means to really love your neighbor as yourself. (Roman 13:9-10)

Closer Challenge: Do you practice humility? Would others testify that you really have their best interest in mind? ***Today***, in every encounter that you have with others, practice humility. In whatever way possible, put others *first*. Through service, conversations, driving, and all other events in your day, practice humility. When you do this, you will see harmony established between you and others. If you find people are shocked by your kindness, that's a good indication you need to increase your humility. Today and forever, be Christ's example of humility.

March 17

Promoting Harmony: Be Forgiving

1 Peter 3:9

Since we live in a broken world filled with people bent toward selfishness, we will be offended and deeply hurt by others. It's not comforting to hear that, but it's true. However, when wronged, there is a way to protect yourself from the poison of bitterness. It's forgiveness. Forgiveness is not the flesh's first reaction, but it's the best. Forgiveness is saying you are giving up your desire to hurt others for hurting you. It's undeserved. It's unnatural. But it's the only way to restore harmony when wronged.

Peter wrote that we must not repay evil with evil, but we must *bless* those who hurt us. (1 Peter 3:9) Wow! That's not the model we often witness. Typically, we see revenge, or at least some form of resentment. Yet as a Christ-follower, your call is to bless those who offend you. This is not natural, so it will take a supernatural strength from the Lord. And to find that strength, it's critical you remember the forgiveness Jesus granted you even though you didn't deserve His mercy. (Colossians 3:13)

Closer Challenge: Are there disharmonies in your life due to unforgiveness? Instead of revenge or resentment, it's time to forgive and bless those who have wronged you. **Today**, search your heart to identify any unresolved conflict with another. If you detect one, work through these steps. Begin by asking God to forgive you for holding a grudge. *Feel* how you have hurt God. Now, with God forgiving you as your motivation, release your desire to get even. Finally, if possible, attempt to reconcile the relationship by *blessing* that person. Even if the person who offended you does not change, it's important for you to work forgiveness in your heart so pain and bitterness don't control your life. Harmony can be restored if you seek reconciliation through forgiveness. Pray for healing.

March 18

Promoting Harmony: Watch Your Words

1 Peter 3:10

There are few things in this world that can create more disharmony than the tongue. David wrote that he needed to put a muzzle over his mouth when his enemies were in his presence. (Psalm 39:1) At times, we need to do the same. However, if we can learn how to use our words properly at the *appropriate* time, we can reserve muzzles for barking dogs. So, how can we tame this wild beast of a tongue? Fortunately, God gives us the necessary instructions.

Being quick to listen, slow to speak and slow to anger is a prescription for taming the tongue. (James 1:19) This verse, when applied, can save you from much harm in life. When you are in a disagreement, quarrel, or even a casual conversation, you must control the words that come out of your mouth by listening intently and thoughtfully before speaking. For, once your words escape, they cannot be returned. If you want to see *good days* filled with harmony, control your speech.

<u>Closer Challenge</u>: Do your words cause more evil than good? Do you listen intently and think before you speak? **Today**, in all conversations, let others speak first. Seek to be quiet until spoken to. Listen to their words carefully, and only after wise thought do you need to respond. Provide less personal opinions and more encouragement. Your words can be your greatest asset if used properly. Promote harmony with what you say.

March 19

Promoting Harmony: Be a Peacemaker

1 Peter 3:11

As you're well aware, you will face relational conflict. Whether your conflict is over a simple matter or a complicated issue, you cannot avoid clashes. But you *can* deal with them in a godly manner. It is critical that in a disagreement, you seek peace even if your flesh tells you otherwise. Peace making is not impossible, but it will take patience, calmness, and determination.

Peace *making* is different than peace *keeping*. Peace keeping involves doing what you can to give an appearance of peace, which may involve sweeping a conflict under the rug or avoiding that person. This is not peace, because inside there is still evidence of discord. Peace making involves understanding that even conflict is an opportunity to worship God. A peacemaker is someone who will approach conflict in a godly manner, which involves gentle confrontation and a humble spirit and doing whatever is necessary to reconcile the relationship for *Christ's* sake. When you do this, you become a peacemaker and promote harmony.

Closer Challenge: Is there someone who you are not at peace with? Have you attempted to be a peacemaker? **Today,** start by viewing your conflict as an opportunity to bring God glory. Determine how you can reconcile the relationship. Maybe you could begin with a loving, respectful letter or phone call to initiate a conversation. Maybe you could calmly approach the person. Whatever the manner might be, in humility seek to be a peacemaker. Do your part, and pray God will work on the other person's heart too. Even if the other person is not willing to settle the conflict, be determined to keep trying, for you are promoting harmony.

March 20

Equality in Christ

Matthew 20:1-16

When reading this parable, you might be stirred with mixed emotions. Is it fair for someone who worked only a fraction of the day to receive the same amount of wages as someone who worked all day? Common sense says no! But if you view this from a heavenly perspective, your attitude will change. We must be mindful that this parable is speaking of salvation, not rewards. Whether you believe and follow Jesus early in life or at the end, salvation is sealed by a profession of faith, regardless of when it happens. Fair or not, that is the mercy of our God. (Matthew 20:15) God desires all people to be repent (2 Peter 3:9), even a murderer in his last hour of life. (Luke 23:40-43)

We typically visualize entering heaven as though we assemble in a vertical line, waiting to be checked in, like waiting in line to purchase a ticket at a movie theatre. However, we need to change this image. Instead of picturing a vertical lineup, envision a mighty *horizontal* line of the redeemed where all God's children take a step into heaven at the same time. Meaning, the last will be first and the first will be last. (Matthew 20:16) We all enter together. There is equality in Christ! Shoulder to shoulder, the most moral saint and the most horrid criminal will enter heaven together when Jesus calls us home. This does not imply there will be equal rewards, for we will all be judged for our good and bad deeds. (2 Corinthians 5:10) But it does mean we are all equally washed in the blood of Jesus when speaking of salvation!

<u>Closer Challenge</u>: Do you have a hard time rejoicing when hardcore sinners repent? Do you have a form of self-righteousness that unjustly views all God's redeemed? **Today**, change your perspective and love all sinners who repent! Reach out today to a believer with a culturally rotten past, and treat that person with a kind act. Be gracious. Understand that you and the worst of sinners are on equal footing when it comes to entering God's Kingdom.

March 21

Fill God's House!

Luke 14:15-24

This parable is a vivid picture of God's longing for salvation for all mankind. Jesus describes the kingdom of heaven like a great banquet. Through the death and resurrection of Jesus, the banquet is now ready for guests to enter. (Luke 14:17) All that is left to do is gather the attendees. We see from this passage that everyone is invited, regardless of background. (Luke 14:21) And it is our job, as Christian servants, to *go* out into the streets, alleys, roadways, and country lanes to *speak* about our Master's love for all people and urge them to commune with God at His table along with us.

In a powerful statement tucked away in this parable, God desires His heavenly household to be *full* with the people of the earth. God wills that there be no empty seats at His banquet table. And since we do not know who is to sit at the table, when every seat will be filled, and when the door will be shut, we continue to GO and share the gospel as long as we have breath. To GO is an expected burden of a Christ-follower that will bring glory to God by drawing both the seeker and the messenger into deeper fellowship with Him.

Closer Challenge: Are you obeying God's command to go? Or are you merely waiting for people to come to you? Are you doing *anything* to point people to Jesus and His banquet? **Today**, view yourself as a *vocal invitation* to all you encounter. Inviting people to God's banquet is twofold, doing good deeds and vocally sharing the gospel. (1 Peter 3:13-16) Provide someone with a good deed, and then use it to voice the gospel. Do your role as God's messenger of the Great Banquet and join the movement to fill His table!

March 22

Stop and Enjoy

---

1 Kings 8:1-11

There are times when God's presence can be so overpowering that you must stop everything you're doing. (1 Kings 8:11) In these moments, even the wonderful, spirit-filled services you perform *for* the Lord cannot compare to His incredible presence when He wants you to know He is *with* you. The priests were faithful servants diligently working *for* God. But when God made His presence known to them and others at the dedication of the Temple, they could do nothing but give Him undivided attention and admire His glorious indwelling.

This must have been a marvelous sight to behold. Yet, why do we rarely experience moments like this? Is it because God doesn't choose to work in this manner anymore? Or is it that we do not expect this sort of magnificent encounter from God? Let us remember that God has not changed. He desires to make Himself known to all generations, but often we are not willing to slow down enough to receive the glorious blessing of His powerful presence. Maybe it is time we raise awareness of His presence and stop everything to enjoy our Creator.

Closer Challenge: When is the last time you stopped and enjoyed God's presence in worship? **Today**, prepare yourself for worship. In the privacy of your home or in a secluded place, stop everything and worship God by listening to some God-centered music. Raise your hands in awe as a sign of surrender to Him. In the next corporate setting of worship you attend, prepare you heart and mind for worship. As wonderful as it is to interact with other believers, make this day solely about God. Concentrate on Him even before the first word is spoken or the first lyric is sung by quietly praying for a fresh encounter with Him. And ultimately, commune *with* God over doing anything *for* Him. Stop everything and enjoy His presence!

March 23

The Foundation of God's Will

1 Thessalonians 4:3

Many ponder, "What is God's will for my life?" That's a difficult question to answer in regard to each person's functional direction for following God. After all, each of us has different gifts, experiences, and passions that will drive His will for our lives. But there is a universal will for all believers that should guide us. It is God's moral will that you be *sanctified*. No matter what your specific calling is, all Christians must adhere to this portion of God's will. When an immoral, unethical situation arises, you know it is *not* God's will, so run from it because God desires you to be sanctified.

What does it mean to be sanctified? In 1 Thessalonians 3:13, sanctification refers to being *strengthened in the Lord*. In 1 Corinthians 1:2, being sanctified describes those in Christ as the *set apart* ones for God's glory. It's being in pursuit to be like Jesus. Even though you will not reach His perfection, it is your calling to pursue it with passion. Two components power us toward sanctification: Being washed in the blood of Christ through salvation, and being daily cleansed by the Holy Spirit through God's Word. There is not a greater will for you to seek than to be sanctified.

Closer Challenge: Are you wondering what is God's will for you? Before you seek the functional will, examine God's moral will. **Today,** carefully review the actions and attitudes of your life to make sure you are morally seeking Jesus. Let the Spirit of God cleanse you by His Word. If you are out of line morally, the functional will of God will suffer. Repent now and be sanctified.

March 24

Facing Opposition

---

2 Timothy 3:12

When it comes to living out your Christian faith, someone will be offended by you. Whether it's intentional or not, you will cause disturbances, especially if you aggressively follow Christ. Paul clearly wrote that if you want to live a godly life, you will be persecuted. (2 Timothy 3:12) He did not say you *might* be persecuted; he said you *will* be persecuted. Even though it is not your desire to cause discord, there is no way to avoid it if you live a godly life.

As a result, since Scripture teaches you will face resistance as you live out your faith, what if you're *not* facing any persecution? This is a serious question that should strike a chord with every Christian living comfortably. Does the lack of opposition mean you're not living a godly life? Maybe. For even Jesus said no servant is greater than his master. If they persecuted me, they will persecute you also. (John 15:20) With this in mind, it's time to evaluate how surrendered you are to a godly life in Christ.

Closer Challenge: Are you surprised when people become offended with your Christian lifestyle? You shouldn't be. You should be more surprised if people aren't offended by your life! **Today**, if you're facing any form of spiritual persecution, be encouraged that you are identifying with Jesus. Do not give up on living a godly life. If you're *not* even remotely experiencing any sort of resistance, it is time to live more like your Master. Today, when an opportunity arises to stand up for your faith when you might normally compromise, endure for Christ. You may face resistance, but you also could experience a spiritual breakthrough. Be strong and use it as a platform to glorify Jesus.

March 25

Controlled?

1 Corinthians 6:12; 10:23-24

Two times, Paul speaks of everything on earth as permissible, but not everything is beneficial. In 1 Corinthians 6:12, Paul instructs us not to be mastered by anything. Even though there are many things God allows us freedom to do and experience, we have to ask ourselves, "Is it beneficial?" In addition, we must ask, "Is there potential that I will be mastered by it?" If we're not aware of all consequences to our actions, something that may seem harmless and fun could potentially misguide us away from God. And as a result, we can become mastered by permissible things and neglect beneficial things, such as spending time with God and helping others.

In 1 Corinthians 10:23-24, Paul alerted us to have in mind the good of others over self. Even though something could be permissible, will it harm others? If what you are doing has the potential to make others stumble into sin, then not only is it unbeneficial to your testimony, but it is harmful for others. As a result, you should refrain from participating in that activity. In both of these instances, we must be careful not to replace God's plan with anything that is of this world.

Closer Challenge: Is there something permissible in your life that has become your master? Is a permissible thing causing others to stumble? **Today**, search your seemingly *harmless* habits. If you have it under control and it's not harming others, continue the activity, but be alert! But, if it's compromising your ministry and causing others to stumble, it's time to drop that habit. At least for a *season*, refrain from doing that permissible activity. Exchange the permissible thing with something that will help others grow in their faith. As you do, you will discover the beneficial thing is more rewarding than the permissible thing.

March 26

Coming to Jesus

Matthew 11:28

What does it mean to come to Jesus? It's been often said by well-intentioned believers, "Just go to Jesus with your problems, and He will carry your pains and worries." Even Jesus taught that we should come to Him, for He will give us rest. (Matthew 11:28) Yet, since Jesus has already ascended to heaven *physically*, how do we actually come to Him? When your earthly parents tell you to come to them, you can physically do that. But in spiritual terms, it becomes a little less obvious how to come to Jesus and offer Him your burdens when He's not physically here.

Since we can't physically make our way to the person of Jesus, here are several ways in which you can sense His presence. 1) Come to Him in *trust*. When you have concerns, simply trust that He will work things out for the good. 2) Come to him in *righteousness*. In all situations, as you seek righteousness, you will find Christ. 3) Come to Jesus by following His *activity*. Wherever God is moving, go there. For you will find Jesus.

Closer Challenge: Do you need to come to Jesus with your problems? If so, **today**, come to Jesus in one of the three ways already mentioned. Are you struggling with a hurt or pain? Come to Him in trust. Is sin causing a disturbance in your life? Come to Jesus by living righteously. Are you confused about direction in your life? Go where God is vividly moving and join His activity. And if you just need some physical arms to hold you as you hurt, confide in a friend who loves Jesus, and you will find Him there. (Matthew 18:20) There are many ways to come to Jesus to commune with Him; practice one today.

March 27

Relational Balance

Matthew 9:9-11 & Mark 6:31-32

Even though Jesus *sat* with sinners and spent precious time with them, He never engaged in their lifestyle. Instead, as He did with Matthew, He called sinners to follow *His* lifestyle. (Mark 9:9-11) Those were important moments in Jesus' ministry, but He reserved His most intimate encounters for His most trustworthy companions. (Mark 6:31-32) It was with His disciples that Jesus shared His greatest pains and deepest teachings. (Matthew 26:36) And at times, He narrowed those moments down to only a few of His disciples. (Matthew 26:37; 17:1) Jesus had great *balance* in His relationships both with unbelievers and followers.

As we learned from Jesus, we must be mindful to spend quality time with those who need to hear about His forgiveness; after all, it is the sick who need a doctor. (Matthew 9:12) However, when it comes to our close relationships, we must surround ourselves with like-minded people. If you plan to grow in your faith and learn the deep truths of God, time with other believers is indispensable. As Jesus did, you must *sit* with sinners to guide them to God, but you must *live* with saints for encouragement and love.

Closer Challenge: With whom do you spend your time? **Today**, evaluate who your closest companions are. Do they build you up or cause you to stumble? It's important that we sit with sinners to point them to God. But unbelievers should not be your closest friends if you aim to mature in your faith. Your closest friends should be those of spiritual like-mindedness. Be careful that you don't have the roles reversed. Create and maintain a proper balance of both touching the lost for Christ and spending ample amounts of time with believers who will build you up spiritually. This might take some rearranging, but follow Jesus' example.

March 28

The One Hour Challenge

Matthew 26:36-40

Jesus had reached the end of His public teaching and healing ministry. It was time for Him to be arrested and face the brutal death of the cross. And even though Jesus was fully God, we must remember He was also fully human. He knew He'd feel every bit of the pain, and the thought of enduring the cross and facing a separation from the Father became overwhelming. As a result, He asked His disciples to pray for Him. Jesus went a short distance away from them, and He also knelt down in agony to pray. (Luke 22:41-44) But when He returned to His disciples, He found them sleeping instead of praying. He said in disappointment, "Could you men not keep watch with me for **one hour**?"

It's easy to cast judgment upon His disciples for falling asleep, but are we much different? It's interesting how quickly we can fill an hour of our time. We have hobbies to enjoy, books to read, work to be done, people to talk to, and so on. But if Jesus asked us to pray for an hour, could we focus that long in communion with the Father? We have 168 hours every week. What would happen if we spent *at least* one hour a week in concentrated prayer? Maybe we'd encounter God on a deeper level.

Closer Challenge: Do you have a time set aside each week where your undivided attention is focused on prayer? Even if you do, try this. **Today**, commit to the *one hour challenge* for at least one month. For the next month, spend at least one hour a week in concentrated prayer. As you talk with God during this time, write down every person and need you pray for so you can stay focused and not fall *asleep* or get *distracted* in your thoughts. If you commit this challenge, you can be certain you will draw closer to God, and you'll likely see God meet needs in unsuspecting ways.

March 29

Pride in Numbers

―――――•―――――

1 Chronicles 21:1-4

Most of us remember David as a man after God's own heart. Yet we know David fell into sin like the rest of us. A less-familiar mistake of David is when he was deceived by Satan to take a census. Conducting the census was a sign of pride in his heart. The great number of fighting men he counted might have made David feel invincible; yet in this brief lapse of judgment, he failed to remember it was the Lord who brought them this far. As a result, the census attempted to steal the glory and fame away from God and place it on David and his men. This displeased God. (1 Chronicles 21:7-8)

It's tempting to seek big, flashy numbers. However, numbers can often mislead you to pride and arrogance. Here are some areas where the pride of numbers can surface: a sizable salary, a high IQ, a cushioned retirement account, pricy possessions, good height, small waist, successful business, solid church numbers, and more. Scripture warns us that when we become prideful, disgrace will follow. (Proverbs 11:2) It's not to say that numbers are unimportant, but watch out that numbers don't become a pride mechanism and tool of Satan to make you self-sufficient and forget God. Unlike David, don't let the pride of numbers create a downfall in your life and influence. (1 Chronicles 21:9-14)

Closer Challenge: Is there an inner voice telling you to attain bigger and better numbers to increase your fame? **Today**, if you sense numbers increasing your pride, it's time to control it before it controls you! Ask for forgiveness as David did. (1 Chronicles 21:8, 17) Then, as a show of humility, truly give God the credit for all successes in your life. Finally, take any measure needed to ensure numbers will not warp your perspective. Do not allow numbers to damage your life and influence.

March 30

Does God Care?

Mark 4:35-41

On a chilly dark night, the disciples faced a monstrous challenge while in a boat traveling across the Sea of Galilee. Even though many of them were professional fisherman, not even they could handle the furious squall they encountered. While they were fighting against this great storm, Jesus was asleep in the stern of the boat. When they could not battle the waves any longer, they rushed to Jesus and said some words to Him that many Christians feel today, "Teacher, do you not care that we are perishing?" At this, Jesus stood up and calmed the storm, and they were amazed at His power.

At times, you may wonder if God really cares for you. When you are dealing with a troubled child, does God care? When your health is failing you, does God care? When you have lost your job, does God care? Many circumstances can cause you to question God's motives and availability, but when you actually look at life from the big picture, you understand that He does care! Who else could have given you the breath in your lungs? Who else is with you every second of the day? Who else would have sacrificed His only Son for your wretched soul? Only God! Even though your circumstances may seem insurmountable, be confident that God really does care!

<u>Closer Challenge</u>: Have you been wondering if God really cares for you? Has a current hardship tempted you to doubt His love? **Today**, be reminded of God's great care. List in your journal at least five memories of God blessing you or delivering you in some way. Meditate on those precious memories of deliverance and be cheerful. (Psalm 63:5-8) Know that if He could do it then, He can do it now! Your God cares for you. Remember His past love and have faith He is with you now.

March 31

Why Complain?

Numbers 21:4-9

As the Israelites did earlier in their journey to the Promised Land (Numbers 11:1), they once again complained about God's provisions. (Numbers 21:4-9) Again, they spoke against God because they had no water to drink or bread to eat. They even despised the generous manna from heaven. (Numbers 21:5) They had lost their faith in God and Moses. As a result, God became angry with His people and sent venomous snakes into the camp. Many died while others were poisoned by the snakes. In fear for their lives, they cried out to Moses for God to remove their punishment. In a show of mercy, God saved the lives of the Hebrews who looked at a bronze snake.

Before we start slamming the Hebrews for their lack of faith, let's remember that they were in a dire situation. They were slowly moving through the hot desert, fending off enemies, living on just enough manna and water each day, and they had no land or home of their own. If we were placed in the same situation, it is safe to say our faith would be stretched too. Yet we learn here that complaining is not the answer. God hates complaining after He blesses. Did God not deliver the Hebrews from slavery? Did He not provide them water from a rock? Did He not provide the miracle of manna from heaven? Sure, it may not have been ideal, but God was their Provider!

Closer Challenge: Are you complaining about an undesirable situation that you're in right now? If so, what is it? **Today**, stop complaining because you're gaining *nothing* productive out of it. In fact, when you complain you lose faith, you become negative, and you influence others to do the same. Whatever you're complaining about, ask for forgiveness and replace it with faith and gratitude for the things you *have* received from God. Instead of complaining, talk with another about one of God's blessings you've received. That will please Him and direct you toward a proper attitude.

April 1

Joking Arrows

Proverbs 26:18-19

Everyone likes a good laugh. We are all created with emotions, and one of the greatest ways to release stress is laughter. In fact, many should do more of it. With that being said, don't let your humor come at the expense of deceiving or hurting another person. In this proverb, your harming words are depicted as deadly arrows. (Proverbs 26:18-19) When you carelessly launch your words in the name of *fun*, you can unknowingly damage another person's image and your reputation.

Sometimes it's hard to know where to draw the line or when you have gone too far with a joke. So as a godly guide, if your gag can hurt someone, hurt yourself, or is contrary to God's Word, refrain from doing it. There are many ways to laugh and enjoy life, but primarily use your words as encouragement. For when you do, they can lift spirits and heal hearts.

Closer Challenge: Do your words often get you in trouble because they bring people down? Are you hurting people in the name of a *joke*? **Today**, watch the way you use your words. If you use lots of sarcasm, refrain from it, and try to replace it with encouraging words. You must be careful not to carelessly wound a person's spirit. And even if you think it is fine that they pull that particular joke on you, remember that our personalities, temperaments, and sensitivities are all different. As a result, someone else may not appreciate it or think it's funny. Your joking words are like arrows. And when an arrow is shot, it wounds whatever it strikes.

April 2

A Foolish Thought

Jonah 3:10-4:11

Jonah had a hot hatred against the Assyrians, especially the ones who lived in the capitol city of Nineveh. They were the despised enemy to the north. It seemed logical that God surely would never send Jonah, God's *holy* prophet, to share His mercy with those evil-doers. Yet, that's exactly what He did. However, in rebellion, Jonah refused and fled on a ship in the opposite direction. As a result, he caused a sequence of unfortunate events. He induced a massive storm, got tossed overboard, and was swallowed by a large fish. Finally, while in the belly of the fish, he repented, returned to Nineveh, and reluctantly warned them of God's judgment. Ironically, Nineveh repented. This caught Jonah by surprise, and he became upset because God did not give them the punishment they *deserved*.

God often calls us to reach the people we want to overlook. He longs to love the sinner, the outcast, the foreigner, and even the betrayer. He desires to hold the prostitute, the cripple, and the murderer. He wishes to embrace the prodigal, the hated, and even the annoying. Why? It's because God created all of them, and He loves them equally. How much do you love them?

Closer Challenge: Do you foolishly think only you deserve God's mercy? Is there someone who you refuse to touch for the gospel due to a selfish root buried in *your* heart? **Today**, think of a person who needs a touch from Jesus, but you deny love. First, ask God to change your heart. Secondly, purposely find a way to reach out to that individual. As you do, pray this person feels accepted, as God accepts you. Most importantly, pray for this person's salvation. And if this person repents, rejoice in God's prevailing mercy.

April 3

In Christ Alone

Acts 4:12

The American culture has a buffet of belief systems. If you believe in strict personal discipline, you might follow Buddhism or Hinduism. If you want a belief system based on personal merit, adhere to the teachings of Islam, Mormonism, or the Jehovah's Witnesses. If you desire to embrace the modern culture, use humanism or secularism as your belief system. Everywhere you turn, there's an option that will appease *your* heart. All these and many more will keep you busy; but in the end, they will not bring you salvation. Furthermore, in moments of crisis, they will leave you empty, searching for *the* Answer.

Of all the belief systems, Christianity is like no other. Christianity isn't based on human achievement; it's built on *grace*. Jesus' selflessness is like no other god. When He died on the cross, He did all the *work* necessary for salvation. As a result, salvation cannot be found anywhere else because no one who has ever lived or will ever live can compare to His matchless *grace* and sacrifice! In Christ is the fullness of the Deity (Colossians 2:9), the perfection needed for oneness with the Father (Hebrews 7:28), and the hope for eternity! (1 Timothy 4:10) You can look elsewhere, but eternity only rests in the name of Jesus!

Closer Challenge: Do you believe there are other ways to God? **Today**, remind yourself of the selflessness and truth of Jesus. Spend some time in the Bible reading some of the powerful truths of salvation. Use an online search tool or concordance to do some word studies on *salvation*, *perfection*, *eternity*, and *atone*. Think of other powerful words to study and better your understanding of God's salvation found only in Jesus, so you can live in light of these rich truths.

April 4

Fleeing Shame

Genesis 2:25

It is hard to imagine our world without shame. Thoughts wouldn't be hidden. Full obedience would be embraced. Life would be void of much suffering. That's how Adam and Eve lived while in the Garden of Eden. They followed the ways of God through righteous living. As a result, due to their sinless life, they were naked without shame. But as soon as they took a bite of the forbidden fruit in disobedience, shame entered the picture, and it has tortured lives ever since.

We can identify with the shame of Adam and Eve, for we have all fallen into similar traps of sin, which have led to embarrassment. So how can we escape this wretched situation? We have only one place to look, the cross. By the cross, Jesus scorned the shame that has entrapped us all. (Hebrews 12:2) His perfect life leading up to the cross became the substitute needed to erase shame. We have victory over shame because of His death! Though we weren't obedient, His matchless obedience reversed our situation and brought glory to the Father. Yet unfortunately, so many fail to rid their shame even though they can.

<u>Closer Challenge</u>: Is shame limiting your joy and possibly controlling your life? If so, release your shame at the cross. **Today**, in a step to rid shame, write down in your journal as a prayer to the Father the sins that bring you the most embarrassment. If you are actively involved in that sin, repent and *flee* from it now! You cannot escape the clutches of shame until you turn from the sin causing it. If you are shamed by a sin of your past, confess it. It would be healthy to confess this sin to a godly friend or spiritual leader. The power of shame is in secrecy. If you talk about your shame, that will release its power. (James 5:16) This confession may open up wounds and result in some consequences, but it's the healthiest option. Do not let the stronghold of shame rule your life any longer. Turn to Jesus and His victory over sin.

April 5

The Armor of Integrity

Proverbs 13:6

Many people in our world gain popularity and wealth through the means of wickedness. Some corporations build empires on fraud. Fame can result from scandalous or questionable living. It may seem that all is going well for them, but there will be a day when sin is exposed, and they'll have no guard or defense because integrity is missing. The characteristic that sets apart the righteous from the wicked is integrity.

What is biblical integrity? Integrity is our armor against a wicked world that wants to have us follow its ways of living. (Proverbs 13:6) Integrity is the discipline in your life that keeps you doing right, even when Satan tempts you to do wrong. (Proverbs 11:2) Integrity is the confidence a believer has when accusations rise against him because he's not contrary to the Word of God. (Proverbs 10:9) Integrity directs you to live correctly, even when no one else is looking. Integrity is the voice of the Holy Spirit reminding you of truth when you're confronted with a compromising situation. Some people live by integrity; others do not. But the ones who do are guarded by the righteousness of God.

Closer Challenge: Are you careful to follow the ways of integrity? Or are there areas in your life where you have compromised integrity? **Today**, examine your life closely. Do you handle shady business deals? Does your word match your actions? Do you secretly sneak sin in your life, hidden from the eyes of man? Choose integrity in every situation, even when the flesh tempts you otherwise. Integrity could save you from false accusations. Let go of wickedness and embrace the shield of integrity.

April 6

Dealing with Debt

Proverbs 22:7

In the present day, we desire material possessions right *now*. And if we don't have the cash, we use credit cards or borrow money from banks, friends or family. Yet when we borrow, we mount up undue stress in our lives. We become slaves to the lender for a material possession that often isn't *needed*. As a result, this lust for stuff is ruining many modern families. Don't blame government; it's a desire that comes from within. (James 1:14)

Throughout Scripture, we see God is concerned about financial issues. In Matthew 6:24, Jesus is clear that we cannot serve two masters, both God and money. If you attempt to serve money, you will find yourself less available for God's work. That's why Peter wrote that a leader for God's work cannot be a lover of money, but he must be eager to serve God. (1 Peter 5:2) Maybe it is time to reexamine who you really serve and make sure it is not money or the things that money buys.

<u>Closer Challenge</u>: Is the drive for more stuff mastering your life? Is there someone or some institution you are neglecting to pay back? **Today**, set yourself on a path to rid debt! Discontinue buying unnecessary possessions. Cut up credit cards you don't need. Sell pointless items you have. Pay off that person you owe. Do what you must so that your only Master is the Father. Next, set up a plan of action for clearing all your debt. You might have an overwhelming amount of debt, so get a good biblical tool to help you chip away at it. Ask your pastor for one. Finally, practice contentment. Trust that God will supply all your needs. Your only Master should be your God. Don't let anything else replace Him.

April 7

Send Me!

Isaiah 6:1-8

Isaiah had an incredible experience with the LORD. In the presence of the LORD, Isaiah observed Him sitting on the throne, witnessed the seraphim in worship, felt the ground shake, saw the temple fill with smoke, and experienced holy cleansing as the Lord forgave his sin. If the experience ended there, Isaiah would have had an encounter with the LORD that he would never forget. However, the Lord went a step further by offering a task that would test Isaiah's gratitude for being cleansed.

When the Lord asked, "Whom shall I send, and who will go for us?" Isaiah yelled like a school boy wanting to answer a question, "Pick me! Here I am, send me!" When God renews through forgiveness of sins, He never stops there. He wants cleansed, *willing* servants to be *sent* out in His name to spread His mercy and forgiveness to others. After **true** repentance, a *willingness* to serve God is an absolute. The second Isaiah heard of a task from God, no matter what it was, he said, "I'm available, let me be the one you send!" Should this not be your response too?

Closer Challenge: Have you experienced the cleansing work of the Lord in your life lately? If so, service should be on your mind. **Today**, examine if you have had true cleansing of sin. If not, fall to your knees and allow God to burn the sin from your life with the coals of forgiveness. Now, after true cleansing, a willingness to serve should be present. Hear the voice of God saying, "Whom shall I send?" Without hesitation, be the one God sends. Look around. What does God need to be done for His glory? Don't wait for someone else to fill that role. If He is speaking, just say "Yes!" As you do, you'll be like Isaiah, communing with God through service.

April 8

Jesus Will Stop for You

Mark 5:21-34

In an urgent moment, Jesus rushed to help Jarius' daughter, who was dying of a sickness. But during His travel to meet her, He was interrupted by another need, one that wasn't involving death. However, Jesus stopped to address this need too. Fortunately, Jesus healed her bleeding issue even in the midst of an emergency for another. With this story in mind, do you ever feel like Jesus doesn't have enough time for you? Maybe you believe God couldn't possibly stop long enough to heal your situation when there seems to be so many larger, more pressing needs.

It's sad, but many refuse to come to Jesus with seemingly minor issues. Sure, when there is a *big* need, we will go to the Lord. But when we have a minor need, we *try* to take care of it on our own because we might believe He's too busy to deal with our simple predicament. In *everything*, all worries, petitions, praises, and thanks, present your prayers to Jesus and the God of peace will be with you. (Philippians 4:6-7) Never believe that God does not have the time for you. He is waiting to reach out to you like He did for this woman.

Closer Challenge: Do you have a simple need you haven't brought to Jesus? Have you only dealt with it on your own? **Today**, reach out to Jesus like the woman in this passage. He will not overlook you. He will take the time to touch your life too. Think of an issue in which you have failed to involve the Lord. Drop to your knees and talk to Jesus about it. Allow Him to touch your life like this woman. He is never too busy for you.

April 9

Rightly Positioned

---

2 Samuel 11:1

It doesn't matter who you are, if you're not in the right environment, you will drift away from God. A great example of this came when David stayed home while his military went out to war. It was customary for kings to go out to war in the springtime. Yet while David's army was battling the Ammonites and besieging Rabbah, he remained idle in Jerusalem. His idleness led to a series of regrettable moments. David slept with Bathsheba (a soldier's wife), impregnated her, set up her husband to be killed on the front lines of war, and as a consequence of his poor behavior, he lost his newborn son. (2 Samuel 11) All these events occurred because David was not where he should have been.

Like David, our most embarrassing moments can often be traced back to times when we weren't where we should've been. If you've recently done something regrettable, ask yourself if you were in the right place. If you weren't, this is a good reminder to constantly be aware of your surroundings. You may think you're strong enough to withstand the temptation, but don't test the flesh. Instead, seek environments that will build you up, not pull you down.

<u>Closer Challenge</u>: Do you often find yourself in the wrong place? **Today**, purposefully situate yourself in a positive environment. If it's Sunday, make sure you go to church. If you're aware of a Bible study going on today, make an effort to attend. Be *somewhere* positive! And above all else, stay away from environments that could lead you to sin. For some, that place could be a bar, club, casino or mall. For others, it could at your computer late at night. Still for others, it could be spending time with that friend who poorly influences you. Always position yourself in environments that build you up, and as you do, you'll draw closer to God.

April 10

Testing Spirits

1 John 4:1-3

As you walk with God, you will hear many different perspectives concerning Jesus' validity of being the eternal Son of God. And strangely enough, these slight variations will come from people who claim to be Jesus followers. That's why it is important that you take the time to test the spirits of those who claim to speak the words of God. Testing spirits involves a simple filter. Ask this question, "Does this 'voice of truth' believe that Jesus has come from God?" If not, then that person has failed the test.

There are other teachings in which people could falsely speak, but Jesus being God is the basic necessity for a messenger of biblical truth. Most people believe Jesus was a *good teacher* and a solid *moral example*, but many have a difficult time declaring that He is God's Son in the flesh. If someone cannot believe this, he has discredited himself as a valid teacher of the Bible and the spirit of the anti-Christ is in him. It is also essential that when you hear or read *truth* spoken, rake the messenger through the coals of high moral character. If he does not practice what he teaches, be aware that his teachings could be faulty too.

<u>Closer Challenge</u>: Are you mindful to test the spirits of those who claim to be speaking truth, or do you casually accept what they say? **Today**, when you hear truth spoken, be sure to test the spirit. Both the content and the character of the voice should match God's Holy Word. Study the Scriptures and determine if what people are saying is accurate. Secondly, examine the actual moral integrity of that person. If that person is not personally applying biblical truths, a red flag of warning should rise. Make sure that what you are hearing is actually biblical truth so your life will be enriched with the things of God.

April 11

Mary or Martha?

Luke 10:38-42

On one special day, Martha invited Jesus to visit her at her house. Knowing she wanted to rightly host Jesus, she hustled and bustled to finish all the preparations. But while Martha worked hard to complete the chores, Mary didn't lift a finger to help as she sat listening to Jesus. This bothered Martha, so she went to Jesus and asked Him a question concerning Mary's lack of help. But Jesus calmly replied to her that Mary chose wisely, for she was communing with the Lord.

From this passage, it's difficult to become too upset with Martha, for she was serving like Jesus wants us to serve. So, what's the catch? The main issue here is choosing what is better at any given moment. Martha had Jesus, God's Son, relaxing at her house! Wow! Instead of communing with Him, she was caught up in all the distractions. There are times we need to stop what we are doing and just sit with the Lord, for that is the better choice when God is making His presence known.

Closer Challenge: Do you constantly serve the Lord without taking a break to adore Him? **Today**, examine your *planned* day. If you have not left room to sit at Jesus' feet, schedule some additional time outside this discipleship tool. Study a Psalm, read a Christian book, or talk with a mature Christian about some deep truths of the Bible. Remove some *preparations* you might have, and do the wise thing. Preparations are necessary, but do not let them distract you from Jesus. If you remember, you read this same passage of Scripture on January 2, but it's necessary to return to it so it sinks in. If you do not take time to sit at the feet of Jesus and commune with Him, you miss His aim to be in close relationship with you. That tops everything else! Make it your priority each day.

April 12

Better with the Lord

Psalm 84:10

Korah was a man in Israel who railed against the direction in which Moses and Aaron were leading them. So in rebellion against their leadership, he gathered elite men in the community to rise up against them. (Numbers 16:1-3) Eventually after the initial words of rebellion, God swallowed them up by a hole in the ground. (Numbers 16:31) It was a sad day for the descendants of Korah. But generations later, Korah's descendants wrote Psalm 84 with a much different attitude. No longer did they want the elite status of leadership; they were content with being *doorkeepers* in the house of the Lord. (Psalm 84:10) What a drastic turn in humility!

Do you struggle with following your church leadership as Korah did with his leadership? Maybe like the Hebrews you're less than satisfied with how they are leading, so it might seem fitting to complain and even expel them from leadership. However, God called Moses and Aaron to lead, and it's critical not to rebel against God's anointed. Any time a leader is called into question, walk with caution and search your heart that you are not trying to overthrow a leader for your benefit. Instead, be like the descendants of Korah and humbly accept any position God may have for you.

Closer Challenge: Do you envy your leaders? Do you secretly want to overthrow them because you don't like their direction? If so, watch the ground! **Today**, take some time to love your leaders. Send them a note of encouragement; contact them with a word of support; or provide something special for them. Leaders carry many burdens, so assist them by displaying your love. If a leader is in sin or is misled, go to him in caution and love with reliable eyewitnesses of his fault. (1 Timothy 5:19) Above all, whatever position or title you have in a church, be grateful for it as the Sons of Korah were thankful for their position as doorkeepers.

April 13

Reconnecting with Family

2 Samuel 14:33

After Absalom had his brother, Ammon, killed (2 Samuel 13:28-29), David disallowed Absalom to return into his presence. For three years, Absalom lived in Geshur, but in David's heart, he longed to see his son again. (2 Samuel 13:38-39) Wisely, Joab devised a plan to allow David to see his own struggle, and through this clever act, David requested that Absalom be brought back to Jerusalem. (2 Samuel 14:1-21) But David still had not let his bitterness fade, so he ordered Absalom to refrain from being in his presence. (2 Samuel 14:23) For two more years, David did not see Absalom. Finally, due to a rash action by Absalom, he was brought to the king, his father, and they exchanged their affection for each other. (2 Samuel 14:33)

It took five years for David to release the bitterness he had because of Absalom's murder of Ammon. Five years they disconnected from each other. Five years they were not able to laugh and enjoy life together. Five years caused more grief and unresolved resentment. Five years were lost between this father and son. Was the pain real that David faced from the foolish act of Absalom killing Ammon? Yes! Absalom was extremely wrong for the murder of his brother, but in a sense, David lost two sons that day because he refused to speak with Absalom. Maybe in a less severe way, have you lost contact with a family member over a dispute? Maybe it is time you attempt to resolve the situation and be a family again.

<u>Closer Challenge</u>: Is there a family member who you're disconnected with due to a disagreement or struggle? How much time has been lost with that family member? **Today**, restore contact with that person and seek to reconcile the relationship. More than likely, if there has been disconnect for a long time, both of you are at fault to some extent. If you need wise counsel, seek that first. Life is too short to waste days apart from family. As with David, you may reopen the wounds with contact (2 Samuel 15:1-12), but displaying God's grace can restore the years stolen by bitterness and hate. Strive to keep a healthy relationship with your whole family, no matter what disputes might have taken place.

April 14

Love the Father, Not the World

1 John 2:15-17

Many people choose or at least are tempted to love the world, but what does John mean when he refers to "the world" in this passage? Is he referring to people of the world, the created world, or something else? Well, it is most consistent with John's writings and the New Testament to conclude John is referring to the world as the *realm of sin*. You are to hate the realm of sin and turn from it because it is not of the Father. There is nothing in the realm of sin that will last eternally. If anyone loves the world (realm of sin), the Father's love is not in that person.

John provides this stern warning because it's attractive to concede to the deceptive ways of this world. The world brings quick but temporary satisfaction, which lures people to it. Many settle in its ways only to find emptiness. It is impossible to both love the world and love God. Something has to give. As a result, we need this strong warning in order to stay away from the sin that disconnects us from God.

Closer Challenge: Do you have a love for the world more than a love for the Father? Are you consistently falling into the pit of sin? **Today**, in your journal, make a list of things you love. Where you spend your free time is a good gage of what you love. In a typical day, rank the activities from greatest to least according to the time you spend in that activity. By assessing where you spend your free time (and extra money), you'll discover what you love. If you're off focus, realign the time to match the love that you have for Jesus!

April 15

Taking Advantage of Authority

───────◆───────

1 Kings 21:1-28

In a twisted story of evil and greed, Ahab and his wife, Jezebel, used their authority to do evil in the eyes of the Lord. Ahab wanted to possess Naboth's vineyard so that he could have a vegetable garden. When Naboth refused to sell his land, Jezebel abused her power by writing a letter to the elders of his city, declaring that Naboth cursed God. The city elders then stoned Naboth for his accused sin. Once Naboth was dead, Ahab promptly took the vineyard for himself, verifying a complete abuse of power.

Corruption of power is a temptation in all walks of life. So whether you are the authority figure over thousands or merely one, you must be careful not to abuse your authority. If God has granted you authority, you have been given a great responsibility. Authority is not a luxury to take advantage of people; it is a privilege and opportunity to influence those under you into a vibrant relationship with Jesus. If you are not being fair and just, you are setting yourself up for judgment. (1 Kings 21:19) Choose wisely the way you lead.

<u>Closer Challenge</u>: Have you been granted by God a position of authority? It could be in a job, church position, or volunteer role. It could be your function as a parent. ***Today***, examine your life to see if there is any abuse in the way you lead. Do you take advantage of your authority to get what you want? If so, change your habits, and look to bring out the best in those you oversee. Do something special today for those who you are over, and watch their lives flourish with gladness. When you do this, you will honor God and give them a picture of Jesus.

April 16

Lots of Action but No Fruit

Mark 11:12-25

When Jesus taught, He often did so in creative ways, such as comparing two objects to give deeper insight about truth. For example, as Jesus was walking with His disciples, He saw a fig tree that was not bearing fruit. So He cursed it. Shortly after that, the group reached the Temple in Jerusalem. In a similar way, Jesus became upset that His Father's house had lots of activity, but it was not doing what it was supposed to do, which was to be a place of prayer and worship. As a result, both the fig tree and the Temple were not doing what they were created to do. They both had lots of action, but they were not fulfilling their created purpose.

It's possible that you could be really busy doing church activity, but are you really focused on what God desires? If you're not careful, you can become somewhat like the fig tree and Temple – lots of busyness, but not the correct action you're created for. As a result, all that activity could potentially produce little to no spiritual fruit. The type of fruit we're created to produce deals with drawing closer to God and impacting others to do likewise. We must be careful that we do what we are created to do.

Closer Challenge: Are you *busy* serving the Lord, but you realize there is no fruit? Have you recently evaluated if what you are doing for the Lord is what you were created to do? **Today**, reevaluate your service to the Lord. Do you find it is the heart of God? Does it create deeper communing between you and the Lord and impact lives for His Kingdom? You must be careful not to become like the fig tree and Temple in the sense that there is much action but no fruit. If you are not doing what you're created to do, seriously consider how you can improve your impact. Start over as soon as possible and make a difference for the Lord's sake.

April 17

Responsive or Reflective?

Proverbs 14:29

You will face conflict. You can't avoid it, but you can control how you deal with it. You can increase conflict with unrestrained responses, or you can minimize its damage with patience and understanding. If you have a natural leaning to respond impulsively, you've probably had your share of experiences when conversations become intense, argumentative, and unproductive. In fact, in those heated moments, it's likely you've said or done things you regret. Sadly, it could have been avoided.

Conflict will arise almost every day. Conflict should not be seen as a problem, but a potential to draw closer to God. When you disagree with another, take the advice of Solomon. Strive to be *patient* so you will gain understanding. As you follow his instruction, two things will occur. First, patience will lead you to listen better so you can evaluate the facts properly. And secondly, patience helps you speak objectively, not emotionally, which typically makes things worse. Strive to be a patient person, not quick-tempered, and you will find your conflicts will resolve with more ease.

<u>Closer Challenge</u>: Do you tend to lose control when you disagree with another? Has poorly managed conflict damaged any of your relationships? ***Today***, what conflict are you facing right now? Instead of retaliation, insert patience in that situation. *Listen* to the person you are struggling with and attempt to gain understanding. Then pause for a discerned amount of time before speaking. (James 1:19) Think about what you'll say as you keep in mind the goal of glorifying God. This simple practice of patience could turn your conflict into a healthy relationship-building encounter. On the other hand, don't go to the other extreme and use patience as a way to avoid conflict. Be patient, but deal with conflict accordingly.

April 18

Identifying with People

---

1 Corinthians 9:19-22

Paul was a true servant of the Lord. Repeatedly, he attempted to identify with *all* people so he could win over to the Lord as many as possible. He sought to identify with the strict religious Jew, the Roman Gentile, the unlawful pagan, and the spiritually weak. Paul was all things to all men, but his inspiration came from his Master, Jesus, who reigns on a mighty throne in heaven, came to earth, birthed by a young common girl and placed in a feeding trough. This doesn't sound like the entry of a king, but He came in this manner to identify with us. If the God of the universe would go to such great lengths to identify with you, how willing are you to do the same for others apart from God?

God has created us all different, so it is quite a task to fully become like your neighbor when you don't seem to have much in common. But you will find that if you make a little effort to enter other people's world, spiritual doors will open. Identifying with others will take you out of your comfort zone, but it's necessary if you are heavenly minded. Strive to become all things to all men without compromising the Holy Scriptures.

Closer Challenge: Are you sheltered in your own world so much that you've been unable to associate with people unlike you? Do you avoid certain people because they are different than you? **Today**, open up your heart to anyone God may have cross your path. You may have little in common with that person, but do your best to join with him in his world and care for him as needed. It will take great patience and increased listening skills. But when you enter that person's world, you will be like Paul, becoming all things to all men so you might save some. Do what you must within the boundaries of God's Word to lead people to Jesus.

April 19

Unsatisfied Eyes

Proverbs 27:20

A sobering fact is that anyone who has lived has died. Outside of a few people in the Bible who were lifted to heaven (Genesis 5:24; 2 Kings 2:11), 100 percent of people have died. There are over 7 billion people alive today who are awaiting their chance to beat death. Unfortunately, they will not be successful. Only if Jesus calls His people up to meet Him in the sky before death will we be able to beat it. (1 Thessalonians 4:17) The grave is never satisfied; death wants everyone, and it will not stop with you.

Solomon makes an interesting parallel with this proverb. Just as death is never satisfied, neither are the eyes of man. Our flesh always wants more! We want more stuff, more money, more pleasure, more of everything! Our lust for *more* drives us to work harder, stay up later, and disobey longer. The lust of our eyes can even damage us sexually if we're not careful. Many people are harming relationships and ruining purity by looking at naked flesh outside of the confines of marriage. Lust of the eyes can lead to many different struggles, so it's important to know your struggle area and be self-controlled to live by the *Spirit*, not by the flesh.

Closer Challenge: Are your eyes out of control? Do you find your lusts are controlling you? **Today**, determine what kind of lust tempts you the most. Do you want more stuff? More power? More flesh? Whatever your struggle is, remove any means of succumbing to that lust before it overtakes your life. Share your lust struggle with a trusted friend. This is an area where most of us need brothers and sisters in Christ to help us. Be bold and expose your lust before it exposes you. When you remove that area of lust, do not forget to fill it with service to God or some other healthy option. Above all, practice contentment. (Philippians 4:11-13) Trust that the Lord will provide for all your needs.

April 20

God Wants Your Sin

Galatians 2:15-16

Many believe that behavior according to the law is what carries them to heaven. The truth is, that would be the right answer if we could live perfectly. However, here's the catch. None of us has lived up to the level of perfection needed to enter the heavenly realm. (Romans 3:10) All it takes is one measly sin, and we've broken perfection. And since we've all broken perfection, we're not able to enter heaven. As a result, we need something outside of ourselves to take the penalty of sin we deserve. We need someone who is perfect to do what we couldn't. Enter Jesus and His mercy displayed on the cross!

But not only does His mercy allow you through the gates of heaven, it also keeps you from falling away from heaven! Even though you might have already accepted God's grace for salvation, you might be living as though you are under the law. What a shame, because it's keeping you from living in the freedom of Christ. If you struggle with trying to be perfect, yet fail repeatedly, remember you are upheld by grace! At this point, what Jesus needs most from you is not perfection but your sin. He has all the perfection in Himself that is needed, but what He wants more than anything is your dirty, gross, and defiling sin.

Closer Challenge: Are you dealing with guilt because you cannot live up to the perfect standard of the law? Even though you should continue to strive for perfection (Matthew 5:48), understand that you are not under the law anymore. You are saved and sustained by grace. **Today**, if you're experiencing guilt due to a particular sin, completely give it over to Jesus. Drop to your knees before you do anything else and lay that sin at His feet. In addition to that particular sin, also confess the sin of disbelief. Disbelief? Yes, disbelief is the sin that is keeping you from trusting that the cross is enough. Guilt's payoff is fully compensated. Jesus doesn't need your additional work to fix the problem of sin. It's done. Just believe it and let that belief flush away guilt. This simple truth can set you free to enjoy Christ on a deeper level. Give Jesus what He wants—your sin!

April 21

Having Real Faith

Hebrews 11:1

The best definition of faith is found right here in Hebrews 11. According to the author of Hebrews, faith is broken into two components. In both components, *confidence* is the key ingredient in spite of the unknown. First, faith is being sure of what you hope for. This is a confidence in the things that have been promised to you, but you have not attained. For example, if you are born again, you have faith that you will enter heaven one day. Though you are confident you will live there, it's not a reality yet, but our faith pushes us toward that reality.

Secondly, faith is being certain of what we do not see. This is confidence in the things we know are real, but we are unable to physically visualize. For example, we know the presence of God is with us at all times. (Matthew 28:20) Though we cannot see Him visually, the effects of His presence are certainly known, much like the wind. As a result, we have confidence that He is with us. Faith is meant to be a simple concept to understand, but living by faith challenges our rational minds. Yet, when we can live by faith, we display a confidence that God is in complete control. Furthermore, we're able to cope better with life's most difficult circumstances.

<u>Closer Challenge</u>: Have you been living by faith or by sight? Are your circumstances dictating your attitude instead of faith? **Today**, embrace the confidence and joy of living by faith. What is the one thing that is greatly consuming your thoughts? Whatever it is that is causing anxiety, move forward in faith. Have *confidence* that God will do whatever is *best* for you according to His will. Maybe it's not what you'd like, but it is best. Do not allow the world to distort the way you live because what you see is often not a picture of future reality. Move forward in faith with confidence! As you do, you'll draw closer to God in sweet communion.

April 22

Representing God Well

Joshua 22:18

We often believe the myth that our rebellion only affects ourselves. That is far from the truth. In fact, God becomes disturbed with a whole community when one person decides to live in sin. It does not seem fair to the community when one person rebels, but if a community labels itself with God's name, it is important that *all* in that community represent Him well.

God does not want anything to defile His name and cause a perishing world to be misinformed about who He is. Each person in the community of God is to reflect God's character, and when one does not do that according to His Word, the outside world obtains a distorted view of God. That does not settle well with a holy God. As a result, if you or someone you know happens to rebel against God and misrepresent Him, gently turn yourself or that person back to God. If God is going to have His name stamped upon the community, then we must do our part to show outsiders the real God.

Closer Challenge: Are you living in rebellion against God? Do you see that your sin is harming others? Do you even care? **Today,** look into your life to see if there is anything that is defaming the Lord's name. As a representative of your Holy God, drop that sin and trust in His mercy to restore you and guide you to reflect His holy character. If you do not want to do this for yourself, do it for the God who has redeemed you and the people who will be affected by your rebellion. As you go throughout the day, represent God with the honor He deserves. Wear your Christian label with integrity and gently point others in the community to do the same.

April 23

Remember This

Isaiah 46:8-10

There are many spiritual disciplines we should seek to apply in our lives, such as prayer, fasting, mediation, and so on. But there's one we often leave out even though it's a very prominent discipline seen throughout Scripture. That spiritual discipline is *remembering*. Remembering is the discipline that keeps us on the right track. When it's not practiced, we forget God, and forgetting God was a major cause of Israel's rebellion. (Isaiah 65:11-12) They forgot God's statutes, decrees, law, love, and wrath. As you choose to remember God, you will walk faithfully with Him.

Remembering reminds you to think on the former things, including that there is no one like Him. (Isaiah.46:9) Remembering causes you to think back on your wretched past condition without God. (Deuteronomy 5:15) Remembering recalls God's past wonders, which leads you to believe He could do it again. (1 Chronicles 16:12) Remembering makes you acknowledge who the Creator of the world is; thus, reminding you of His sovereignty. (Ecclesiastes 12:1) Remembering points you in the direction of Jesus being crucified and raised to life for your benefit. (2 Timothy 2:8) Remembering is also the key element of the Lord's Supper. (Luke 22:19) When you forget these things and more, you lose focus on the things that should drive and sustain your life.

<u>Closer Challenge</u>: When was the last time you sat down to remember God and His greatness? When you do, it will add spiritual fuel to your life. **Today,** make a list of at least ten things God has personally done for you or taught you. Some of the things may be exciting past victories, while others may be defeats or failures that you learned not to repeat. When you choose to remember your lessons and experiences from God, you will gain hope and direction for all your present and future situations. Choose to remember the greatness and power of our God!

April 24

Praying for World Missionaries

Romans 15:30-33

Paul often faced great struggle as he delivered the message of truth to regions that had not heard of Jesus. While in Judea spreading the gospel, Paul encountered unbelievers who were causing him much grief and problems. Yet it was the prayers of the saints from other regions of the world that helped sustain his ministry and deliver him from many close calls.

Think about the many missionaries around this world. There are missionaries in Africa, Asia, South America, Europe, Australia, and even in our homeland. Missionaries all over the world are striving to bring hope to people who do not have the saving message of Jesus Christ. Your prayers are desperately needed for them, so when they return, like Paul, they will be able to return with joy and refresh us in the process. Do not underestimate the power of prayer for these individuals. Fervently pray for those who are serving the Lord in spiritually dry areas of the world.

Closer Challenge: Do you often pray for God's servants around the world? Do you know some of them by name? **Today**, if you do not already have a few missionaries in mind, find two to three missionary family units you can pray for. Make a commitment to pray for them with regularity, starting today. If you already have missionary families in mind, today send a digital message or write a letter to bring them support as they continue their work. Even if you are not physically on the mission field, your calling is to support and love those slaving for Jesus. Do this with prayer and encouragement.

April 25

Good and Bad Fish

Matthew 13:47-50

Throughout the gospels, Jesus provides many pictures of heaven. In this particular depiction, Jesus tells us the kingdom of heaven is like a net that was dropped into a lake. This net was pulled up with many kinds of fish. In the end, the Lord will separate the good fish from the bad ones. The good will go with Him, and the bad will be cast into judgment. To make things clear, a good fish is someone who has confessed Jesus as Lord and believed in his heart that He was raised from the grave. (Romans 10:9-10) A bad fish is one who has not made that commitment. Trusting in Jesus will be the mark that distinguishes between who goes where in the final separation.

It is important for all believers to understand that this separation is not done now. As of right now, we live with all saints and pagans. While we have time on earth, believers continue to love the saints and desperately seek to persuade lost souls to Jesus so they also can inherit eternal life. Our role on earth is not to do the final separation. That will be God's job. Knowing this reality takes the pressure off of us. Our fervent focus is pointing people to Jesus with love, and God will do the judging at the appropriate time.

<u>Closer Challenge</u>: Have you falsely believed you are to separate pagans from believers? Have you even looked down upon those who do not love Jesus? Though like-mindedness in Christ is lacking with these individuals, we still need to love them enough to tell them about Jesus so they are not cast into final judgment. **Today**, while there is time before the final separation, commit to love such individuals. Take some time to think about what it would be like if you were on the other side. Would you want someone to tell you about Jesus? Practice showing love to an unbeliever who is in your circle of influence. This person could be a neighbor, coworker, family member, etc. Be creative so you can start a conversation with that person. Use your voice and life to lead a *bad* fish into being a *good* one. As you do, you will please God and draw closer to Him.

April 26

Connect Your Life and Doctrine

---

1 Timothy 4:16

Throughout 1 Timothy 4, Paul provides some important instructions to his apprentice, Timothy. And in the last verse of this chapter, he sums it all up. Watch your *life* and *doctrine*. Those are the two things we must constantly keep sharp. First, keep your life sharp because it is the first thing outsiders see. Your life deals with the outward, visible actions of who you are. When you live rightly, you honor God and display His wonders. When you live poorly, you misinform people of who He is. Your life is an open book for the world to read, so watch it carefully.

Secondly, keep your doctrine sharp. Your doctrine deals with the inward, unseen components of your being. Many will become lazy when it comes to rightly knowing doctrine because it takes time and effort. You must search the Scriptures and watch out for the traps of false teachers. Listen to wise, godly people who have been there before you, but always filter their words through the unchangeable Word of God. It is your doctrine that will drive your life and actions, so be careful to correctly divide the truths of God.

Closer Challenge: Are you carefully observing these two components in your life? Do people see a life that is driven by correct doctrine? **Today**, start with examining your doctrine. Are there one or two truths that seem puzzling? Spend concentrated effort today studying these things in God's Word to strengthen your doctrine. Do not be lazy in learning doctrine! Once you obtain a proper doctrine, apply these truths to your life. Life execution of these truths is essential. So *live* with discipline once you have correct doctrine. Life and doctrine are closely connected; never separate the two.

April 27

In Love

---

1 Corinthians 16:14

This one little verse sums up our attitude in Christ. Paul simply writes that we are to do everything in love. (1 Corinthians 16:14) This calling may not seem profound with a casual glance, but if you unpack the reality of that one statement, your entire world changes around you when you apply this principle. Love defined is an attitude from within that produces a demonstration of sacrifice for others. Once love is displayed, it increases trust, intimacy and unity. But when love isn't expressed, the manifestations of jealously, hate, indifference, and selfishness are produced.

Now, with this understanding of love, from the way you treat your family, interact with your church, speak to outsiders, and even view yourself, do you do *everything* in love? Odds are you have some work to do. But the more you practice love, the more natural it will become to love all people. For this reason and more, it's important that you intentionally adopt a biblical view of love so that you will be able to share God's love with others. After all, the greatest picture of love resides in our heavenly Father, who loved us even before we knew what love was. (1 John 4:19) He gave us the true picture of *demonstrated* love when He sent His Son to die for our sins. (Romans 5:8)

<u>Closer Challenge</u>: Are you doing everything in love? Are there some particular areas of life or people you find more difficult to love? **Today**, though you are to do *everything* in love, focus on *one* person who needs to experience the love of God. Even if you find it difficult to love that person, go above and beyond the call of duty to show him you care. For when you do, your reward will be great. (Luke 6:32-35) In all things, emulate your Master by demonstrating love to all people.

April 28

No Fault Found in You

---◆---

Daniel 6:3-4

Daniel was an upright man. Scripture teaches that Daniel had distinguished himself among the rest due to his exceptional qualities. He found favor in the eyes of King Darius because of his loyalty and character. However, the other administrators who served alongside Daniel were jealous of him. So they conspired to have him killed through a decree set by the king himself. Since Daniel would only worship God and not man, David was thrown into a lion's den for his reluctance to follow the man-made decree not to pray to God. But God shut the mouths of the lions and rescued Daniel from death.

In your life, good character and a positive reputation may be the one thing that saves you from disaster. Our world is filled with evil, including people who would like to see you fail to give them extra leverage in life. As a result, sometimes evil will seem to get its way. But if you hold firm to the conviction of an unwavering integrity, you'll remain in peace. Daniel separated himself from the rest by the way he lived and followed both God and the law of the land. But even when it came between following God or the law of the land, he followed God; thus, keeping his ultimate loyalty intact. If he would have died that night in the lion's den, he would have gone to the grave with the peace of doing what's right. That should be your aim too.

Closer Challenge: Do you sense the world trying to bring you down? Are you confronted with compromising situations? If so, hold firm to the truths of God's Word! **Today**, practice living your life above reproach. Hopefully, you already live this way, but for this day, go above and beyond the norm to keep your life distinguished among the rest. Publicly show your loyalty to God when given the opportunity. This is not to be done in self-righteousness, but in humility and respect for your God. Make a habit of this kind of living by finding ways to eliminate any questionable behaviors. Be bold to live your life without a hint of fault found in you.

April 29

Ask God

Luke 11:5-11

This short parable is about a man who did not help his friend late at night. Though it may be justified why the man did not assist his friend in need, our God is not that way. The disciples wanted to learn how to pray, so Jesus provided this parable after He illustrated the Lord's Prayer. Jesus used this parable to explain that God will not be like this heartless friend. Whatever time of day and for whatever need, your Father will be there to listen and help out. All you must do is "ask, and it will be given to you; seek, and you will find; knock, and it will be opened to you." (Luke 11:9-10)

We all have needs. But often we turn to our own strength or the strength of others to meet those needs, instead of turning to our gracious Father. He desires to extend His hand of mercy into your life and touch you with love. However, you must *ask* Him to provide. Interestingly, the original language concerning these verbs denotes perseverance in coming to Jesus. You must "keep asking, "keep knocking" and "keep seeking." He knows what is best and that involves providing for your *needs* just at the right time. So keep asking and wait for Him. As you do, you will draw closer to your Maker.

Closer Challenge: Do you have a specific need that has been unmet? Be sure it's a true need and not a want. **Today**, turn to God in prayer for Him to meet that need. And if God doesn't answer immediately, keep asking, keep seeking, and keep knocking on God's door. Be patient. Rest in God and continue to live righteously as He answers your request in His time and in His way. He will come to you at just the right time and in just the right way to bring glory and honor to His name. Do not give up on God, but trust that He loves you deeply, and He will supply what you need in due time. So, what's your need? Come to God in boldness and with patience. Your God is gracious; rely on Him in faith as you commune with Him in prayer.

April 30

Receiving Correction

Proverbs 12:1

Solomon was wise to know you can only gain knowledge if you are humble enough to take correction. Correction is not an end in itself; it is to turn you toward knowledge. When children are disciplined, it is to teach them that they should not repeat poor behavior. Discipline helps us mature and learn more of what is right. However, when you do not receive it well, you verify that you do not desire to obtain knowledge. Instead, you demonstrate that you're more concerned with sticking to old, poor habits than developing righteousness in your life.

No one likes to be wrong; so our pride often keeps us from receiving discipline well. Whether good or bad, self-image is very important in our culture. When someone stands corrected for a statement or action, more often than not, he will become defensive toward correction no matter how wrong he is. This is sad; for that person is more concerned with how he is perceived than godly maturity. We must change our perspective on righteous discipline. View it as a tool to develop you into the image of Christ.

<u>*Closer Challenge*</u>: Do you find yourself quite defensive when corrected? Are you humble enough to stand corrected when you are wrong? **Today**, begin to receive discipline well. If you have been corrected in your recent past and have not received it well, revisit that experience and receive it the right way. Go to the person who corrected you and thank that person for being honest. This will take humility, but use correction as a tool to point you in a holy direction.

May 1

Staying in God's Presence

Exodus 33:7-11

Being in God's presence is the absolute best place you can be. For when you're in His holy dwelling, nothing else matters. When Moses would enter the tent of meeting, a pillar of cloud would lower from the sky and cover the entrance, moving everyone to worship the LORD. When Moses would leave the tent of meeting to take care of community matters, young Joshua would stay. Whether he was there to guard from intruders or not, Joshua constantly remained in the holy dwelling place of God.

Staying in God's presence causes great change in us. Whether Joshua knew this or not, God was shaping him into a future, godly leader. Joshua could not help but morph into godliness as he remained at the tent where God rested. It's an example we should follow. Do you often dwell in the holy place of God? You might ask, "Where would this be?" Well, God does not solely dwell in man-made structures. Instead, He resides in the lives of those who choose righteousness. And when God's children gather in purity of mind and heart to worship Him, His presence is strongly felt. Do not neglect these times, for they will grow you into God's likeness.

Closer Challenge: Do you crave to be in the God's presence? Are you positioning yourself to hear and be with God at all times? ***Today***, remain in the presence of God. Remember that your body is the temple of the living God. (2 Corinthians 6:16) As a result, wherever you go, God is with you. However, He will manifest Himself more vividly when you choose holy living. As you move throughout the day, consciously picture the Lord with you at all times. It will greatly impact your decisions in that day by keeping you from sin and focusing you on righteousness.

May 2

A Picture of God's Love

Psalm 91:14-16

Those who are regularly in church have heard repeatedly that God is love and His love is stronger than anything else on earth. It is a precious bond that the Father has with His children. Yet do you actually know what this love looks like? According to the words written in Psalm 91:14-16, *if* you love God, He will love you like this: He will rescue you from harm, protect you from evil, answer your calls to Him, be present with you to deliver you during troubled times, honor you, bring you satisfaction, and provide salvation! Amazing! What can be more loving than that?!

His love has a wealth of riches waiting for you, not necessarily worldly riches, but spiritual riches that satisfy your deepest longing. However, you must realize that the fullest extent of experiencing God's love is conditional on your part. Psalm 91:14 starts with a conditional phrase, and tucked away in the following verses are two expressions of love we should give to God, which sets into action the full extent of God's love. As *we love* Him and *acknowledge* Him, we will experience His love when we call upon Him. (Psalm 91:14-15) Complete love always involves two parties. Follow through with your part to love God, and He will grant His matchless love to you.

Closer Challenge: Do you understand the depths of God's love? It's absolutely stunning; but do you love Him? **Today**, build up your love for God by spending ample time with Him. A love relationship, filled with intimacy and reverence, can only be built through consistent, intentional time. Make sure you do not quickly brush over your time with God each day. Spend quality time listening to Him and calling out to Him in dependence. When you do, you will experience His grandiose magnificent love in return, which is the mark of a close relationship.

May 3

Broken Before God

Nehemiah 1:1-4

Nehemiah was a man who honored God and loved his fellow people. When he heard the news that the remnant of Hebrews still in Jerusalem were in distress because the walls of Jerusalem were torn down, Nehemiah fell to the ground, wept, prayed, fasted, and called out to God. He was broken over the wickedness of Israel since the days of Moses. (Nehemiah 1:7) Nehemiah did the greatest thing he could for his people. He was vulnerable before God. And in his brokenness, God heard him and did not refuse his request to rebuild the wall and protect those Hebrews living in Jerusalem.

Is there something in your life producing in you extreme brokenness? Maybe your marriage is suffering. Maybe your children are being defiant. Maybe your church is losing focus concerning the Lord's work. Maybe *you* are being unfaithful to God? Whatever is causing you anguish, realize that godly sorrow is a good thing. (2 Corinthians 7:10) For God will draw near to the brokenhearted (Psalm 51:17), and as in the case with Nehemiah, your brokenness can be a catalyst for healthy change!

Closer Challenge: Is there something in your life that is causing you great brokenness? **Today**, identify at least one thing. Now, are you broken enough about this issue to weep, pray, and fast? If so, start with fasting at least one of your meals today. During that time of fasting, spend quality time with God, exploring His Word so you can hear from Him concerning this matter. In privacy, pray specifically about this situation, and if necessary, let your brokenness move you to tears. God is close to those with contrite hearts. (Isaiah 57:15) Wait on God and rest in His ability to heal any crisis.

May 4

Removing Question Marks

―――――•―――――

2 Corinthians 6:3

Paul was very particular about the appearance of his character to both Christians and non-Christians. He knew one of the greatest ways to defend his preaching was by living His message clearly. Paul understood that if there was something in his life that would hinder someone from receiving Jesus or growing in faith, he would become a stumbling block to that individual. As a result, Paul viewed his life and ministry as a high calling to righteousness. In his witness, he removed any question of sin in his life.

We must do the same. We must be careful not to cross over to legalism. If our attitude is right and our heart is focused on lovingly leading people to Jesus, we live holy for the correct reasons. Paul was careful not to point to himself in self-righteous arrogance; his mission was always to point people to Jesus so they would receive salvation and follow Him wholeheartedly. Adopt this attitude and remove all doubt of sin in your life.

<u>Closer Challenge</u>: Are people skeptical of your claim of being a Christ-follower because your witness is weakened by a poor behavior? If so, work hard to remove that stumbling block. **Today**, identify one thing that might be considered a stumbling block to others. It could be something that seems insignificant. Yet, that one subtle thing may hinder someone's spiritual growth. Even worse, it could the beginning of a major setback in another's life or yours! Live with high character so others will not make poor decisions based on your actions. Remove any question of sin and encourage those who you encounter.

May 5

A Form of Godliness

---

2 Timothy 3:1-5

As we approach Jesus' return, the final days are described as being terrible, filled with confusion. False teachers will speak with loud, convincing voices; Christians will become less tolerated; and people will become lovers of themselves (along with the long list of other characteristics described in 2 Timothy 3:2-5). They will have a form of godliness (that is, they know the lingo and do some things consistent with the Holy Scriptures), but they will not have the Spirit of God within them because they've never truly received Jesus for salvation. They know just enough to be dangerous with their knowledge; but without acceptance of Jesus, they are void of His power and love.

You may know some individuals like this. They speak highly of God and may even go to church, but they are not genuine. It may be hard to accept, but Scripture teaches that we should avoid such people. (2 Timothy 3:5) These people seek to please the voice of the majority in the culture, not God. As a result, they fail to follow the Word of God with integrity. We should have *nothing* to do with them, because they claim Christ but really defame Him.

Closer Challenge: Have you been spending much time with someone who has an appearance of godliness but is really more loyal to the world? And in the process, are you overlooking someone who might be ripe for salvation? **Today**, decide to have nothing to do with fake Christ-followers who have knowledge of truth but continue to deny it. This may appear to be unloving, but trust God's Word. Don't necessarily unfriend that person, but shift your focus to those who are ready for change and will encourage you in your faith. Nothing is impossible for God, so always leave room for the defiant to change. But spend the bulk of your time investing in true seekers. By faith, release contact with imposters so they might feel ashamed and turn their *form of godliness* into real faith. (2 Thessalonians 3:14-15)

May 6

Shining Like Stars

Philippians 2:14-15

While in this spiritually dark world, our role is to shine like stars among the pagans. And in Paul's beautiful letter to the Philippians, he gives us a specific way that we should shine as a star, which is to do everything without complaining and arguing. Even though the world may operate in a grumbling manner, this is not the mode of living according to God. When we have a problem, we communicate, but we do it in such a way that brings glory to God and respect to other individuals.

What causes people to respond to conflict with arguing and complaining? They believe their *rights* have been violated, so they lash out in defense of a subjective point of view. But according to God, your rights belong to Jesus. You were bought at a price! (1 Corinthians 6:20) When you surrendered to Jesus, you also surrendered to His way, which is not burdensome. (1 John 5:2-3) Therefore, your life belongs to Him and your rights fall under His authority. Since God says you should do everything without arguing and complaining, that is how you are to react in all circumstances.

<u>Closer Challenge</u>: How do you respond to conflict? Do you react in complaining or arguing? **Today**, put your money where your mouth is. Each time you complain or argue, give a dollar to your local church. If you're financially stable, commit to a higher amount. As you do this simple practice, you're more likely to watch your words more carefully. And if you stumble, you'll provide a little extra for your church. As always, your spiritual growth is a work in progress, but never use the process as an excuse not to change. Complaining and arguing don't show people Christ; they show people the ways of evil. Be a bright star for Jesus by not complaining or arguing!

May 7

Open Up

Psalm 81:10

We *open up* our lives to many things. We open up to the thoughts and philosophies of the entertainment industry, including what's online. We open up to foods and other pleasures. We open up to people we love and even those we should avoid. We open up to sports or other kinds of hobbies or activities. But do we fully open up ourselves to the Lord? Do we lay out our lives completely exposed to the Lord and allow Him to fill us in ways that only He can? So many things attempt to fill our emptiness, but only God can fill us to the brim and make us completely satisfied. (Psalm 103:5)

God declares, "I am the Lord your God." (Psalm 81:10) There is NO other god who can fully satisfy you. Only God can supply *peace* when you face troubles, bring you *hope* in the midst of despair, and provide *salvation* for eternity. Those promises cannot be obtained by the things of this world. Yet many people endlessly search for those things and come up disappointed. Until we refrain from opening up to the world and completely open up to God, we cannot experience the peace He has waiting for us.

<u>Closer Challenge</u>: Are you fully open to the Lord, or just slightly? If you're not wide open to the Lord, what is in the world that you're relying on to fill your innate longing for Him? **Today**, determine what you use to fill the emptiness in your life. If it is not the Lord, you will never be satisfied. If you turn to substances, carnal pleasures, or any other worldly activity, you might gain temporary satisfaction, but only God can bring you eternal satisfaction through His Son, Jesus. Open up your soul to God today by turning to Him in prayer and Bible study. Be filled with Him and not the vices of this world.

May 8

Whose Side Are You On?

Jude 6

In God's great created universe, there are two forces: good and evil. Even though we cannot visually see the spiritual world, the forces of both can be felt. At one time, all heaven was in unison, praising the Creator. But as explained in Jude 6, rebellion took place from a seditious sect of the angels. As a result, their judgment awaits them in the end. But until then, their destructive influence will continue to confuse the weak and draw the undisciplined away from God.

Like a good movie, the story of God is the greatest chronicle of good and evil. In fact, all stories stem from God's story. And whether you like it or not, you're on one side or the other. You might be quick to confess that your allegiance is to good. But what do your actions say? If you embrace sin, you are influenced by evil and you're fighting for Satan's kingdom. But if you cling to righteousness, you are on God's team. Be very careful that you do not subtly change teams. A simple act of disobedience can make you a traitor to the faith you claim.

<u>Closer Challenge</u>: Who are you fighting for concerning spiritual matters? Do you fight for Satan or Jesus? Even the smallest degree of support for Satan gives him a foothold to promote his influence. Extinguish that action or thought immediately! **Today**, as you go throughout the day, watch carefully all your moves. Purposefully promote goodness. Find ways to score for Jesus today! Give to, love, or encourage someone out of the ordinary, even if you might have a hard time doing so. And refrain from promoting evil at all cost. Make it vivid whose side you are on.

May 9

Jesus Can

Mark 9:21-24

In this passage, the disciples came across a boy who was violently overtaken by an evil spirit. The disciples could not drive out this spirit and heal the boy because they had lacked praying in faith. (Mark 9:29) Knowing that Jesus had performed great miracles, the boy's father turned to Jesus, requesting that *if* He could do anything, please take pity on them and help. Jesus replied, "***IF*** I can?" For Jesus, the question should never begin with *if*, for He *can* help. But, the request should come in faith.

We often limit the power of Jesus. There are many times when we encounter a seemingly impossible situation, and like this father, we question whether or not Jesus can really come through. Yet, your attitude in a challenging situation should always assume that Jesus *can* help. Whatever He chooses to do in the situation is up to Him (Isaiah 55:8), but He definitely has the power. So come to Jesus in complete faith and wait upon Him to see what He will do.

Closer Challenge: Do you have an impossible situation you're responding to in doubt? If so, like this father, come to Jesus and ask Him to help you overcome your disbelief. (Mark 9:24) **Today**, in a seemingly dire situation that you're facing, turn to Jesus by *believing* in your heart that He CAN come through. He responds to faith, and if you don't possess it, you may miss out on an incredible miracle coming your way. Throughout the day, at least ten times exclaim, "Jesus can!" Create a perspective believing that Jesus can come through in any circumstance. Even if your desire isn't His will, miracles start from prayer in faith.

May 10

Who Do You Say Is Jesus?

———————•———————

Matthew 16:13-16

Many people have attempted to make Jesus who they want Him to be instead of who He really is. Some call Jesus a fake, a liar, the devil (Matthew 12:24), a blasphemer (Matthew 26:65), and many other offensive names. These are the same people who will not let Jesus reach into their lives and touch them with His wonderful mercy. And as they remain in their disbelief, they never experience full life with the Creator.

Yet there are some who view Jesus in a different light. Like Peter, this group of people acknowledge in faith that He is the Son of the living God. If you can confess this, then you have the marvelous King of Kings watching over you. There is something very special in a name. When you misspeak a name, you misrepresent who that person really is. Jesus is the Son of the Living God. He is the Christ, and He is the Savior! Never misuse Jesus' name, for it points directly to the very person He is.

<u>Closer Challenge</u>: Are you hesitant to speak the true name of Jesus? Can you say His name to anyone and not blush or think twice about it? **Today**, do not shy away from speaking the wonderful name of Jesus. When an opportunity arises to encourage someone, speak His name and tell of His wonderful works. The mere name of Jesus can bring great encouragement to those who are weary and in need of help. Just as you would speak the name of any close acquaintance and not think twice about it, declare Jesus today.

May 11

Do Not Let Your Hands Hang Limp

Zephaniah 3:15-17

When we fail, we often become discouraged. Discouragement can come from many different areas of life. A failed marriage. A failed attempt at a job. A failed ministry. A failed test. A failed relationship. A failed attempt to follow God morally. Discouragement will enter our lives from time to time, but we need to understand that it's not the end. There is much, much more to look forward to.

In these three beautiful verses, we find the encouragement needed to face every failure. Though Israel had deserved punishment for their collapse of obedience, God removed their judgment and pushed back their enemies. God could have stopped with the release of punishment and that would have been enough, but instead, He went further. He admonished Israel not to let their hands hang weak in discouragement. Instead, He urged them to **lift** their hands in praise because God was with them and loved them very much. As a mother sings over her precious children before bedtime, our God sings over us with love songs from heaven. No matter how badly you have disappointed God, you have a Father in heaven who rejoices over you with singing!

Closer Challenge: Have you failed God in the last several days or weeks? Are you still dealing with the pain of that failure? If so, pull away from that discouragement that is pinning you down. **Today**, open your heart and allow God's love to rejoice over you with singing. Next time you are in a corporate worship setting, like a flower receiving rain in full bloom, stretch out your arms in full worship to God. Allow His sweet mercy to flow over your life. Do not let your hands hang limp to your side when the King of Kings is focused on you. Receive His love and respond in worship!

May 12

Such a Time as This!

Esther 4:14

Esther is a prime example of how God can take an ordinary person and do extraordinary things. She was a young peasant Jewish girl living in captivity during the reign of Xerxes in Susa, Persia. Through various events, she rose to be the queen while keeping her Jewish identity silent. A decree was sent throughout the land to kill her Jewish people. But just at the right time as the decree was about to be sent out, she went before the king without being summoned, which was an unlawful act that could lead to death, even for her. Yet the king found mercy for his bride and asked for her request. At this, she revealed her true identity and pleaded for her people's lives. The king granted her request, and because of her great courage, she helped save the remnant of Jews left throughout the land.

Similar to Esther, you may be in a position to rescue someone in great need. In fact, you may be the *only* person who can do anything to help a situation. Have you recognized that God has placed you in your position for such a time as this? Possibly, you have the skills or resources to deliver people in need. You could be the one who can reach an individual for Christ due to a similar upbringing or some other life experience. Be like Esther, and use your position and experiences to continue God's work to glorify Him.

<u>Closer Challenge</u>: Have you taken the time to evaluate the position in which God has placed you? Who needs your help? **Today**, observe what God is doing around you. You could be the *one* to answer a specific call and make a great move for God's glory. The risk of consequence might be great, too (Esther 4:16), but if God has raised you for such a time as this, find the courage to move forward in obedience. Do not miss this opportunity to impact lives for Christ. In fact, this very thing might be the reason why you were born. What is God asking of you? Bring glory to God!

May 13

Speak Up!

Luke 18:35-41

Each of us has needs, but this comes with good news and bad news. The good news is that the Creator of the universe is bending His ear toward His children. The bad news is that more often than not, His children don't speak their concerns to their all-powerful Father. A blind man had heard Jesus was coming. So instead of swimming in a pool of self-pity, he called out to Jesus for help. Jesus did not respond to him at first, and the people around him rebuked him for speaking. But then, instead of giving up, he shouted even louder! Due to his courage to shout even louder, Jesus stopped and spoke with the man.

Unlike this blind roadside beggar, many of us do not speak up when there is a need. Instead, we attempt to handle our needs in our own strength, or we simply believe there is no hope. You do not have to live this way. Jesus desires for you to commune with Him in conversation. Like the blind beggar, maybe it is time you shouted out loud to Jesus for Him to hear you and respond accordingly.

Closer Challenge: Do you have a specific need? Have you spoken to Jesus concerning this need? Maybe like the blind beggar, you've called out to Jesus, but He has not responded. **Today**, be determined to make your voice heard by the Lord. In the privacy of your home (or publicly, if you choose), audibly voice your request to Jesus. If you must, literally, *shout* to Him for help. It may seem silly to do this, but try it. You might discover this to be very liberating as you turn to heaven in dependence. Spend some quality time speaking out loud to Jesus as though He were physically in the room with you. Do your part to make your request known and allow Him to do His part. In the process, you'll find yourself communing with God.

May 14

Accepted by Jesus

John 8:3-11

The effects of personal sin can create excessive discouragement. Whether you have a past sin haunting you or a present sin distracting you from God's best, the pains of guilt can be quite overwhelming. This can tempt you to believe that even God couldn't love and accept you. Yet, this is far from the truth, for Jesus extends His love to every sinner no matter what the crime!

A woman was caught red-handed in the act of adultery. Possibly naked, she was taken out into the city streets by the religious leaders to be humiliated and stoned according to the Mosaic Law. (Leviticus 20:10) Then, they asked what Jesus would do. Calmly, Jesus knelt to the ground and wrote something in the sand. (Maybe in her sight, He wrote, "Watch this!") When He stood up, He said, "Let him who is without sin among you be the first to throw a stone at her." (John 8:7) Again, He knelt down and wrote something else in the sand. (Maybe this time He etched, "Busted!"). Slowly but surely, these proud men dropped their stones and walked away. Then, Jesus turned to this woman and pointed out that her accusers were gone and so were her sins. In that moment, guilty as can be, she experienced acceptance and love from the Savior!

Closer Challenge: Are you feeling the guilt from a past or present sin? If so, **today**, read this passage over and over again until you realize the depth of Jesus' acceptance. No matter what you have done, He looks you in the eyes and forgives you. However, like this woman, He will call you to leave your life of sin. Ask a close friend to help support you and keep you accountable as you turn away from this sin. Don't be discouraged, for you have received compassion from our loving Savior! Jesus accepts you!

May 15

The King's Table

Revelation 3:20

Many well-intentioned Christ-followers use this passage as a tool to share with unbelievers. But in reality, Jesus is speaking to the *church*. Jesus is knocking on the door of His church because they had become self-sufficient, shutting the door on Him. (Revelation 3:17) They had neglected to grow their relationship with Jesus. So, Jesus says to them that He stands at the door and knocks, and if anyone hears His voice and opens the door, He'll come in and *eat* with them. Even though His bride, the church, pushed Him aside, Jesus gave them another chance. This is an invitation for them to sit and dine with Him at a table and strengthen their relationship together.

Throughout the Bible, the table is a symbol of high honor, which includes love, care, and fellowship. Sitting at the table is a sign of relationship. If you fail to share life with those you love, you'll drift further apart. Likewise, if you want to tighten your relationship with Jesus, you must daily sit at the table and commune with Him.

<u>Closer Challenge</u>: Do you steadily sit and commune with Jesus? If you're daily staying in God's Word through this devotional, you're on the right track. But this devotional can only bring you so close. **Today,** if you want to draw nearer, possibly start reading through the Bible or begin reading a book that will deepen your walk with Jesus. Maybe launch or join an existing Bible study. Maybe begin or join an existing prayer group. Devote time to sit with your Savior who loves you! Take a seat at a table for two with Jesus and talk with your Friend. (John 15:15)

May 16

The Valley of Eschol

Numbers 13:17-14:9

In this passage, Moses had led the Israelites to the edge of the Promised Land. Before they would enter, he sent twelve spies to survey the land. When the men returned, they found it to be full of rich blessings just as the Lord described. But ten of the spies returned with anguish, for they feared those living in the land. Their terror struck fear in the rest of the nation. But two of the spies, Joshua and Caleb, stood with courage and reminded Israel that God was with them. Their brave influence wouldn't prevail until years later after Moses' death; but eventually, Joshua and Caleb led Israel toward a new beginning by overtaking the land of Canaan for God's glory.

We all have our opportunities to enter the Valley of Eschol. (Numbers 13:23-24) Like Israel debating whether or not they should face their fears and take on this new adventure, you also face decisions that involve risk. When confronted with a new opportunity, you have to decide if you will step out in faith or return to your same life. If God is leading, move forward in spite of any fear. For when you step out in faith after God speaks, you will grow your faith and experience God in a fresh way.

<u>Closer Challenge</u>: Do you sense God urging you in a new direction? But after assessing the opportunity, are you filled with fear? **Today**, IF God is calling, start moving forward in faith. Rarely will you experience great success in life without the element of risk and faith. Be wise in all that you do. Survey what needs to be done to take this leap of faith, but do not shrink back because of the obstacles. For when God calls, He completes His end of the promise. You simply need to obey. Determine your Valley of Eschol and march forward in faith!

May 17

The Valley of Dry Bones

---•---

Ezekiel 37:1-14

When Israel was cast into Babylonian captivity, God illustrated for them their national condition. Figuratively, Israel was a valley of dry bones. They were dead as a nation. There seemed to be no hope for them. But God called Ezekiel, one of God's prophets, to preach His Word to these dry bones. So Ezekiel obeyed, and to his amazement, the bones rattled to life again. Even though the nation of Israel was dead, they were brought back to life through the power of God's Word!

Symbolically, you might feel as though you are *spiritually* in the valley of dry bones. If you find yourself in a rut of spiritual dryness, you need to hear a fresh Word preached to you to bring you back to life. (Ezekiel 37:4) God has ordained many godly individuals to stand before you and expose the treasure of God's Word, but you have to make time to hear it. For when you hear the spoken Word, you will find pools of fresh water that will awaken your soul. Don't delay in positioning yourself to heed His powerful Word.

<u>Closer Challenge</u>: Are you spiritually dry? Do you need a fresh Word from God? **Today**, outside of your weekly visit to hear your pastor preach, listen to a sermon of choice that will awaken your soul. This could be a past sermon from your pastor or a strong *biblical* preacher on the Internet or television. (Ask your pastor for guidance.) Be faithful not to neglect the preaching of God's Word. For it can bring life to a dried up soul.

May 18

The Valley of Achor

Joshua 7:1-26

In one of the more recognized valleys of the Bible, we're reminded that one man's sin can have a negative effect on an entire community of believers. Achan was a brave soldier, who fought for his nation well. But after Israel defeated Jericho, he rebelled against strict orders. He took some of the plunder for himself. (Joshua 7:1) His sin tainted the entire house of Israel, and as a result, God refused to fight for them. Without the Lord's presence, they lost their next battle with the much smaller city of Ai. When the leaders determined it was Achan who had sinned and caused their defeat, his consequence resulted in his death and those of this family too.

A clear take away from this tragic story is the cold hard fact that sin is serious to God. Achan's one sin was so serious that it caused many deaths on the battlefield, and it even resulted in the death of his family. (Joshua 7:25) Though we may not face the immediate consequences of our sin like Achan did, our sin will be judged. (2 Corinthians 5:10) In fact, sin is so serious that God the Father had to send His blameless Son to die in our place. Next time you are tempted to sin, hopefully you will weigh the consequences so you won't hurt yourself and others.

Closer Challenge: Do you consider the seriousness of sin before each questionable action you take? It's probable you will be tempted to sin today. So **today**, each time you are tempted to sin, pause for a moment and think of both the immediate and long-term consequences you will face if you execute that thought or action. From a casual hurtful word to a blatant wrongful course of action, think before you do anything. If you can get in a *habit* of measuring the effects of sin, you will increase your strength to refrain from practicing it. After you deny that sin, immediately replace it with something godly and experience the presence and power of God flowing through you!

May 19

The Valley of Baca

---•---

Psalm 84:5-6

Jesus warned us that in this life we'll have trouble. (John 16:33) Sorrows are an unavoidable part of life. There will be times where you'll find yourself directly in the middle of the Valley of Baca, the valley of sorrows. It's a place of testing. It's a place where hard lessons must be learned. It's a destination you never choose to visit, but while you are there, it's important you seek what God is teaching you.

The Sons of Korah, who faced much sorrow themselves when their clan was swallowed by the earth (Numbers 16:31-33; 26:10-11), understood some important realities about the valley of sorrow. First, they knew it wasn't *if* you pass through the valley, but *as* you pass through the valley. Everyone will have sorrows; it's just a matter of *when*. However, secondly, this valley is not a final destination. You will pass *through* the valley of sorrows. Sorrows will stay behind you as healing takes place. Finally, the dry, lifeless valley of sorrows can transform into refreshing *springs* and deep *pools* of blessings. Though it isn't a path you'd probably choose, your sorrow can glorify God and bring you great meaning in life.

Closer Challenge: Are you in the Valley of Baca? Are you confronted with great sorrow? **Today**, adopt the perspective of the Sons of Korah. Believe you will pass *through* your sorrow and refreshing springs will burst forth! Kneel down before God today and claim the words of Psalm 71:20 as your prayer. Say several times right now, "You who have made me see many troubles and calamities *will revive* me again; from the depths of the earth you will bring me up again." You will pass through this valley. Don't build camp there. Open your eyes to how God is drawing you closer to Him.

May 20

The Kidron Valley

Matthew 26:14-16, John 18:1-2

One of the gloomiest stories in the Bible leads us down the trail of betrayal. Jesus had spent over three years pouring into the lives of His twelve close friends. He taught them, prayed with them, rebuked them, cried with them, and He probably laughed with them from time to time. He had a deep bond with the twelve He called friends. (John 15:15) But in His final days, He experienced something very painful. One of Jesus' twelve companions, Judas Iscariot, betrayed His friendship for a measly thirty silver coins. As a result, Judas turned Jesus over to soldiers to be killed.

It's natural in the flesh to point a finger of judgment at Judas and scream, "You traitor!" But be honest with yourself. Have you betrayed Jesus? Have you sinned when you knew better? Have you not spoken up for Jesus when you should have? Can you see traces of Judas in you? If we're not careful, we can head down a trail of betrayal similar to Judas. Be firm to stand your ground and not to turn your back on Jesus when an opportunity arises. Be self-controlled to steer away from another Kidron Valley betrayal.

Closer Challenge: Even in the slightest sense, have you become a traitor to the One you call King? You might be quick to condemn others when they fail Jesus, but what about when you fail? Examine your life to determine if you're having or recently had a Kidron Valley experience like Judas. Sure, Jesus is not here in the flesh, but you can betray Him just as violently in the spirit. **Today**, if you have betrayed Jesus, fall to your knees and turn from your waywardness. Be grateful that even though you've betrayed Him, His mercy is greater than our sin! (Romans 5:20) Going forward, hold firm to the One you love.

May 21

The Valley of Aijalon

Joshua 10:1-10

Israel had established a peace treaty with Gibeon. But five other kings in Gibeon's region didn't respond well to their peace with Israel. So, these five Amorite kings and their armies attacked Gibeon. Gibeon sent word to Israel for help. Israel was outnumbered, but they knew that God was never out-manned. So in faith, they came to Gibeon's rescue. And in a display of God's power, several miracles occurred. God threw the enemy armies into confusion; He cast hailstones down upon them; and He caused the sun and the moon to stand still so Israel could gain victory. These mighty miracles occurred because Israel trusted God to deliver in spite of the poor odds to gain the victory.

There will be times when you realize you need a miracle. And when you face a challenge with insurmountable odds, never doubt God's ability to overcome. God can deliver! It's never a question of His ability; it's a question of His will. And since you can't always see God's plan unfolding, your role is to ask Him for help, persevere through the trial, and trust He can deliver as He chooses. The need for a miracle will arise in your life; and when it does, lean upon His understanding and power!

Closer Challenge: Are you in need of a miracle? If so, have you turned to God? **Today**, cry out to God for a miracle! If you do not need one, then it's quite possible you know someone who does. Intercede for that person's situation. In the process, remember that Israel received the miracle as they were doing all they could to win the battle. (Joshua 10:10) They *pursued* their enemy and took action by doing their part. If you need a miracle, trust God, but also do all you can to help the situation. When you do, a miracle could be coming your way soon.

May 22

The Valley of the Shadow of Death

―――――•―――――

Psalm 23:4

Whether we like it or not, death is unavoidable. Not just personally, but we will also face the deep pain of losing loved ones. Yet, as we trust God, there is nothing to fear. Psalm 23:4 paints a beautiful picture for us to dwell upon as we face death. The valley of the shadow of death can refer to shepherds leading their sheep through dark ravines created by steep cliffs where no sunlight could creep in. The shepherd would have to guide his sheep through these frightening valleys. Danger lurked everywhere, but there was no need to fear, because the shepherd was there to protect the helpless sheep with his staff and constant presence.

When you approach death or experience death through the tragedy of losing someone close to you, you have no reason to fear. Though the pain of loss is real, if the Lord is your Shepherd, He will walk hand-in-hand with you. Rest in the fact that your caring, ever-present Shepherd is near to guide and protect you through this dark and difficult valley in life. (Hebrews 13:5-6) Since death is a certainty and you gain nothing by going through it without Him, turn to the Shepherd and let His tender mercy calm your fear and ease your pain.

<u>Closer Challenge</u>: Have you recently faced the death of a loved one? Does the death strike fear in your mind? **Today**, focus your attention upon the caring Shepherd. Our Lord does not want us to fear death because He has conquered it with His own death! Use a Bible app, concordance or some other online Bible tool to conduct a study on the word *protect*. As you'll discover, the world has nothing in it to fear, for the Lord is our Great Protector, even in the face of death!

May 23

The Valley of Jericho

Deuteronomy 34:1-4

Have you ever had something wonderful in your grasp, only to let it slip away? At that moment, the feeling of failure may have led to a great amount of disappointment. When you experience this, know that you are not alone. At the end of Moses' life, he faced devastating failure. As he stood atop Mount Nebo, looking over the Valley of Jericho, thinking he was about to lead his people into the Promised Land, God delivered a demoralizing blow. Due to Moses' sin (Numbers 20:8-12) and Israel's constant complaining, Moses and his generation would not enter the Promised Land. How painful! After all the toil to make it from Egypt, they were denied access to complete what they started. Moses saw the land, but could not possess it.

All people have stumbled into the valley of failure. And if you claim you have not, then you will someday. The important thing to remember is that your failure does not forfeit your future. Sure, your course may change, but since you still have life, you can bring glory to God! Use your failures as valuable experiences to launch you into new adventures.

Closer Challenge: Have you been crushed by life's failures? If so, **today**, change your perspective. Lean on God's grace to give you a restart. Tell a close friend of a failure you've experienced, and discuss ways in which that failure could launch you in a new adventure to glorify God. Pray together and take action. Watch your life blossom into something special in spite of your past. Listen to God and go in faith.

May 24

Valley of Mizpah

Joshua 11:7-15

Most people are not remembered as much for how they started as they are for how they finished. After the death of Moses, Joshua took the reins of leadership over Israel. He was the chosen man to lead them through the Promised Land and attain it for God's glory. After several great victories, he came to the final battle against all the remaining kings and their armies. Together, these kings formed a massive military force. It was decision time. Would Joshua stop the mission and be satisfied with what they accomplished, or would he finish the mission and battle against this impressive army? Joshua confidently chose to finish the task with courage!

Many of us have noble plans and even start tasks with great ambition. But only the courageous and determined ones will finish with the confidence they had at the beginning and complete the task. Obedience to the end and a drive to finish strong will separate Christ-followers to receive greater rewards in heaven. Each of us has been given a God-ordained mission in life. It is up to you if you will discover your mission and finish strong.

Closer Challenge: Have you started a task but find yourself slipping away from completing the goal? ***Today***, pinpoint your current mission or project for the Lord. Now, find ways to revive your calling by injecting a renewed commitment into it. Explore new ways to stimulate it. Whatever you feel called to do for the Lord, finish strong. Trust in the Lord that if He started this work with you, He will complete it. Like Joshua, accomplish the mission God started with you!

May 25

Reflecting His Ever-Increasing Glory

2 Corinthians 3:18

The Bible teaches that God is glorious. (Psalm 102:15) Nothing in the universe can compare to the splendor of His greatness. God is all-knowing, all-powerful, ever-present, abounding in love, perfect in justice, and rich in mercy. No created being can come close to His brilliance and perfection. Yet, even in man's known inadequacies, our temptation is to exalt self over God. How foolish! Our role is not to absorb glory for personal fame, but to reflect His glory and make Him known for what He has done!

Those who choose to exalt self will find emptiness because there are limits to human greatness. In fact, our capabilities are rather small. But there are no limits to the glory of our Lord. Reflecting God's glory is the key to spiritual growth and significance. If you are not reflecting, you will become trapped in the prison of self that leads to meaninglessness. But as you reflect God's glory, you will find a never-ending fountain of purpose, both in this life and the life to come. Furthermore, you will gradually be transformed into His likeness forever and ever!

Closer Challenge: Are you seeking personal glory? Do you take credit, seek attention, and shun God during successes and blame God when things don't go your way? If so, you are self-absorbed. **Today**, as the moon reflects the light of the sun, do your best to reflect the Son. If someone needs a kind word, send an uplifting message in a way that excludes personal recognition. If someone needs a kind act, serve anonymously so that all attention is directed to God. In every way possible, reflect God so He will receive the fame He deserves, and in the process, you'll be transformed into His likeness!

May 26

Glory Exchanged

———————⁂———————

Jeremiah 2:11-12

God is adamant that His people do not exchange their precious relationship with Him for anything less. But Israel had consistently done just that. Even though they had experienced great wonders and unconditional love from God, they repeatedly turned their backs on Him by adoring gods of no eternal value. They exchanged the glory for something incomparably less. And due to their transgressions, they faced the consequences of their actions. They were flushed out of the land God set before them and sent into captivity under foreign leadership.

Worthless idols surround us all. Money, sex, narcotics, material possessions, and many other things of this world seek to capture our affection. Everywhere you turn, there is the temptation to reach for something of no value, and worship it. And if you do, you exchange the glory for something worthless. It sounds inconceivable that you would serve something insignificant and empty, but that's what happens if you replace God with anything else.

<u>Closer Challenge</u>: Have you exchanged the glory for anything in this world? The way you spend your time and resources will help you determine if you have replaced the glory for something less. **Today**, write down a detailed list in your journal of the way you spend your time, money, affection, and strength. Ask yourself these questions (be honest): Am I devoted to the Lord with my time, money, affections, and strength? Is there something I place as greater value than God? If so, like going to the store with a defective product, exchange it for the greatest God of all. May the *glory* be reflected in all you say and do!

May 27

Hanging on a Word

―――――•―――――

Luke 19:47-48

Scripture teaches that Jesus taught *daily* in the Temple courts, and people listened to His every word. Having an opportunity to hear the Savior of the world each day was priceless to those who followed Him. His words are like spiritual gold. They are precious jewels for the heart and fine treasures for the soul. Even when the religious leaders looked for a way to kill Jesus, they feared uproar because His followers hung on every word He spoke!

You can fill your heart and mind with foolish words of the world; but when you do, you will miss out on the precious, soothing comfort and correction of Jesus' words. It would be enough to experience His marvelous miracles, but to add His amazing teachings that baffle even the wisest of all is priceless. His miracles help physically, but His words bring hope to the hopeless, peace to the anxious, and salvation to all who call upon Him. Hang on His words for they bring sweet tranquility to your life.

<u>Closer Challenge</u>: Are you anxious about anything? Is your soul lacking rest? **Today**, go on a treasure hunt. Read through several passages of Jesus' teachings in the gospels. Do a word study on what He says about trust, faith, hope, or love. Whatever you need, look for that idea in Scripture and hear God speak to you. If your Bible has red letters, be drawn to those words. Allow His soothing words to calm your spirit and renew your mind. Like the disciples of the past, hang on every word Jesus speaks.

May 28

Finding Peace

Psalm 131

Peace can be a slippery virtue to grasp. Just when you think you have it, something circumstantial can enter your life and attempt to rob it from you. Though circumstances can't always be changed, you can keep internal peace. In this short Psalm, David provides the secret to maintaining peace. Peace comes with embracing a set of *attitudes*. Drop your pride (Psalm 131:1), release your concern for uncontrollable matters (Psalm 131:1), and place your hope in the Lord. (Psalm 131:3) If you can embrace these attitudes, you will find God is more than enough to bring you the peace you desperately desire.

David describes peace like a weaned child near his mother, receiving protection and love. (Psalm 131:2) As a child, you believe your parents can protect you from anything, so your trust in them is great. As we mature, our need for earthly parental protection decreases. Yet with our Heavenly Father, we should never outgrow His everlasting arms of protection and love. In His arms, you will find peace for your soul in the midst of any uncertainty.

Closer Challenge: Has the world attempted to steal your peace? Do you fully know the peace of the Father? **Today**, change your attitude to receive peace. If you're stressed from a relationship due to your pride, choose to drop it by humbly lowering yourself to resolve the situation. If you're concerned with things uncontrollable, simply trust in God to intervene. If you're placing your hope in anything other than God, release that false hope and rest in Him alone. Speak to a Christian friend about what you need to do to restore peace in your life. Like a child, curl up in your Savior's arms and find the peace you desperately need.

May 29

The Self-Esteem Cycle

Isaiah 66:2; Proverbs 22:1

Self-esteem has become a buzz word in the 20th and 21st centuries to describe people's need for self-approval. But *self*-esteem is not a word used in the Holy Scriptures. Self-esteem develops from how you view or praise yourself. Often, it grows or diminishes by the way *others* perceive you. However, when you depend on others' perception of you, you become a vacuum, seeking to consume acceptance. And when the acceptance is not there, you feel defeated, depressed, and your confidence shrinks because your confidence is not in the Lord but in how others perceive you. (Proverbs 29:25)

Your focus should not be on how you or others view you, but on pleasing your God who esteems you as you honor Him. (Isaiah 66:2) When you please God, you will not have to work on *self*-esteem, for you will receive *God*-esteem, which is much more valuable! Since our culture has lost its touch with God, self-esteem makes sense to them because it places people at the center of the universe. But if you have God as the top priority, He is in the center and you seek to gain His esteem and praise over anything else! (John 5:44)

Closer Challenge: Are you often looking to others for acceptance? **Today**, change your mindset. As you go throughout the day, look to find confidence from the Lord, not others. There is not enough time in this devotional entry to adequately address this topic. So, if you need extra reading about *self*-esteem (or as Edward T. Welch says, *the fear of man*), read Welch's book, **When People Are Big and God is Small**. It could biblically revolutionize your thinking concerning the Americanized concept of self-esteem. Remember, if you are a child of God, you have been accepted by the King and His esteem is more important than man's! (Galatians 1:10)

May 30

The Reach of God's Arm

Numbers 11:23

Israel complained about the manna because they wanted to eat meat. (Numbers 11:6) So God responded by telling Moses He would supply so much meat that they would loathe it. (Numbers 11:18-20) Then, Moses questioned whether or not God could provide enough meat for 600,000 men for a whole month. (Numbers 11:21-22) And God replied with a simple question, one that also pertains to us when we doubt His ability. God simply asked, "Is the Lord's hand shortened?"

There are times when you might doubt whether or not God has the *ability* to do something humanly impossible. As Moses did, you might respond to God with reservation that He could actually provide for a massive need. But you must not forget that with His outstretched arm, He created the earth and all that lives in it! (Jeremiah 27:5) Nothing is impossible for God! His arm can reach into your dire situation and turn things around in a flash. With the command of His voice, He can take any worrisome circumstance and turn it into awe. (Deuteronomy. 4:34) No, the Lord's arm is not too short; our faith is often too shallow.

Closer Challenge: Have you doubted God lately? Do you disbelieve that God could actually reach into your life and change things for the good? **Today**, if you have doubted God in any capacity, exchange it with faith. With a heart of trust, write down in your journal a situation where you have doubt. Explain to God your true feelings, and then in faith, boldly proclaim that God's arm is not too short. His reach is limitless, so walk in expectation throughout the day that God will provide. Whether He will answer your request or not, it's never a question of ability.

May 31

Setting Yourself Apart

Numbers 6:2

There are times in your life when you may need to commit a selected amount of time to strictly focus on the Lord. In the Old Testament, a Nazirite would make a vow of holiness by setting apart a period of time for Him. It was not meant to be a never-ending lifestyle; but for a season of life, a Nazirite would consecrate himself to the Lord. (Numbers 6:8) He did this by abstaining from unhealthy foods (Numbers 6:3-4), refraining from an unwholesome appearance (Numbers 6:5), and staying away from unholy associations. (Numbers 6:6-7) Once the time of separation was over, he would make a thank offering to the Lord. (Numbers 6:13-14)

Living in the New Testament era, the particulars of a Nazirite's vow may not be necessary, but the exercise of setting yourself apart to the Lord for a period of time is a healthy one. Deliberate consecration to the Lord can help cleanse you spiritually and set your mind wholly on His desires. So, from time to time, set apart a special season of time to the Lord so you can keep your mind in focus and your heart fully devoted to Him.

<u>Closer Challenge</u>: Do you need to consecrate yourself to the Lord to hear from Him more clearly? **Today**, take a vow similar to that of the Nazirite. Determine what you can abstain from for a period of time to focus more attention on the Lord. It could be television, a certain food, an association, a behavior, etc. After that period of time is over (the amount of time is up to you), present an offering of thanks to the Lord. You could sing with or listen to a worship song. However you decide to conclude this season of time, make the focus communing with your Father.

June 1

Money Issues: Accounting

Proverbs 27:23-24

It's likely that you don't own flocks and herds, but the principle from these verses can be applied to all resources you have been entrusted with by the Lord. Accounting is nothing more than keeping track of where your possessions and finances are. It is making sure you are not cheated when you spend money, and understanding if you have enough for the next expense. Accounting is important, because as God's Word teaches in these verses, if you are not keeping up with your finances, it will fly away fast!

With the resources you have, you must be wise to keep track of them. After all, keep in mind that the earth is the Lord's and everything in it. (Psalm 24:1) You are a *manager* of God's riches. You *own* nothing. So it's vital that you manage God's wealth well. How money is administrated in your life will show a true sign of your commitment to Jesus. Therefore, watch carefully where your money goes so you will be deemed faithful.

<u>Closer Challenge</u>: Are you keeping good record of your resources? If not, **today**, find a biblical approach of accounting where you can record all your financial gains and spending. Great tools are at your fingertips. Research well and commit to a method that honors God. If you don't take initiative on this matter, you'll slip into mismanaging God's resources. As you show you are trustworthy and faithful with little, you can be entrusted with much more. (Luke 16:10)

June 2

Money Issues: Tithing

Malachi 3:8-10; Proverbs 3:9-10

The Old Testament principle of tithing can be experienced as one of the greatest blessings. Everything on the earth is the Lord's, including everything you've earned, and even yourself! (Psalm 24:1) So when you refuse to give back to God the small portion He requests, you are seen as a thief. (Malachi 3:8) This small portion is called a tithe or a tenth of your earnings. The tenth is supposed to be returned to God's storehouse for ministry purposes. The blessing comes in knowing that when you give your tithe, you will see ministry accomplished through your efforts, and the floodgates of heaven will open wide to take care of you and His work!

It was understood in Old Testament times that saints would return to God the firstfruits of their labor (Proverbs 3:9-10). The firstfruits were considered the best portion of their crop. It was the ripest and best of what they grew, not leftovers. They would return it to the storehouse to provide for ministry, in part for the priests to be able to live. (Numbers 18:12-13) When you rob God of His tithe, you hinder ministry in your local faith circle, and ultimately, you will rob yourself of greater future blessings. And though the tithe is not extensively addressed in the New Testament, Jesus deemed tithing as a noble act not to neglect. (Matthew 23:23) As a result, it remains a healthy standard for cheerfully giving back to God.

Closer Challenge: Do you tithe to your local church? The application is quite simple to understand here. ***Today***, determine your earnings for each paycheck. Now, simply take at least 10 percent of that and give it routinely to your local church. Trust that God will use that money for the furthering of His kingdom. Remember, the tithe is not a membership fee to a club. The church does not *owe* you anything. The tithe belongs to God; you're simply to manage it. And finally, in regard to finding motivation to tithe, do it out of an overflow of love because of the salvation Jesus brought you through His death! What could you possibly give to equal that?

June 3

Money Issues: Budgeting

Luke 14:28-30; Romans 13:8

Jesus tells a simple parable about a wise builder. A builder must first evaluate his finances before he takes the initiative to begin building. If he starts and cannot complete it because he did not have enough resources, he will be considered a fool in the eyes of others. Consequently, it can be concluded that this man did not budget his finances well.

In a world where debt is constantly holding people captive financially, the need for budgeting is at an all-time high. A secret of the affluent is to live well below their means, but many people refuse to do this. Instead, they charge credit cards and request higher loans than they can afford. Impulse buying has driven people into suffering. The Bible is clear that debt is not advised. (Romans 13:8; Proverbs 22:7) One of the primary ways to steer clear from debt is creating a firm budget with the resources you have. Receive the Word of the Lord and *think* before you spend.

<u>Close Challenge</u>: Do you have a plan for spending the money you have been entrusted with, or do you merely spend at will? **Today**, examine how you spend. First, determine how much you earn. Then, break down your necessary spending into different line items. (Make sure you include your tithe.) Avoid debt at all costs; but if you already have outstanding debt, do your best to rid those debts quickly. Ridding debt will mean you must refrain from *unnecessary* spending. Stick to a manageable, planned budget and your finances will not fly away.

June 4

Money Issues: Saving

Proverbs 21:20; 13:22

It is a common belief that we all want to be deemed as wise. In Proverbs 21:20, a wise person is one who appropriately stores resources for a later use. Yet a foolish person is one who has not considered the future and the needs it will entail. This foolish person will take his earnings and waste them in a short amount of time, thus crippling him and his family when special future needs arise. But the wise will practice saving.

Many may argue that saving resources is unnecessary because Jesus may return to take His redeemed home at any moment. That is possible, but it does not take away the responsibility to be prepared for the future. In fact, Scripture gives us motivation for why we should save. Proverbs 13:22 states that a good man will leave an inheritance for his grandchildren. This takes both a plan and the discipline to save a portion of your finances for later use. However, you cannot go to the other extreme and hoard money. (Proverbs 11:26) So, adopt a healthy balance between saving, spending and giving.

<u>Closer Challenge</u>: Have you adopted a savings plan with your finances? If so, wonderful! Stick to your plan! But if you do not have a plan, start with your next paycheck. **Today**, determine an amount you can store. It is understandable if you must start small and grow the amount over time; but the main issue is to consider the future. As you save, carefully determine how you can invest it and make it grow over time. (Matthew 25:27) Be wise with what you have been entrusted with, and you will honor God.

June 5

Money Issues: Contentment

1 Timothy 6:6-10

Money, including all resources, has been given by God for our good. Yet, when we become a lover of money instead of a lover of God, destruction is around the corner. Paul reminds young Timothy (and us) that many people who once loved Jesus have sold their souls to grief because they were not content. (1 Timothy 6:10) And on the road to grief, they wandered from the faith. The love of money leads to greed, greed leads to a lack of contentment, and a lack of contentment leads to ruin.

Paul states that if you have food and clothing, you should be content. (1 Timothy 6:8) Yet, because we are inundated by the love of money in our culture, we are daily tempted to want more. Your neighbor may purchase something new, and the temptation to covet arises. The primary way to fight covetousness is to practice contentment. Rejoice in the many blessings you currently have instead of being sour over the things you don't.

<u>Closer Challenge</u>: Are you in a race to keep up with the person next door? Is there a root of sin leaning toward the love of money? **Today**, begin to dig up that root. The only way to practice contentment is to change your mindset. Make a list of the things that bring you joy. When you examine this list, you will find you are very blessed! Your list will most likely go well beyond the food and clothing Paul speaks of. Be grateful and begin to focus on what you can *give*, not receive! When you think about giving, you will better learn contentment.

June 6

Dealing with Disputes

Matthew 5:21-22

Jesus often encouraged His followers to be above reproach. It was understood in the Old Testament that God-fearers should not murder. (Exodus 20:13) If they did, they would be subject to judgment. Yet Jesus raised the standard by saying if you're even *angry* at your brother, you will be subject to judgment. He simplified the sin to a thought, for it is the thought that leads to the sin action of murder.

Each of us has been angry at someone. In fact, there's a good chance you're angry at someone right now! According to Scripture, you are subject to judgment. Yes, your one small, sinful thought warrants punishment. Since God's standard for heaven is perfection, you deserve the wretched flames of hell. (Matthew 5:22) What a horrible predicament! However, due to the willing sacrifice of Jesus to bear upon Himself all the sins of the world, He became the substitute for your punishment. Hallelujah! And with this overflow of joy, steer away from anger so you don't abuse the mercy He freely gives.

Closer Challenge: Do you have an angry thought against someone? Have you clearly understood the ramifications of that one small, heated thought? **Today**, carefully determine if anger is stirring in you. If so, release it by thinking of what Jesus has done for you. (Colossians 3:13) He died for both the sin of your offender and the sin of your anger. Allow the peace of Jesus to reside over you, not the bitterness from disappointment. As you release your anger and your offender, you'll be able to rightly worship and commune with Jesus. (Matthew 5:23-24)

June 7

Reflecting Jesus at Home

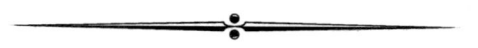

―――――•―――――

Mark 5:19-20

Being godly at home can be the most difficult place to practice your faith, because it's where you're often tempted to let your guard down. At times we are politer to strangers than we are to our own blood-related family. What a shame! When Jesus healed a demon-possessed man, the man wanted to go along with Jesus and His disciples. But in a strange response, Jesus did not allow him. Instead, He encouraged the man to return *home* and share with his family the great mercy that Jesus had granted him and extend it to those close to him. The man was to be a living testimony in his home and community concerning the love and power of Jesus.

Most Christ-followers will not become foreign missionaries or full-time ministers of the gospel as a paid occupation. The vast majority of Christians are to follow Jesus like the redeemed man in this story, being a living testimony of Jesus' grace in and near home. It's very likely that God is calling you to be like this man, which is to passionately see *your* home and community as your mission field in spreading the character and love of Jesus. Your familiar setting (home, occupation, marketplace, etc.) is your first calling. As a result, strive to be a witness for Jesus where you are right now!

<u>Closer Challenge</u>: Do you see a pattern in your life of letting your guard down at home? Do you often slip in your character toward those who you know well? **Today**, reverse that mindset. To those who you are closest to, do your best to display integrity, holiness, genuine care, and trust. In your home and to those who you consider close friends, do something today surprisingly nice to them. Watch your words and cherish your loved ones as Jesus loved His disciples. Go home and show Jesus' character to the people closest to you.

June 8

Making Music to the Lord

Psalm 108:1-3

Music has a way of stirring us emotionally, and it especially touches the heart of God when it's directed to Him. No matter what style you prefer, when your music is offered to Him, it's special to His ears. Throughout the life of David, he presents music to the Lord as he plays his harp and lyre. Singing and making music to God was something he cherished. It was a way in which David could express his gratitude and give praise to God.

Though you can worship God through service, prayer, Bible study and many other methods, music is often paired with worship. Because when you sing and make music to the Lord, you express adoration and devotion in intimate ways. Worship songs induce heartfelt affection toward your Creator and Master. As a result, continually be in the habit of making music to the Lord so you can share your love with God.

Closer Challenge: Have you recently made music to the Lord? **Today**, set aside some time when you can worship God with music. If you can play a musical instrument and sing, spend some quality time making music to the Lord in that manner. If you cannot play a musical instrument, simply find some recorded praise music and sing along with it. Sing alone in your car or in the privacy of your home. Whether you sing well or not, it doesn't matter. Most importantly, listen to the words you are singing and direct them to the Lord you love. God is your audience, and He awaits your worship! Commune with your Father through music.

June 9

Viewing Life Like the Ostrich

Job 39:13-18

All creation has received the unique creative touch of God. Each animal, each plant, each snowflake, and each person has been distinctly crafted by the hand of God…even an ostrich. As we read from the mouth of God in this passage, the ostrich was **not** endowed with feathers to create flight, nor blessed with sweet motherly instincts, nor granted great wisdom and good sense, but it was given strong legs to run fast. The ostrich is not like the stork, but to be fair, the stork is not like the ostrich. Each is uniquely different.

In life, you will come across many people who do not seem *normal*. When you see someone who you might think is *strange*, remember we are all created differently. No one is alike. In fact, no one is even like you. *Normal* is a word that can only be understood by our Maker. Instead of focusing on people's strange behaviors or looks, change your perspective to see their unique characteristics ordained by God. God does not make mistakes; He creates people uniquely.

<u>Closer Challenge</u>: Have you found yourself looking down upon those who are not like you? Do you overlook those with special needs? **Today**, move outside your comfort zone and speak with someone who you would typically overlook because of your differences. Provide that person the gift of encouragement by writing a letter, sending an email, or giving a nice compliment face-to-face. If possible, spend some time with that individual so you can understand your differences better and praise God for His creativity in each of us!

June 10

God Will Come Through

Isaiah 30:18

Quite often you might find yourself looking toward heaven, wondering when God will rescue you from a time of need. The time of waiting can be unbearable, especially if you feel a sense of desperation. As you read Isaiah 30:18, be reminded that God longs to be gracious to you. But you must keep in mind that His timing is perfect. He sees the world from a different perspective, lining up all experiences and encounters for His glory. At just the right time, He will come through to gain the greatest amount of glory.

The keyword for us is *patience*. Your time of waiting is really a special gift. Do not see waiting on the Lord as idle time, but time when you can build your faith and trust in Him even more. If God did not call us to wait from time to time, we would rarely need to depend upon Him in faith. In addition to the gift of faith building, you will also gain understanding in your situation as you wait upon the Lord to move. (Proverbs 14:29) So, be patient with the Lord, and discover how you can draw closer to Him during your time of waiting.

Closer Challenge: Have you recently called out to God for help, but you still find yourself waiting? **Today**, see it as an opportunity to build your faith. Share your need with a friend and pray together for the endurance to patiently wait upon God. Honor God as you wait and reflect His glory in all ways. Hold on tight to the faith you have in Jesus, for at times, it's all you have. But, that is more than enough!

June 11

God's Signet Ring

Haggai 2:23

In the Old Testament, a signet ring was often used as a signature. Just as we commit to an agreement with our signature in writing, the signet ring guaranteed a vow of commitment from the one who gave the ring away to another. In Haggai 2:23, God placed a signet ring on the finger of Zerubbabel to signify a promise that God had chosen him, and he would not be harmed. Furthermore, the ring was also a guarantee that the Messiah would come and redeem His people. Jesus fulfilled this promise in the days to come.

Since Pentecost, believers have also been given a signet ring of sorts. Our signet ring is the seal of the Holy Spirit. (2 Corinthians 1:21-22) As a born again follower of Jesus, the Holy Spirit is evidence of the Lord's comfort, protection, and correction in your life. The Holy Spirit is also the seal of your salvation. You know you belong to the Father by the Holy Spirit actively working in you. You have been given a signet ring in the Holy Spirit to wear proudly and confidently, so be mindful of this marvelous promise!

<u>Closer Challenge</u>: Do you recognize you are sealed in God's love through the work of the Holy Spirit? **Today**, rest assured that your Father in heaven will never let you out of His grip. Be conscious of the Holy Spirit working in your life by jotting down in your journal the ways He has spoken to you in the last week. If you have not noticed much action, maybe it is because you haven't been observing too well. Starting today, keep your spiritual eyes open to see how He is moving in you. As you see Him work, be joyful that our seal of God's love is forever placed in your life, further amplifying His great desire to draw closer to you.

June 12

Justified by Grace

Romans 4:4-5

In our "earn it or don't receive it" world, salvation by grace is hard to accept. Every religion except for evangelical Christianity has some sort of justification by works. However, as we see in Romans 4:4-5, if you *earn* salvation, it is not a gift. Thus, Jesus' sacrifice would be diminished to a mere noble example. But Jesus' death is much more than a noble example, He *is* the free gift of God offered to all who choose salvation. There is no way to earn eternal life; you must rely upon grace through the gift of Jesus' sacrifice.

If you believe producing good works earns you a spot in heaven, you're sadly misled. All it takes is one sin to miss God's standard of perfection. And we've all done that! (Romans 3:23) Even if you somehow remain perfect from this point forward, the sins you've already committed separate you from God, and those sins lead to death. (Romans 6:23) As result, if you are to avoid death, something perfect must die in your place for God to remain just. Enter Jesus. His perfect sacrifice becomes your free ticket to eternal life. If you believe in Him, you are not only saved by grace but also sustained by it. Never substitute with works the power of God's grace to save souls.

Closer Challenge: Since the day of your conversion, are you still *living* under justification by grace? Some fail to remember they are under grace; hence, when they fail, they constantly feel unworthy before God. **Today**, determine if bad doctrine is causing you to depend upon good works to gain God's love. Renew your mind by believing justification by faith. Remember, your good works—which should exist (James 2:17)—come from an overflow of gratitude because of Jesus' **free gift of eternal life**. Trust in His grace and let it motivate you to serve Him well.

June 13

Sabbathing

Hebrews 4:9-10

Today's culture is very fast-paced. Just about every day, you frantically rush to your next obligation, barely having enough time to stop and enjoy life and your Creator. God knew His people would struggle to slow down, so He set an example of resting after the sixth day of creation. (Genesis 2:2-3) The seventh day was set aside for admiring His good work. Likewise, God has ordered us to set aside a day of rest to draw closer to Him and admire His wonder in creation.

Our key passage today reminds us that the Sabbath-rest still remains for the people of God. Be very diligent to work hard throughout the week, but also be certain to pause for a day before you get started again. The Sabbath-rest is needed to refocus your mind on God and the things that really matter in life. If you choose not to take this rest, you might fly through life, confusing priorities and losing touch with your precious Savior.

Closer Challenge: Are you consistent to take a day of rest so you can focus on God and other important matters in life? Or are you plowing through life without concern for the Sabbath? ***Today***, on one day this week, schedule a Sabbath day to rest. If it cannot be Sunday, choose a day you can set aside. During this day, find ways to connect with God and focus on the most important things in life. Most notably, do not perform your normal routine of work. If you do not routinely set aside this day, you will soon burn out. Follow the example of your Creator and simply rest.

June 14

A Time to Laugh

Ecclesiastes 3:4

In all of Solomon's wisdom and earthly power, this might have been one of the simplest but most-needed statements we need to hear. Understand that there is a time to laugh. At times, we can take life too seriously and miss out on the enjoyment God has intended us to have. Jobs are pressure-filled, families can produce stress, and relationships can be a strain. Life is filled with areas that can result in anxiety, so it is extremely vital you take the time to laugh and enjoy life.

Outsiders to the faith often view Christians as being too uptight because we may look as though we cannot have fun. Though there are certain activities you should refrain from due to your convictions, there are still plenty of ways you can enjoy life and produce laughter that is good and healthy. As a precautionary note, there is a time to laugh, but there is also a time not to laugh. Use wisdom to know the difference.

<u>Closer Challenge</u>: When was the last time you had a good laugh? **Today**, here is your permission to go and laugh. In good taste, watch a funny movie, play an interactive board game with others, go to a humorous show, etc. Find ways you can add laughter to your life. In fact, your marriage or other relationships might need some laughter to spice them up again. Life is too short to miss the opportunity to enjoy it. So regularly find ways to experience the most of it through laughter.

June 15

Stop Worrying

Luke 12:22-23

As you start to read this devotional today, first determine if you're even slightly worried about something. It's likely you're wrestling with at least one matter of uncertainty. Each day, you are bombarded with anxious concerns, many of which will never materialize into real issues. Our Lord understands our tendencies to worry; so in a firm response, Jesus guides you to place your burdens upon Him.

Walking by faith is a calling for every believer. (2 Corinthians 5:7) But if you fill yourself with worry, you eliminate the very faith nature in which you are to live. The Old English word for *worry* means to kill by strangulation. Worrying strangles faith to death and leaves you empty and dead. So instead of worrying, seek first the Kingdom of God in faith, and your worries will fade. (Luke 12:31)

<u>Closer Challenge</u>: Are you a person who is often filled with worry? Do you realize your worry is a form of doubt in God? **Today**, recall a worry you have. Instead of focusing on your uncertainties and false perceptions, flip it around and view the situation from the perspective that God will deliver. Confess your worry to a close friend; but after confessing, talk *more* about how you trust God to carry you. Removing worry does not mean you take life flippantly, but it places your burdens in the hands of Him who can overcome. Give your worries to God and feel His closeness.

June 16

Pray Without Ceasing

---

1 Thessalonians 5:17

As you journey through your day, challenges are all around you. But instead of worrying, pray. Paul urges us to pray continually throughout the day. (1 Thessalonians 5:17) There is never a moment in the day when you can't pray. In fact, as you pray, the Spirit of God is interceding for you (Romans 8:26-27), and even Jesus is at the right hand of the Father, speaking on your behalf. (Romans 8:34) God is ready to move through prayer. Are you ready to pray?

Many factors may keep you from praying. Busyness, self-reliance, and distractions keep you off your knees, but none of them can compare to what could happen if you actually prayed continually. Each day, you pass people who need prayer. Behind every face you encounter, there is a deep need for a touch from God. Sometimes you know the need; other times you don't. Just as the Spirit and Savior intercede for you, do the same for others continually.

<u>Closer Challenge</u>: Are you engaged in prayer throughout the day? **Today**, within the next seven days, choose at least one day when you can make a conscious effort to intercede for others. In this day, as you pass by every person you encounter, pray for that person. Whether you know that person or not, say a quick silent prayer. Even as you engage in conversation with another, in the back of your mind, be praying for that person. Do this for a full day, and if possible, fast from food. As you pray and fast, you will sense great impact in the lives of many people and draw closer to God. Pray without ceasing.

June 17

Exposing the Light

Ephesians 5:13-16

As you woke up this morning, you probably flipped on a switch to bring light into a dark room so you could see clearly. Without light, vision is impaired. The gospel works in a similar way. Without the light of the gospel, life is dark, and it is impossible to see or understand this world. Yet once you are exposed to the Light, your world is brightened and you are able to have spiritual visibility. Now, as a child of the Light, you are to reflect the Light so others can see too.

Our world is full of darkness and Jesus is the only source of light that can help others see well. (John 14:6) If Christ-followers fail to flip on the spiritual switch for those in darkness, many will walk blindly in this world. Therefore, as Paul alerts each believer, make the most of every opportunity, so others can see God's goodness too!

Closer Challenge: Are you reflecting the great and glorious light of our Savior? Are you intentionally attempting to flip on the switch for others to see spiritually? ***Today***, pay attention to who God places in your path. Make a valiant effort to strike up a conversation with that person and move the discussion toward whether or not they have faith in God. Then turn on the Light of the Gospel by speaking the truth of Jesus in love. As God's children, we are to talk passionately about our Daddy and point others to the Light.

June 18

Waiting on God

Genesis 40:23-41:1

The story of Joseph is a fascinating tale of tragedy and reconciliation. Joseph was sold into slavery by his brothers, falsely accused of adultery, and thrown into jail. Then, to make matters worse, while in jail, he interpreted the dream of Pharaoh's cupbearer. The cupbearer promised he would remember Joseph, but he did not. Two years later, Joseph was still in jail. Finally, when Pharaoh needed his dream interpreted, the cupbearer remembered Joseph. After Joseph correctly interpreted the dream, he was elevated to second in power over all of Egypt. Joseph's path to influence wasn't ideal. Yet through it all, he kept his faith and waited on God.

It is hard to imagine the anguish Joseph must have felt while on his unusual path to glorify God. Though probably very few of us have faced the extreme case of isolation and suffering that Joseph did, we all have had our share of affliction as we followed God. And during that affliction, there has normally been the temptation to become angry at God or possibly even deny God. Yet in our distress, we should model Joseph's faith and wait on God during those dark moments of life.

Closer Challenge: Has your faith been shaken due to uncontrollable circumstances in your life? Are you a victim of unpredictable tragedy? If you have not already, implement the attitude of Joseph. Remain faithful to the vow you made to God when you committed to Him. **Today**, if you are facing a difficult situation, determine how you can bring glory to God through it. And if your situation does not improve immediately, as Joseph did, *wait* on God and keep your faith. God is faithful.

June 19

Bringing Hope to the Masses

Exodus 14:14

There are times in your life when *you* will need to be the pillar of faith for a group of people. Bringing hope to the masses isn't easy, especially when people tend to focus on obstacles. Moses was in this kind of dilemma. With the Egyptians quickly pursing them on the banks of the Red Sea, Israel was stricken with fear and doubted God's protection over them. So Israel wanted to give up, but Moses strengthened the masses with his words of encouragement. (Exodus 14:11-14)

Whether you are in a leadership position or not, God may use you to bring a message of hope to a group wedged in doubt. This group could be your family, friends, or even your church. If you observe any group you're connected to struggling to find hope, maybe God is calling you to remind them of His great power. God graciously displays His power to those who come to Him in faith, but often it's the zeal in one person that can spark hope in the masses. Be that person!

Closer Challenge: Is your church or family at a crossroads? Are you associated with a group who simply needs to trust God? **Today**, be the one who models the faith needed to move the group forward. Wisely discern what is needed, and then charge your group to seek the face of God and trust in His power to intervene. It may not be easy, because not everyone is willing to have faith in God. But in the best way possible, speak with a confident voice and heart of faith and pray that it motivates others.

June 20

Making the Right Decision

Exodus 28:29-30

In the Old Testament, when decisions needed to be made, the people turned to their priest. The priest wore a breastplate made of gold and precious jewels, bearing all the names of the tribes of Israel. Symbolically, he was to represent the whole nation in the decisions made. Also within the breastplate were the Urim and Thummim lots. It is traditionally understood that the Urim was the *no* lot and the Thummim was the *yes* lot. It was the belief of the time that when a question was asked, if the Urim dominated when cast, the answer was no. And if the Thummim dominated, the answer was yes. Whatever the answer was, Israel believed it was God's desire.

Each day you are filled with countless decisions. Some are easy and less stressful, such as deciding whether or not to brush your teeth. But major decisions need more focus and thought, because each decision you make bears an outcome. So you must carefully determine if what you decide is from the Lord. (Proverbs 16:33) We are not commanded to cast lots by God, but there are other ways in which you can discern God's will. Specifically, we have the treasure of God's written Word.

<u>Closer Challenge</u>: Are you on the brink of a major decision? **Today**, move toward making the right decision. Wisely consider the following steps. Read Scripture to make sure the decision is moral. Ask godly advice from someone who faithfully seeks God. Carefully watch your circumstances. Spend ample time in prayer, and possibly even fast. At the right time, confidently make your decision. Know the heart of God and passionately move toward Him. God will direct you if you seek and commune with Him

June 21

Living in the Present with Purpose

James 4:13-17

It's important to prepare for the future, but in reality, you live in the present. James rebukes those who merely think about future activities and gain without doing good in the present. We have little time on earth to really make a difference, and if we waste that time on frivolous, uncertain activities, we can possibly miss out on our created purpose in the present. As a result, it's crucial that you seek out the Lord's will *today* and passionately run toward it. You are here to make a difference for God *right now* by doing good things. (James 4:17)

If you're not careful, you can become distracted by worldly matters and fail to see God-ordained appointments. It is very wise that just as you would prepare for the distant future, you should plan today activities. Today is the only day you are guaranteed; and even today has surprises waiting to be revealed. So it is important to make the most of today and live your life in the present with purpose, bringing glory to God as you make a difference in another's life. Let your mind be on today, and good things can happen.

<u>Closer Challenge</u>: Are you primarily planning for the future without giving much thought to making a difference in the present? **Today**, before you get started, map out your day with purpose. Strategically process and organize at least one activity in which you can do good. This can be as simple as taking a hurting person to lunch as you listen to that individual's struggles. You can visit a hospital, nursing home, soup kitchen, or some other place with needs. Creatively plan something today where you can draw closer to God and meet a real need in the present.

June 22

The Great Forgiver

Micah 7:18

Our God stands alone. No being in the universe has the power to forgive sins but Him. He stands solo in that category. And to enlarge His greatness, God never gets exhausted in regard to distributing forgiveness. For every person who confesses sin and believes in Jesus as the risen Savior, godly compassion is reserved at all times. It's a divine gift you don't deserve, but if you are wise, you will receive it cheerfully.

God is not obligated to forgive your sins, for He is just to refrain from it. But in a radical response to your rebellion, He *delights* to pardon your sins and provide you mercy. Within His being is compassion only He understands. He longs to reunite you into fellowship with Him. If you're feeling guilty due to a sin you have committed, reach out to the God of mercy and allow Him to be the Great Forgiver He is.

Closer Challenge: Have you forgotten the great mercy God has for you? Are you ashamed to approach Him due to sin? ***Today***, come to God in humility and let Him renew your heart. Determine if there is a sin keeping you at a distance from God. Symbolically kneel down and lay that offense at the feet of Jesus. Rest assured that He deeply cares for you, for He will not turn away from you. It is time for you to live in freedom because the Father delights to show you mercy. Thank God for His never-ending mercy!

June 23

Breaking the Cycle

---

2 Chronicles 27:1-2

Even good parents make mistakes that children should not repeat. Uzziah was a good king and lived an honorable life for God. (2 Chronicles 26:4) However, he made one critical mistake of burning incense in the Temple, which was a task only for the priest. Azariah and eighty other priests rebuked him. But Uzziah let his pride produce anger against them, and he decided he wouldn't leave. At that moment, the Lord afflicted Uzziah with leprosy, and he lived in isolation the rest of his life. (2 Chronicles 26:16-21) Jotham, Uzziah's son, learned from his father and was honored in Scripture for not making the same mistake.

Scripture teaches that you should always honor and respect your parents. (Ephesians 6:1-2) But it never encourages you to make the same mistakes as your parents. In fact, Jotham was commended for *not* making the same mistake as his father, Uzziah. Jotham learned from his father that he should never allow his pride to challenge the sacred mandates of God. He had a role as king, and he was not to extend his role to that of the priests. There were many good things Jotham learned from his father concerning doing what is right in the eyes of the Lord, but he also learned a lesson of what *not* to do.

<u>Closer Challenge</u>: What have you learned from your parents? You can probably recall both good and bad lessons. **Today**, without disrespecting your parents, choose to follow God's ways and not your parents' mistakes. Consider their mistakes and make a vow not to repeat them in your life. This might be a sobering reminder that your parents do not follow God. But it is important that you break the cycle of unrighteous living, so these mistakes are not continued in your children. Furthermore, if your parents are living, pray they can break the habit in them too. These patterns of sin must be broken for you to feel the closeness of God.

June 24

Your Inner Circle

Proverbs 13:20

Each of us has an inner circle of people where we spend much time. This group of people could be your close friends, church members, co-workers, or family. Though it may not always cross your mind, your inner circle has great influence upon your spiritual growth as a Christian. Your inner circle has the potential to build you up with encouragement and love or bring you down, causing disaster in your life.

This simple proverb has deep meaning. It does not imply you should stay away from foolish or wicked people, because you must share the love of Jesus with outsiders. But it does mean you should spend a good percentage of your time with those who will sharpen your faith and keep you on track following God. As you do, you will grow wise in all your ways.

Closer Challenge: Who are the people you spend most of your time with? Are you mainly with people who cause your faith to become stagnant, or are you with those who will build you up? **Today**, if you do not actively participate in spending time with godly people, make adjustments to your calendar. If you need help doing this, start with discovering opportunities in your church. Most churches have some sort of small group system in place. Find the group that fits **you** and join it. It may take time to develop deep friendships, but commit to them by being a godly friend. If you are already in a small group, reenergize your commitment by possibly helping someone in need within your group. Just as friends are present for you, be there to encourage them.

June 25

Your Salvation Story

Acts 9:1-19

At one time in his life, Paul hunted down Christians to kill them. While on his way to receive a list of believers from the high priest in Damascus, he had an unprecedented spiritual encounter. In a radical display of God's presence, Jesus met Paul on the road, spoke words to him, and struck him with blindness for three days. Then, Jesus directed Paul to be taken to one of Jesus' disciples in Damascus. When the disciple, Ananias, touched Paul's eyes, his sight was restored and immediately he believed and was baptized.

Paul's conversion story is proof that God can take any person, despite being aggressively defiant toward Jesus, and bring salvation. Odds are, you're not seeking to kill Christians, but you also have a story of redemption to tell. On numerous occasions in Acts, Paul retells his story to different groups of people. His story is powerful because no one can refute his experience of a changed life. Your story of redemption is powerful too, so be ready to share it at any given moment.

<u>Closer Challenge</u>: Have you carefully processed your story of redemption? **Today**, write an outline of your salvation story, preferably in a digital format. Share what life was like before Christ, when you believed, and since your conversion. You don't need to explain every detail, but add whatever you think is necessary to help people understand your changed life. Now, share it with your devotional partner or a close Christian friend to practice telling it. If you discover your story is full of holes, it could be an indication you've never truly *believed*. If so, place your trust in Him today. Make today your spiritual birthday! (John 3:3) No matter how radical or simple your testimony is, be prepared to let people know about your changed life! Pray for an opportunity to share this week.

June 26

Finding Courage to Share

---

2 Timothy 1:7

As a Christ-follower, you're called to share your faith with outsiders, but due to fear, you might lack confidence. Mix in the culture's desire to keep you silent, and your courage could be lost quickly. But you have a God-given weapon to bring you courage. It's the Spirit of God in you! The Spirit clothes you with power, love, and self-discipline to share confidently. (2 Timothy 1:7) These gifts supply you with what's needed to make a difference in an unbeliever's life.

The *power* of the Spirit is the strength needed from God to change the heart of someone who does not know Him. The *love* of the Spirit is needed to convince that person that God deeply cares for him or her. The *self-discipline* of the Spirit is needed for you to share even if you feel timid about presenting the gospel. With your personal story to tell and the Spirit equipping you, you have all you need to share effectively and courageously.

Closer Challenge: Have you lacked the courage to share Jesus? Yesterday's *Closer Challenge* was just practice, as you shared your story with another believer. **Today**, share with someone who does not know Jesus. You may have a family member, co-worker, or neighbor who needs to hear the gospel. With the power, love, and self-discipline available to you through the Holy Spirit, take a step of faith and tell your story of redemption. Invite that person to your house or go out to lunch or dinner, but whatever you do, speak your story and give that person the opportunity to respond. Take courage and spread the good news, and you'll feel God's closeness as you do.

June 27

Wanting God or the World?

───────•───────

1 Samuel 10:17-19

Throughout history, God had been the king Israel needed. But Israel coveted other nations and wanted a man-king instead of God. The miracles and deliverances that Israel experienced were overlooked as they sought to be like other nations. Surprisingly, God granted their request. (1 Samuel 8:22) But unfortunately, they would pay for it dearly. This began the process of Israel's decline, culminating in exile from the land God had provided for them. (2 Kings 17:23; 25:21)

Looking back at history, it can be tempting for us to condemn Israel's action without seriously considering our own waywardness. But if you're honest with yourself, you would agree that your tendencies aren't much different. If you take your eyes off of Jesus and fix them on the world, you can be tempted to become like it and seek what it has. As Israel desired to be like other nations, you may want what the person next door has without realizing that it's slowly leading you in the wrong direction. You must be careful to seek God, not the world.

<u>Closer Challenge</u>: Are you peeking at those in the world, asking God for what they have? If so, stop before God grants your request, resulting in a load of regret! **Today**, closely examine if you are coveting something others may have. Name that desire and completely turn away from it. Don't be misled by its subtle, negative influence. It can lead to great danger! In place of your worldly passion, fill your desire with pursuing God. Your worldly desire could be a root of destruction if you are not quick to cut it out.

June 28

Free to Receive, Costly to Follow

———————◆———————

Luke 14:33

To receive eternal life, there is nothing required of you. (Romans 6:23) You simply confess Jesus is Lord and believe He was raised from the dead. (Romans 10:9) However, the cost to follow is much higher. If you are not willing to hate your family (Luke 14:26-27), calculate the sacrifice (Luke 14:28-30), and humbly release control (Luke 14:31-32), you cannot be a disciple of Jesus. You must be willing to give up *everything*!

This is a hard teaching to accept because many believe *free* also implies entitlement to live as you please. Not so. If you think like this, it's probable that you haven't really understood salvation, because a genuine conversion experience compels you to live differently! Once you declare that Jesus is Lord, you transform from the world's pawn to God's soldier. Your life is no longer controlled by your desires but by what pleases God.

<u>Closer Challenge</u>: Have you freely received the gift of salvation but recognize little change? He gave all for you; are you willing to give all for Him? **Today**, revisit the cost to follow God and take action. The Spirit might be leading you to change friends, disappoint family, or restructure your finances to follow God. These are just a few costs to consider. Whatever He leads you to do, listen closely to His guidance and follow steadfastly.

June 29

Looking Out for Each Other

Genesis 4:9

The first murder in creation came from a very unlikely suspect. Cain took the life of his brother, Abel. It is hard enough to believe Cain committed this horrible crime against his own flesh and blood, but what was even more chilling was the response he gave the Lord. When asked of Abel's whereabouts, Cain replied that he didn't know and questioned God, "Am I my brother's keeper?" The sheer callousness of Cain's heart oozed ill-fated indifference. When a person's heart moves from care to indifference, fallout is looming in that relationship.

Your brother, sister, family, and any close friend are your business! You *are* your brother's keeper. Not in an eerie, nosey sense of the meaning, but you should be concerned about your loved ones and do all you can to help them in times of need. Being indifferent about their lives isn't an option. Know what they are doing and wisely intervene when crises arise. Be your *brother's keeper* and gladly show it.

Closer Challenge: Have you lost contact with a family member or former close friend? If distance, busyness or anger has separated you, it's time to reconnect. **Today**, make a phone call or set up a visit with someone who has drifted away from you. Listen closely to that person and ask questions about his or her life. Discover if there is something you can do to show you care. At the very least, ask how you can pray for him or her. If possible, pray with them right then. Make every effort to show love by being your *brother's keeper*. As you do, you'll model God's love.

June 30

Caring Like a Mother

―――――•―――――

Isaiah 66:13

When a mother gives birth, she is deeply moved to love that child. Though times of slight or extreme adversity between the two will exist as time passes, her overwhelming compassion for her child will never depart. This deep, affectionate love is the type of love Paul had for the church at Thessalonica. (1 Thessalonians 2:7-8) He knew and we know too that there is no earthly love as strong as the bond a mother has for her children.

Throughout Scripture, God's care and comfort are depicted as a mother's ceaseless interest for her children. (Hosea 13:8; Luke 13:34) Even when Israel faced discipline from God, the divine care He had for them was like the unyielding affection of a mother. (Isaiah 66:13) Yet, even a mother's love isn't as complete as God's love for you. (Isaiah 49:15) You have a God who thinks of you above all other endeavors. Rest assured that God can never forget nor relinquish His incomprehensible love for you.

<u>Closer Challenge</u>: Have you pondered that the depth of God's love for you is like a mother's? Though you *may* have a distorted view of a mother's love due to the failures of your mom, believe that God has a perfect, matchless love for you. ***Today***, your challenge is two-fold. First, regardless of the relationship you have with your mom, if possible, verbally thank her for raising you. Her mothering isn't flawless, but she is still your mother. Show her your appreciation. Secondly, rest peacefully in knowing God has a perfect love for you. Crack a smile today because God loves you more than you can ever comprehend!

July 1

Turning to Friends

Proverbs 27:10

Family is a wonderful blessing when they are nearby and can help when you are in need. But in our day in time, it is not uncommon to have immediate family spread out across the nation or even the world. Furthermore, you may have damaged relationships within your family, or they may have passed away. Though bloodlines run thick, family may not be your first response. That is why it is critical for you to have quality friendships nearby who can act and love like family.

Our lives are filled with moments of stress, fatigue, and surprises that can turn our lives upside down in a flash. In those moments, you are in need of godly individuals who can comfort you, lift your spirit, and provide you a helping hand. If you have not established these relationships, difficult situations will be even harder to overcome. Spend time building these family-like relationships before disaster strikes, so you can have a healthy support system in place before tragedy.

Closer Challenge: Do you have close friends who you can depend upon when you are in dire need? **Today**, draw closer to those individuals. Identify a few people with whom you have a mutual friendship. Express your gratitude for them by doing something special. You could write them a card, take them out for lunch, or invite them to your house for dinner. Continually show loving-kindness to your friends, because you never know when you will need their support during an emergency, tragedy, or disappointment. Also, go out of your way to comfort them when they are in need. Having a friend and being one is a special treasure.

July 2

Expressing Love to the Messenger

Acts 16:13-15

Lydia was a common woman, who by divine appointment met Jesus through conversation with Paul and his missionary crew. Immediately after she began to follow Jesus and was baptized, she felt compelled to express her gratitude to the messengers of the gospel. As a result, she invited them into her home and hosted them with great care. A forever bond was established as the gospel was transferred.

The promise of your salvation is the greatest gift you have ever received. Words cannot express the gratitude you ought to have for Jesus. But you should also be thankful to the one who brought you this message. You were not born with the knowledge of Christ. Someone played the important role of imparting the redeeming story of Jesus to you. A parent, a pastor, a friend, or a stranger came to you with beautiful feet and influenced you with the message of salvation. (Romans 10:15) And as an overflow of gratitude, it should be natural for you to return much love to this angel of truth.

<u>Closer Challenge</u>: Can you recall the person who shared with you the great news of Jesus? If so, **today**, attempt to reconnect with that person and express your love. Provide a meal, send a card of encouragement, make a phone call, do something to say, "Thank you." It is possible you may have read the Bible and began to follow Jesus on your own. Even so, there was probably someone who was instrumental in drawing you toward Jesus. Do something special for that person. Give back to the one who introduced you to the Savior.

July 3

Stop Grumbling Against Leaders

Numbers 17:1-13

The people of Israel had a reputation of grumbling against leadership. This grumbling caused Korah and his clan to be swallowed by a hole in the ground. (Numbers 16:31) In response to this rebellion, God reaffirmed Aaron's leadership. He had all tribes represented with a staff. They placed all staffs in the Tent of Meeting, and the staff that would sprout at the top would be the sign of who to follow. Aaron's staff not only sprouted but budded and produced almonds. This was affirmation that God's anointing was on Aaron, and if the people did not trust his judgment, they would face judgement as Korah did.

Even for the people of God, disagreement can arise. Many times it is unwarranted. As a precautionary word of advice, take notice if you are joining the cause against God's anointed, especially if your complaining is against frivolous, preferential matters, not doctrinal error. God has ordained leaders to hear His voice and move people in that direction. When you create disunity against such leaders, you are hindering the work of God. As best as possible, support and encourage God's anointed leaders.

Closer Challenge: Are you grumbling against a leader in your church? Is this a biblical matter that merits a loving confrontation, or is it a dislike due to personal taste? **Today**, follow God's anointed leaders without grumbling. As long as it's biblically sound, participate in a direction you have been reluctant to go. In addition, do something kind for the leader who you struggle to follow. And if you must approach your leader to discuss a matter, come with gentleness, prayer, Scripture, and love. But ultimately, yield to the anointed leader's direction. If you continue to complain, you could be the negative seed that causes disunity in your church. Stop it before it gets out of hand. Promote goodness in all things, not harm.

July 4

Independence Verses Dependence

Isaiah 50:10

Declaring independence can be healthy for you if you need to break away from a certain group of people or you need to take personal responsibility in a matter. Yet you should never declare independence spiritually. If you choose to be independent, everything will begin to unravel at the seams in your life. An oracle of the Lord through the pen of Isaiah states that you should rely upon on the Lord in times of distress. (Isaiah 50:10)

Due to pride, spiritual dependence is something we do not like to admit. We would rather be noticed for our independence. For in our culture, the one who stands alone is often admired. But the greatest position for you is the place of full dependence upon God! Since God is all-powerful and all-knowing, it would be foolish not to turn to and rely upon God in every situation you face.

Closer Challenge: Are you attempting to handle life on your own? Do you trust the way of God or do you follow your own methods? **Today**, declare your dependence upon God. *Believe* in your heart that God is your source of strength and knowledge. As you face any difficult situation today, declare your dependence upon God by simply saying, "In God I trust." Pledge allegiance to God and His great power, and as you do, you'll point others to the Savior through your dependence upon Him.

July 5

Wisdom in Action

James 3:13

Wisdom is not just a mental exercise. You can have all the knowledge in the universe, but if it's not supported with obedience, it's useless. True wisdom produces action. Many people's image of wisdom is an old man sitting in a rocking chair, speaking slowly in response to a particular question. Though he might have sage words to speak, James reminds us that biblical wisdom leads to action. (James 3:13)

Execution to do right is always the most difficult part of your Christian walk. Much of how you should live is clearly described in Scripture. So you know what is right and wrong in most cases, but a person full of wisdom is one who will take biblical knowledge and follow through in obedience. This is precisely what separates the wise and foolish in our world. (Proverbs 14:16) You have a call to proper action in all you know from God. When you do, you will be deemed as wise in the eyes of our Lord.

<u>Closer Challenge</u>: Have you minimized wisdom to a mere mental exercise? Do you have a circumstance in which you know what you should do, but you haven't executed it? **Today,** seek true wisdom that comes from heaven (James 3:17-18) and follow through with it. Think about a decision you must make today. Assess what is right from Scripture, and then, do the hard part...*take action*! Often, doing what is right takes sacrifice. Whether you must sacrifice time, money, or pride, be wise by taking action.

July 6

Finish the Race

---

2 Timothy 4:7

Many Christ followers face serious temptations of quitting the faith. When circumstances appear overwhelming, those believers often blame God for not delivering as they desire. Paul had faced much suffering in his life. He was flogged, imprisoned, stoned, and constantly in danger of additional pain and agony for the cause of Christ. (2 Corinthians 11:23-28) Yet, near the end of his life, Paul was able to say, "I have fought the good fight, I have finished the race, I have kept the faith."

Paul visualized the Christian life as a race. No lengthy race is won without constant toil in your body, mind, and soul. You will take a beating in some way or fashion. But, if you want to say like Paul, "I have *finished* the race," you must persevere until the end. Many have given up on the faith and have turned to things much less promising. This has brought even more pain on their lives. As for you, will you finish the race?

Closer Challenge: Is a dire situation tempting you to leave the faith? Do you want to continue but need inspiration? **Today**, view the day as a mini-section of life's race. In spite of possibly feeling alone or mistreated, stay loyal to Jesus by wining today's small segment of the race. Endure. Stay the course. Hold tightly to biblical teachings in spite of what you see. Through all the battles Paul faced, he was confident of a crown of righteousness waiting for him in heaven. (2 Corinthians 4:8) Starting with this day, finish today's section of the race. And as you do this *daily*, clarity can come even in a fog of doubt and uncertainty.

July 7

Returning Your Mother's Love

Luke 2:51

Like most mothers, Mary had a soft spot in her heart for her Son. When Jesus deserted His parents to teach in the Temple, she was deeply concerned about His whereabouts. (Luke 2:48) But even in her anguish, Mary treasured this event in her heart, knowing there was something very special about her Son. And as every mother should, she gradually released her parental supervision as He aged and matured.

Mothers have a difficult task in life. They hold helpless infants against their chests, completely giving themselves to their children. But as their kids mature, mothers must continually let go and let God direct their children's lives. That is precisely what Mary did. Even as she watched her Son die on the cross (John 19:25), she sorrowfully yielded to the Father's plan for Jesus. Only a caring mother can know the grief related to this experience. Even as you age, never miss an opportunity to show your mother love. (John 19:26-27)

Closer Challenge: Have you recently expressed a deep appreciation for your mother? When was the last time you let your mother know she is loved? **Today**, if your mother (or mother figure in your life) is still living, do something very special for her. Make a surprise visit, call her on the phone, or bring or send her a gift. It will brighten her day. If you've had a rough past with your mother, try to heal some of those hurts by taking a small step toward reconciliation in this manner. Regardless if she deserves it, thank your mother for the gift of life and the sacrifices she has made for you.

July 8

Repaying Greater

Luke 19:1-10

Zacchaeus is often remembered for the size of his stature instead of the size of his heart. For years as a tax collector, Zacchaeus used poor judgment by cheating many people into overpaying taxes for his profit. But when Jesus called him by name and sat with him at his house, Zacchaeus changed his ways. Not only did he give back what he owed to everyone he cheated, but he paid back four times more! His outward display of repayment was a sign of an inward change in his heart.

It's nearly impossible to go through life without cheating someone at some point. You may not have been as abusive as Zacchaeus, but it's highly probable you too have deceived another. Do not live any longer with this guilt hanging over your head. If your heart has changed, let your actions show it. Like Zacchaeus, it's time to repay those who you have wronged.

<u>Closer Challenge</u>: Who have you cheated without repayment? Maybe it wasn't with money, but you simply used someone to get what you wanted. **Today**, first repent of your sin. Then, acknowledge who that person is and find a way to repay him/her. If you cheated with money, give back. If you took advantage of someone's time, give your time and strength in return. If you damaged another's reputation, try to restore it. However you cheated or abused that person, show a changed heart and attempt to make things right. When you do, the burden of guilt will flee and a relationship can be strengthened.

July 9

The Refreshed Person

———❖———

Proverbs 11:25

This world is full of need. It doesn't take long to find someone requiring a meal, a coat, shoes, a job, etc. Needs are abundant in our communities, and God has allowed poverty to exist to display His goodness. Without poverty and need, there would be no reason to practice giving and sharing. Your resources, whether great or small, are provided by God for you to use as a way to glorify Him by pointing others to His kingdom.

But not only do your resources provide assistance to others, they help *you* be restored spiritually. If you desire to be refreshed continually, be a person who gives freely. When you give and then encounter a frown slightly turned upward from a person who has faced hardship, you experience more renewal than if you would have received an unneeded gift. Allow a giving spirit to reign in you so that you can glorify God and experience refreshing!

Closer Challenge: Would you like to be refreshed today? If so, don't seek it by attaining something, but instead by giving. **Today**, open your eyes and heart to the needs of those around you. Without hesitation, when you see a need another has, do your best to meet that need. It could be someone you know or a stranger. As you do this, you will impact someone's life, and you will be refreshed in the process. Make spontaneous giving a common practice in your life.

July 10

Encouraging People to the Lord

Acts 11:22-24

It is recognized throughout the Acts of the Apostles that Barnabas was known for being an encourager. He was the one who believed Paul's conversion was authentic, encouraging Paul to grow in the Lord. (Acts 9:27) Barnabas was also chosen to travel to Antioch to further imbed the teachings of Christ into the hearts of those living there. As a result, being filled with the Holy Spirit, he brought many people to Jesus through the influential act of encouragement. (Acts 11:22-24)

When you encourage people, you fill them with confidence to move forward in their lives. It offers people a positive perspective instead of a pessimistic one. We constantly need to extend and receive encouragement, because our world is filled with confusion, negativity, and hopelessness. Furthermore, as with Barnabas, encouragement could be the influential tool the Spirit uses to bring people to faith in Jesus. Never miss an opportunity to encourage those around you.

<u>Closer Challenge</u>: Are you a deliverer of spiritual encouragement? **Today**, be aware of those who need to be encouraged. Without being overzealous or insensitive to the needs at hand, direct that person to Jesus with hopes of lifting his/her spirit. You could possibly handwrite a note or simply text a message; but if possible, deliver your words of encouragement face to face. As you do, include Scripture in your encouragement. Like Barnabas, you could be the voice that bridges him/her to eternity with kind, uplifting words about Jesus.

July 11

Death Produces Life

John 12:23-26

When Jesus predicted His death in John 12, He used an agricultural analogy to expound upon His reasoning for dying. Unless a seed is detached from its life source (the branches) and then buried in the ground, it cannot produce new life. Only after it is in the ground can it grow and bear new fruit. After Jesus was put to death on the cross and buried in the tomb, He was then raised to life again, bearing new life for all who believe in Him. (John 6:29)

This analogy also applies to our lives. Only after you die to yourself and bury your will, can you be a living, breathing disciple for God, able to guide others to new spiritual life. (Luke 9:23) If you long to produce new life, you must put to death your personal desires and follow Jesus to the cross. Thankfully, you probably will not need to follow Jesus to the literal, physical cross, but you must die to your will and serve Him so others can see Jesus and repent. That is the only way you can bear new, spiritual life in this world.

<u>Closer Challenge</u>: Are you willing to lose your life for the sake of Christ and eternal life for others? If not, what is keeping you from dying to yourself? **Today**, decide if you really want to bear new life. If so, put to death at least one of those lingering personal desires that is holding you back. Share it with a close friend or pastor. Now, fill that void with something of God. Find a service, mentor someone, do something that can produce life in others. Producing life takes sacrifice; so remember the sacrifice Jesus provided for you and follow in His footsteps.

July 12

Treasured Memories

—————•—————

Luke 2:19

Jesus' birth was accompanied by great awareness. Shepherds were minding their business when suddenly an angel of the Lord appeared to them along with a great heavenly host, praising God for the entrance of the Savior. The shepherds immediately rushed to Bethlehem to observe this marvelous sight. All were greatly amazed at the coming of the Savior, but Mary carefully stored away in her memory this wonderful experience.

One of earth's greatest treasures in this life is the memories that you have with loved ones. They are more precious than any jewel you can attain. When a house burns down, outside of life itself, the loss of pictures and sentimental possessions create the most grief, because they represent precious memories. When you face difficult times, these memories can serve as a refresher to your soul. Keep your memories safe and close to your heart and recall them when you need to be lifted up.

<u>Closer Challenge</u>: What are your treasured memories? **Today**, spend some time reflecting upon the delightful memories you have received in this life. Look through a photo album, dig through an old treasured memory box stored away, or simply tell a few old stories with loved ones. Do not let the memories slip from your mind. They can bring comfort to your soul and peace to your mind. Be thankful for these treasures in life.

July 13

Your True Crown

---

1 Thessalonians 2:19-20

While living in a culture with a vast array of earthly treasures, you can become misled about what is true reward. Paul sought a different kind of crown. His prized possessions were the people he had helped see Jesus and grow in their faith. As written in 1 Thessalonians 2:19, Paul's hope and joy rests in the faces of those who he would see with Jesus in the eternity. We can't take anything material with us into eternity (Job 1:21), but we can meet up with people who we've influenced to Jesus. Thus, people are our crowns!

If you are truly in Christ, you can't avoid positively influencing some to respond to the gospel. It's likely you have led another to believe in Jesus. Possibly you have discipled someone in the faith. Maybe you don't even know what a kind deed or an encouraging word did to help someone, but when you get to heaven, it will be credited to you and you'll be filled with joy. These are the crowns you should seek with all days God gives you!

Closer Challenge: Have you reminisced about the people you have touched for the gospel? **Today**, strive to attain eternal "people crowns," for they are rewards that will last. For encouragement sake, make a list of people who you have influenced in their walk with Jesus. Pray for them. Now, reach out to at least one person in written form, similar to Paul in 1 Thessalonians 2. Explain in your message how this person has brought you joy. Encourage this individual to continue strong in the faith! Your letter might be a timely word of encouragement. Keep striving for the crowns that will last!

July 14

Overflowing with Thanks

Psalm 119:171; 2 Corinthians 4:15

Many Christ-followers limp into worship services each week, torn and battered from the past week's challenges. As they enter the doors of the building, they hope and pray a pastor, a teacher, a mentor, or a friend can say something to spiritually rejuvenate their souls. Though the church is there for the sick, this should not be a pattern. Corporate gatherings of believers should primarily be a place of overflowing worship, regardless of circumstances. (Job 2:10) Because of the cross, you should always have a deep reservoir of thankfulness ready to spill over into adoration.

Each day is filled with blessings that can result in an overflow of praise to the Lord. You have life; you have breath; you have hope; you have the promise of salvation! Life doesn't always go as planned, but it should never steal the joy of your salvation. (Habakkuk 3:17-18) Like a brimming pond flowing into a stream, be a child who has unceasing praise for his Father.

Closer Challenge: Are you allowing hardships to obstruct your worship of God? Do you often find it difficult to thank God? **Today**, in your journal, write down some blessings you've received and begin to store up praise in your heart. Now, when you attend your next corporate gathering of worship, express love for God from the overflow of these blessings! Fill your God-shaped reservoir with gratitude so a ceaseless flow of praise will gush from your heart.

July 15

Responding in God's Presence

John 12:1-8

In John 12:1-8, besides Jesus, *four* people are named in this passage. All four were in the direct presence of Jesus, yet all four responded quite differently. *Martha was distracted.* It is noble to serve, but instead of being centered on Jesus, she was distracted by duty. *Lazarus was disengaged.* He was positioned in Jesus' presence, but instead of expressing his affection, he merely observed while reclining. *Mary was devoted.* She sacrificially and affectionately worshipped Jesus, regardless of anyone else. *Judas Iscariot was divisive.* He became critical at Mary's response; thus, he failed to worship and crushed the spirit of the moment.

There are times when you will enter God's vivid presence like these four individuals. Yet *how* you respond is up to you. You might be like Martha, too busy or distracted to really worship. You might be like Lazarus, in God's presence, but disengaged, doing nothing. You might be like Judas, observing with a divisive attitude while others actually worship Him. Or, you might be like Mary, a devoted worshipper of Jesus. It's up to you to decide how you'll respond in the presence of God.

Closer Challenge: When you enter God's distinct presence, who are you most like? Martha? Lazarus? Mary? Judas Iscariot? **Today**, determine who you most resemble. If your tendencies are like any of them but Mary, repent. Next time you are in a corporate worship setting, respond like Mary. Sacrificially and affectionately love Jesus. Let your motivation come from understanding the depths of your forgiveness. And since Scripture teaches we can't escape His presence (Psalm 139:7-10), choose in this very moment to be a worshipper like Mary.

July 16

Second Chances Rewarded

---•---

Matthew 21:28-32

In this parable, the first son made an unwise decision to disobey his father. Yet after a while, he realized his wrong and eventually yielded to his father's directives. Though the first son started poorly, he finished strong and was rewarded. The second son started well by telling his father he would obey him. Yet when it came time to execute, he betrayed his word to his father. Thus, the father was disappointed, and this son was not rewarded.

Many people have made poor decisions early in life, yet by the grace of God, they realize their mistakes and change. God has mercy for such people, and they will be richly rewarded in heaven. (Matthew 21:31) But those who claim obedience, yet do not walk in His ways, will be denied His blessings. Even though it is not ideal, it is better to obey late than never. No matter how you have started in your walk with Christ, be overjoyed that God has precious mercy waiting for you if you confess you're wrong and let the Spirit cleanse you and sanctify you. Always remember that it's not how you start, but how you finish.

Closer Challenge: Have poor decisions from your past filled you with guilt? Has this guilt kept you from walking closer with God? **Today,** think about a sin you had committed earlier in your life that has caused great grief. Has that sin been a stumbling block for you to feel God's acceptance? If so, confess your sin and be done with it. After all, once you confess it, God is done with it! (Psalm 103:12) Now, think of that last thing He told you to do. Though you may have stumbled out of the gates of obedience, obey Him now as a display of your love for Him. Rewards are waiting for those who finish strong.

July 17

Bow to Nothing but God

Deuteronomy 8:19-20

God is jealous of your worship. (Deuteronomy 4:24). He cannot tolerate you devoting your time, strength, and commitments to anything other than Himself. For He knows there is nothing that compares to His greatness, and when you bow to anything else, you are demeaning who He is and selling yourself short of the best. That is why He becomes jealous of your devotion.

God gave Israel a warning that if they forget Him, they would be destroyed. There are direct consequences for our choices to serve something other than God. Even as a devout Christian, if you are not careful, you can subtly allow religious acts to assume control over your life and worship. Various enjoyments, concerns, and even people can pull us in every direction but toward God. Keep God first (and only!) in your love and priorities, and all things will work together for the final good. (Matthew 6:33; Romans 8:28)

<u>Closer Challenge</u>: Are you neglecting God in your devotion? Is there some area of your life that has been exchanged for anything but God? **Today**, determine if you are worshipping something other than God. It could be a job, a material item, a hobby, a spouse, a child, or even Christian service. If any of these things are taking the place of God, you are worshipping an idol. Some of those things are fun to enjoy while on earth, but never allow them to take the place of God. He is your highest enjoyment and satisfaction. Never replace the true supremacy of God with anything else! Take the necessary measures to place God back on the throne of your life.

July 18

God Can

Jeremiah 32:17

How often in a week do you hear the statement, "I can't"? How often are you the one saying it? Truth is, there are many things you cannot do, which can create discouragement in your life. However, life is not dependent upon your ability but God's capability. Jeremiah lifted up a prayer to God that began with one of the greatest verses in the Bible. He acknowledged God's mighty creative hand, and then, declared God's power by saying nothing is too difficult for Him. (Jeremiah 32:17)

You may not be able to overcome a difficult situation currently in your life, but you know *Who* can! Your difficult situation may involve someone who is terminally ill. It may be the pains of a wayward, calloused family member or friend who doesn't want to turn to Jesus. It is quite possible you have done everything you know in your power, but you are still unable to resolve or change your situation. Do not fret. Turn to the One who can!

<u>Closer Challenge</u>: Are you discouraged about something in your life? Have you examined all possible angles and now you're left seemingly hopeless? **Today**, turn to the One who can intervene in your situation and deliver with power. Even in the direst situation, God can rescue and draw you closer to Him. Share your concern or situation with another believer or prayer partner. Even if it's over a phone call today, spend some quality time in prayer with that person. Rest in your capable God and trust that He knows best!

July 19

Changing for Future Good

Matthew 9:16-17

Jesus taught in this parable that old systems and forms cannot coexist with the new ones. Just as the law was good for a period of time to bring the acknowledgement of God's perfection and the way to live, the new covenant brought further clarification that should not be continued in the former ways. God does not change; but with the fulfillment of Jesus, our godly lifestyle did. The old rituals performed by the Pharisees and other religious groups needed to adapt and yield to the newness of Jesus' teachings.

While living as the body of Christ, there are significant events and sentimental possessions that make us want to cling to the past. Though these memories and ministries can always be kept close to your heart, they are not always to be continued. If the church is to embrace new generations, the Bride of Christ must be sensitive to the culture and make changes when necessary. The message and doctrine of the gospel must always remain the same because God does not change (Malachi 3:6), but the modes and methods to carry the gospel should be as fluid as the culture. Be sure you are supportive of your church as it moves forward in keeping itself alive with the next generation of Christ followers.

Closer Challenge: Have you been supportive of your church to move in new directions to reach future generations? If not, what do you fear? Is it a preference from the past that you desire to coddle, or is it a real doctrinal issue? **Today**, investigate what your church is doing to reach the next generation of believers. Now then, determine what you can do to embrace it. Don't be idle or too casual with this! Maybe you need to be a leading voice with your peers. Maybe you need to support the move financially. You definitely need to pray for direction. Do not put new wine in old wineskin. Help the charge to continue God's Kingdom on earth.

July 20

Astonishing Jesus

Matthew 8:10

Jesus, knowing every thought, was astonished by the request of a Roman Centurion. The Centurion had a servant who was paralyzed and suffering at home, so he came to Jesus, asking for help. When Jesus replied that He would *come* to his house and heal his servant, the Centurion humbly did not feel worthy of Jesus' presence in his home. Instead, in faith he simply believed that if Jesus just said the words, his servant would be healed. This display of faith and humility amazed Jesus. It was the greatest faith He had seen in all of Israel. As a result of the Centurion's faith, Jesus healed the servant just as he requested.

What astonishes Jesus? You might have thought it was an impeccable righteous lifestyle or a large amount of people receiving salvation. Those are wonderful things, but what really astonishes Jesus is great faith! For when you have great faith, other godly acts will follow. As your faith increases, so does your obedience to Him. Therefore, great faith, like this Centurion, is what really astonishes Jesus.

Closer Challenge: Do you want to astonish Jesus? Would you like Him to speak well on your behalf like He did for the Centurion? If so, practice the faith of the Centurion. **Today,** pray with great confidence for a burden you have. Your request could be for an illness, a financial need, a relational conflict, etc. As the Centurion did, offer your request to Jesus in humility and faith. If your request is not granted quickly, keep the faith and continue to ask. Wait upon God, for He will answer in His time. Have great faith and astonish your Lord.

July 21

House to House

Acts 5:42

The early church didn't have historical examples to follow in regard to living as the body of Christ. Sure, they witnessed the words and events of Jesus' life; but once He ascended, they were left to start a new mission for generations to follow. So they did what they thought best; they committedly traveled from one home to the next, telling their neighbors about Jesus. It was their mission, and they never stopped it.

This mission still exists today! Regardless of your job, your upbringing, or the political climate, your role as a part of the body of Christ is to never cease sharing the gospel. You are on a missionary's journey right now. God has placed you in your neighborhood and at your job to present the gospel to those around you. You are surrounded by people who need to be introduced to the Savior. Daily, go house to house, never stopping the mission.

Closer Challenge: Have you looked around to see who God has placed on your path? There are many people who surround you, but have you introduced them to the Savior? **Today**, determine how you can be polite to your neighbors to bridge the gospel to them. Provide a dinner, assist with a chore in their yard, be a source of transportation, or merely lend a helping hand. Find a way to be nice; but more importantly, go the extra mile to share Jesus. If you really want to be like the early church, make it your mission to interact with everyone who lives on your street and speak to them all about Jesus. Like the early believers, go house to house, sharing Jesus.

July 22

Adhering to God's Warnings

Luke 13:34

Israel had a problem of not minding God's warnings. God had sent prophets to voice His decrees and law, but the leaders often killed His messengers due to a lack of belief and understanding. When this happened, God was saddened because He longs to protect His children as a mother hen shields her chicks from danger underneath the guard of her wings. But since Israel would not stay under God's protection, they became exposed to harm and were left to fend for themselves without the defense of God.

God longs to protect us! He has given us plenty of warnings concerning how to be shielded from harm. By His Word, we are alerted to the many dangers that can destroy our lives. God has established boundaries for marriage, conflict, church order, thinking, speech, and much more. All His instructions are written down so you may live under His protection. These boundaries and warnings are not there to restrain you but to protect you. Find peace underneath the shelter of His wings.

<u>Closer Challenge</u>: Have you paid attention to God's warnings? Do you adhere to these boundaries, or do you drift away from His wings of protection? **Today**, examine your life to determine if you have avoided God's warnings in any matter. If you have gone beyond His boundaries, change your lifestyle in that area and rush quickly back under the care of God. Turn from your disobedience and run again to Him. Speak about your disobedience to a close friend whom you can trust. Accountability is in order for this. Like children protected by their mother, flee to the loving guard of God.

July 23

Releasing to God

———————•:•———————

Exodus 2:1-10

Around the time Moses was born, a decree had been sent throughout the land to kill all newborn Hebrew boys. (Exodus 1:22) Moses' mother couldn't bear the thought of her son being killed, so she hid him as long as she could. But when he became too old to hide, she put him in a basket and released him to float down the river, hoping God would rescue him. In God's providence, Moses drifted into the hands of Pharaoh's daughter, who had pity on him and kept him. In a remarkable turn of events, Moses' mother was able to nurse her son, too! However, after Moses' mother weaned him, she had to release him *again* into the care of Pharaoh's daughter. (Exodus 2:10)

Two times in this story, while her son was young, Moses' mother had to *release* Moses into the Lord's hands and trust He would do what was best. If she failed to do so, Moses could have lost his life. She made a tough decision, but it was the right one. Each of us has matters to release to God so He can display His glory. You might need to release a child, a job, a dream, a relationship, a possession, or a habit. If you don't release that one thing, you may miss God's best for your life, and furthermore, you could harm yourself or someone else.

<u>Closer Challenge</u>: Is there something in your life you should release to God? **Today**, name at least one thing, and in faith, take the necessary steps to release it to God. This is not easy; more than likely, fear is present. But do not allow fear to interfere with God's will. It is possible you may need wise counsel in this matter. Go to a pastor, teacher, leader, or Christian friend. It is wise to receive advice. (Proverbs 12:15) But most importantly, trust that God is sovereign. Believe God is providentially moving and release what you must over to Him.

July 24

Fighting Bitterness

Proverbs 14:10

As you journey through life, people will disappoint you. Some will insult you, ridicule you, and even attempt to crush your spirit. The god of this world is at work, blinding eyes and enticing people away from the gospel. (2 Corinthians 4:4) As a result, you will be disheartened by people. However, you cannot allow your hurts to fester into bitterness. Only you know the depths of your bitterness. (Proverbs 14:10) Therefore, you must dig into your own heart and see if resentment exists.

Bitterness is an evil tool of Satan. It's allowing the actions or words (or even perceptions!) of others to control you, even without that person's awareness. Furthermore, bitterness is one of the few sins that can worsen over time without ever encountering your offender. Without constant alertness, your heart can be infected with this spiritual disease. Your only defense against bitterness is forgiveness. (Ephesians 4:31-32) When you are offended by another, you must forgive or trouble will rule your life. (Hebrews 12:15)

<u>Closer Challenge</u>: Do you have a root of bitterness growing in your heart? If so, have you fed it with **anger** or starved it with **forgiveness**? **Today**, right now, drop to your knees and ask God for the strength to forgive your offender. As you do, consider how God has forgiven you! (Colossians 3:13) Forgiving someone is not easy according to the flesh, but it is possible when you walk in the Spirit. After you forgive from the heart, *comfort* the one who has disappointed you. (2 Corinthians 2:5-7) This will help *you* and *that person* heal. And if your pain resurfaces, forgive again. (Matthew 18:21-22) Do not allow bitterness to rule any longer.

July 25

God Is So Big!

---

1 Kings 8:27

When Solomon was dedicating to God the magnificent, man-made Temple, he understood that this glorious structure could *not* contain Him. In fact, nothing can contain Him! Solomon declared that even the highest heaven cannot extend enough territory to go beyond God's reach and rule. He is everywhere and is able to interact in every activity on earth and in heaven. The heavens declare His glory and the universe shouts His praise! (Psalm 19:1) God is everlasting with superior authority in all kingdoms. (Psalm 102:15)

On a regular basis, it's wise for us to stop and admire God's greatness. Too often we become absorbed in the smallness of the world and lose perspective of who He is. If we're not careful, we can perceive God much smaller than He is. When this happens, fear of creation will increase as fear of God decreases. Keep God big in your mind! Remember that He is all-powerful, and He has full knowledge of everything you could possibly encounter. Your God is big, so leave Him that way!

Closer Challenge: When is the last time you paused long enough to admire God's greatness? Have you taken a step back from life and realized that you are part of something extremely magnificent? **Today**, set up a day this week when you can go outside on a clear night and gaze at the universe. When you find a nice place to reflect upon God's greatness, read *Psalm 19* as you sit beneath the stars. For a few moments, let your cares be released and just bask in the glory of the Lord. Your God is big, so big!

July 26

Pray Specifically

―――――――•―――――――

Genesis 24:12-15

In Genesis 24, Abraham sent his servant to his native land to find Isaac a wife. After the servant *positioned* himself where he needed to be in Abraham's homeland, he precisely asked God for help in finding the right woman. In his prayer, he was very specific and confident. He didn't mince words; he directly asked God for what he needed. And before he was even finished praying, God had answered his plea.

Like Abraham's servant, you will be called to complete various missions that are challenging to accomplish. Picking a wife for another man is not a simple task! So the servant did what he knew best, *pray*! When you are confronted with a mission that is stretching your competence, *pray*! And even if you *think* you have the competence necessary, *pray*! For even your own heart can lead you astray. (Jeremiah 17:9) The greatest tool you have for completing a mission is praying specifically. And as you do, you'll be able to watch God's mysterious and marvelous plan unfold before your very eyes!

<u>Closer Challenge</u>: Are you on the verge of beginning a new assignment or are you in the midst of one, but your next step is causing confusion? **Today**, as Abraham's servant needed direction from God, position yourself in the right place, and ask God specifically what you need. In ministry, if you are unsure how you should serve, pray specifically. In business, if a project is creating stress and confusion, pray exactly for what you need. In your family, if you are facing struggles, pray directly for what is needed. Boldly approach the throne of God and wait for His answer. (Hebrews 4:16) God has the solutions; turn to Him! And in the process, you'll experience His closeness.

July 27

Gaining Full Understanding

Philemon 1:6

Gaining a fuller understanding of who Jesus is doesn't merely come from reading His Word and other great Christian writings. That may sound blasphemous, but there is more to gaining understanding than *head* knowledge. While reading God's word and fearing Him is the *beginning* of wisdom and understanding (Proverbs 1:7), *experiencing* God's Word through action and sharing your faith is how you gain a fuller meaning of who He is and how He works. (Philemon 1:6) If you desire to see God with more clarity, you must experience His truths by actively sharing your faith.

Sharing your faith brings extraordinary spiritual depth to your life. For when you attempt to explain Jesus to an unregenerate person, you are driven to recall the accumulated truths you know about Jesus. And the more you share, the more compelled you will become to know more of Him so you can be better prepared for all types of people. (1 Peter 3:15) If you want to gain a fuller understanding of who Jesus is, tell people the truth about Jesus!

<u>Closer Challenge</u>: Are you actively sharing your faith? **Today**, discover an approach that best fits you. Start with a bridge to the gospel, such as service, hospitality, giving, teaching, leadership, or compassion. These can give you an open ear for conversation, but make sure you actually *explain* the gospel. So, along with one of those bridges, have a *plan* ready to speak the gospel story. You could use a tract, a website, app, or simply share your conversion experience. But no matter what you use, always include Scripture. There are many tools available. Ask a pastor or a spiritual leader for guidance. As you share your faith, you'll gain a deeper understanding of Jesus and draw closer to Him in the process.

July 28

One Sacrifice for All

Leviticus 16:5

From the beginning, our sin has been the wedge between God and mankind. (Genesis 3) Yet, God has always provided a way to make atonement for His prized possession and draw us closer to Him again. In the Old Testament, God forgave sin on the Day of Atonement. On this day, the High Priest would take two unblemished male goats. The first goat was sacrificed to allow its blood to take the punishment for the sins of man. (Leviticus 16:15-17). The High Priest then took the second goat, called the scapegoat, and laid his hands upon its head to transfer the sins of Israel upon it. The goat was then released into the desert. The live goat removed the sins of Israel from sight and eliminated any lingering guilt. (Leviticus 16:20-22)

In regard to the New Covenant, Jesus symbolically fulfilled the role of both goats. (Hebrews 9:12-14) Jesus, being unblemished, shed His blood to remove the punishment of sin and death, and He became the scapegoat by removing guilt from our sight forever. He did what no other sacrifice could do. With one sacrifice, He substituted both the *sacrificed* and *live* goats with Himself! No other sacrifice can compare to Jesus' ultimate ransom, for there is no need for additional sacrifices. (Hebrews 10:9) By this once-and-for-all act, Jesus secured salvation for those who *believe* in Him! (John 3:36)

Closer Challenge: What more can you say to Jesus than "thank you"? Praise God there is no more need for yearly ceremonies! Jesus has become both the forever High Priest and the one and only sacrifice! **Today**, confess to God any sin you might be harboring. As the High Priest of the Old Covenant would have laid his hands on the live goat to transfer sin, drop to your knees in prayer and transfer your sin to Jesus. You have direct communication with the Savior, so let Him rid you of your sin and guilt. Now, thank Jesus for forgiveness of sins and live gratefully because of His mercy!

July 29

Doing Your Part

1 Corinthians 12:12-13

Scripture teaches that all believers make up one body, forming one unit to function and bring glory to His name. Though a body has many parts, it magnificently works together to perform properly. Without certain parts of your body, dysfunction occurs. If your feet told your eyes, "I do not need you," life would become more difficult for your body. It could still function, but it would be missing one of its key components.

The church is compared to the human body, for we are called the body of Christ. (Romans 12:5) Christ is the head, and those who believe in Him make up the rest of the body. (Ephesians 4:15) Each of us has been gifted by the Spirit with a variety of roles. (1 Corinthians 12:4) If you are not doing *your* part, you hinder the entire church body. Many churches are functioning in a handicap-mode because some of its members are not functioning. This is unfortunate because though the church will continue to function, it is not operating in its full functional capacity. And eventually, faithful members will burn out.

<u>Closer Challenge</u>: Are you faithfully doing your part within the body of Christ? Have you even discovered what your function is? **Today**, evaluate your giftedness and decide what you believe is your role. (This is often affirmed by others in your church.) Now, after it's been affirmed, are you doing it? If not, it's time to step up! Be helpful to your church by adjusting your life to your function in the body of Christ. If you are doing your part, discover ways to improve it. You have a divine purpose. Execute it, and you'll draw closer to God as you do.

July 30

Being Grateful

Luke 16:19-31

In this terrifying story, there is a ray of hope for Christ-followers. The parable is about a rich man who was cast into hell for his lack of belief in Jesus. From his experience, we receive a glimpse of hell. According to this account, hell is full of torment (16:23); it's far away from love (16:23); it's extremely hot (16:24); it's a permanent separation (16:26); and it's a reality for all who do not believe in Jesus (16:27-31). There is nothing pleasant about hell.

Unfortunately, some Christians need frequent reminders of what they'd face if it weren't for Jesus. Distractions from the world can cause a loss of focus, resulting in forgetting about being spared from eternal separation from God. A healthy, biblical view of hell can help keep gratitude at the center of our beings. (It also becomes a motivation for sharing our faith!) Hell is not a popular conversation topic to the ones deceived about its existence. But if you are a believer, it brings joy and gratitude because you know it is not your eternal resting place.

Closer Challenge: Are you secure in knowing you will not be in hell when you die? If so, you have reason to celebrate! **Today**, be reminded of your deliverance from hell. No matter what struggle you are facing, it is not as bad as the eternal punishment in hell. If you are a believer in Jesus, your current situation is temporary, so you can rejoice in the future bliss of heaven. Drop to your knees in gladness and tell your Savior, "Thank you." If gratitude is in your heart, it will be reflected in your actions and countenance. Show gratitude for heaven in the way you live today.

July 31

Happiness Verses Holiness

Hebrews 12:10-11

The pursuit of happiness is a goal for many people. They structure their lives in such a way that will increase *short term* enjoyment by generating large incomes, owning a wide variety of material possessions, and experiencing events that will bring temporary satisfaction. Though temporary happiness can be achieved through these endeavors, they cannot fulfill the deep longing of your soul. The hunt for happiness will leave you searching for answers, but the quest for *holiness* will teach you the ways of God and bring peace. (Romans 6:21-22)

When happiness is the aim of your life, hardships don't make sense. But if your target is holiness, understanding is possible, for you can assess that every difficult situation is used by God in His sanctifying process. Without fire, you cannot be refined. Only when you accept God's refining, leading to holiness, can you begin to understand why there is suffering. Set your mind on chasing holiness, and the amazing part is you'll also find happiness by peacefully trusting in God's will.

<u>Closer Challenge</u>: Are you confused why you are not *happy*? Are you disappointed that the stuff of this world isn't healing your brokenness? If you have not already, change your perspective to seek holiness instead of happiness. **Today**, when you encounter a blessing or adversity, *thank God* for moving you toward holiness. Your current circumstance is part of His plan for maturing you. His hand is on the pulse of your life. He knows exactly how He can use you for His glory. So, in this day, chase after holiness, not happiness. As you do, you'll draw closer to Him, resulting in true inner joy.

August 1

When God Delivers

Exodus 13:17-14:31

After Pharaoh freed Israel from slavery and they were marching to the Promised Land, God hardened Pharaoh's heart, and he chased after Israel to destroy them. While on the banks of the Red Sea, Israel began to lose confidence in Moses' leadership. (Exodus 14:11-12) But Moses challenged his people to keep their faith because God could once again deliver them. When Moses raised his staff and stretched out his arms in obedience to God, the water parted and a way of deliverance was provided for Israel. God saved them just in the nick of time to receive the glory He deserved and the trust He desired.

There are certain breakthrough moments all believers experience as they trust God to deliver in a crisis. The timing might not be what you would desire, but when God delivers, great joy fills your soul. Praise for God inhabits your body and you can't help singing and dancing! (Exodus 15:20-21) Every bit of the waiting and worrying is gone in a flash, and you are left with an inexpressible amount of gratitude. When you experience times of rescue, don't hold back the joy waiting to burst forth from your heart!

Closer Challenge: Has God recently delivered you? If so, have you given Him the praise He desires? **Today**, meditate upon a recent deliverance you've experience from God. It may have been a simple turn of fate or a dramatic lifestyle change. Regardless of the extent, God deserves equal praise. First, in privacy, kneel down and praise God by lifting your hands in adoration as you pray with gratitude. (Psalm 63:4) Secondly, during your next corporate worship experience, be motivated to express adoration in singing because of this liberation. Never forget God's precious moments of deliverance, for they are wonderful expressions of His power and presence.

August 2

God Works through Your Weakness

---•---

Judges 6:16

During one of Israel's periods of rebellion, God raised up Gideon as a judge to return Israel back to Him. Gideon was from the tribe of Manasseh. Manasseh was not a highly favored tribe of Israel. In fact, they were seen as a weak tribe; and within the tribe of Manasseh, Gideon's clan was viewed as the weakest of clans. From a worldly perspective, it did not make sense that God would call Gideon. But God often calls the weak to perform wonders so His power can be seen more vividly.

If God only uses the mighty to carry out His work, we could be quick to judge that it is not God who works through impossible situations, but man. This would be a tragic misrepresentation of God! Therefore, God often uses the weak so we are left with no other explanation but God. Paul boasts in his weakness alone because in his weakness God is made strong. (2 Corinthians 12:8-10) As a believer, you must believe your weaknesses are good for the sake of Christ. For when you are weak, God is able to show His power through you as He did with Gideon.

Closer Challenge: Are you avoiding a divine call due to a weakness? It is quite possible God is calling you to this task to display *His* strength. Do not miss this opportunity for God to present His power and build up your faith in Him. **Today**, determine what God has been calling you to do but you have refused because it removes you from your comfort zone of giftedness. *Name* that one thing and write it in your journal. If God is leading, move forward in faith and trust that God's strength will overmatch your weakness, and He will be exalted through it. As you trust God, you will draw closer to Him as you lean upon Him to carry you.

August 3

Dealing with Divisive People

Titus 3:9-11

There is no way around it. You will encounter divisive individuals within the body of Christ. Such individuals should be dealt with as Paul instructs in this passage. (Titus 3:9-11) First, seek to avoid foolish arguments. Such confrontations are unprofitable and useless. You gain nothing from conversations that constantly end in dissention and irresolution. Do your best to avoid these situations.

But there are times you cannot avoid divisiveness. When you encounter such situations, Paul says to warn the divisive person of this warped perspective. This is a potential volatile, emotional process, so guard your flesh with humility and meekness. Seek the greater good of the individual as you confront this brother or sister in love. (Ephesians 4:15) If this person remains spiteful after the first warning, Paul says to warn again; but this time, have nothing to do with that person until change is evident. Your disengagement with this person will create healthy shame; hopefully, it will turn this person back to God. (2 Thessalonians 3:14-15)

<u>Closer Challenge</u>: Are you entangled with a divisive Christ-follower who is causing ongoing conflict within your church? If so, seek to heal the situation. **Today**, first determine if you can avoid divisive conversations (not people). If not, pray that God would change the divisive person's heart and ask God to reveal any sin in your life *before* you give the first warning. (Matthew 7:3) In a *scheduled* appointment (not in the flesh), have a candid, loving conversation with that individual. If this person heeds the warning, rejoice that God has returned a sinner to Himself! If this person continues to stir up conflict, remove your fellowship until that person repents. This can be very difficult, but follow God's formula and watch how He will be glorified through it. (<u>Note</u>: *Only confront like this if the person claims to be a believer in Jesus. Paul's letter was to believers, not unbelievers. Believers are to keep each other lovingly accountable. If you are dealing with a divisive unbeliever, attempt to lead that person to Jesus.*)

August 4

No Fear in Death

Luke 20:38

Fear of death is a common but unnecessary emotion for a Christ-follower. If you are born again, God already views you as eternally alive with Him. (1 Corinthians 15:22) It makes no difference whether you pass through the door (John 10:9) today or live longer. For if you believe in Christ, a seal of infinity has been placed over your life. Death is nothing more than a portal to the next stage of life in eternal bliss with the Lord. There is nothing to fear!

But for the unbeliever, hope of eternal life eludes their mind. Trust in anything other than Jesus Christ will deny access through the door of heaven. Therefore, fear is present in the unbeliever, and it should be. But for a believer in the Son of God, who became the substitute for death (1 Peter 3:18), you have no legitimate reason to fear while you live on earth. You are alive, and it will never be any different! Live your life excited about the future, making the most of every day you have on earth. (Galatians 6:10)

<u>Closer Challenge</u>: Are you frightened of your next move, fearing death around every corner and allowing that to steal your joy in the present? If so, remember that as a child of God, you are infinitely alive in His eyes. **Today**, refrain from living as though you are dead! Take life by the horns and give it your all. Plan something you have always wanted to do but refrained from it due to fear. Do not live a cooped-up life, unwilling to experience all God has offered here on earth. You are alive; live life to the fullest!

August 5

The Deaf Ear Famine

Amos 8:11-12

Throughout the book of Amos, God reveals His displeasure with Israel because they turned away from Him. So He delivers a set of warnings that will be executed if they do not return their devotion to Him. One of those judgments, possibly the most terrifying, is the removal of His Word from their ears. The *deaf ear famine* is a consequence that no child of God desires to receive. It's a dreadful circumstance for children of God to receive the silent treatment from their Father.

The oracles of God are food for the soul. Just as physical food for the body is vital for nutrients, health, and growth, God's Word is a believer's source of food for spiritual health and development. When it is removed, you will become parched, famished, and weak as you trudge through life. Unfortunately, due to complacency or blatant rebellion towards God, many Christians are starved spiritually. They have received God's punishment of the deaf ear famine. When this happens, there is only one way to receive God's Word again...*repentance*. Any time you sin, admit your flaw and return to God before you shrivel up and become spiritually frail.

Closer Challenge: Has it been a long time since you heard a direct word from God? If so, sin and rebellion might be present. **Today**, specifically locate the last time you had a definite word from God. If you struggle to trace it, maybe you have been experiencing the deaf ear famine due to unconfessed sin or deliberate rebellion. If so, search your heart, and if there is any wicked way, repent *now* to regain spiritual strength from God. Your constant line of communication is vitally important for spiritual health, so steer away from sin and receive God's Word to keep you spiritually fit and close to Him.

August 6

Never Doubt a Sowed Seed

Acts 18:5-8

Paul was devoted to preach the gospel of Jesus to the Jews in Corinth. Yet when they became defiant and spoke harshly against him, he moved his ministry focus away from the synagogue. He refused to waste time at the synagogue where stiff-necked religious people resisted believing in Jesus. He simply took his message next door to the house of Titius Justus. However, though Paul's synagogue ministry seemed like an utter failure, a seed of the gospel took root in one man. Crispus, the synagogue ruler, followed Paul to Titius Justus' house, and he and his household believed in Jesus and were baptized. (Acts 18:8; 1 Corinthians 1:14)

There are times when it seems like your Christian witness is failing. Though you are faithful to speak God's truth, it appears to fall on deaf ears and hard hearts. Yet, never underestimate the growing power of a sowed gospel seed! Beneath the surface, deep within a soul, it can wiggle in the crack of a heart and the Holy Spirit can draw people to belief in Jesus. Who would have thought this synagogue ruler would have followed Paul to the house next door and become a believer? Only the Holy Spirit knows the inner dealings of each person! Only the Holy Spirit can make a seed grow. (1 Corinthians 3:7) As a result, keep preaching Jesus and never doubt the penetrating power of the gospel.

Closer Challenge: Have you sowed seeds of salvation but were disappointed in the results? Be motivated by Crispus' testimony. **Today**, reach out to an individual who has received your invitation to believe in Jesus but hasn't committed to Him. Provide an encouraging phone call, email, text message, or meet this person for lunch. Do not let discouragement stop you from believing God can do a miracle where you have sowed a seed of the gospel. Keep sowing seeds, and let the Holy Spirit do His part in drawing people closer to Jesus.

August 7

Loving Others Heals Wounds

Romans 13:8-10

No era in history has more people on medications for symptoms of depression than today. Though some cases may require the advice of trained professionals, there is a spiritual prescription that can help reduce the pains of depressions. The prescription is *love*. More specifically, it's the act of *giving away* love, which helps peel away layers of despair.

Often, depression is caused when there is too much focus on self. It can be quite depressing when you dwell upon unmet expectation and constantly analyze your failures and hardships. So, if you desire to leave your place of depression, trust in God's sovereignty and grace to give you the gifts of perspective and forgiveness. (Ephesians 2:4-9) Then, begin to look outside yourself to love others. (Ephesians 2:10) When you love your neighbor, you will redirect your focus from your hurts to the needs of others. You will regain purpose, increasing a drive for life. So first, receive the love of God through His mercy, and then, give it away as a gift. It will not only help others, but you too!

Closer Challenge: Depression is a complex issue to address. But God's Word is clear: love one another! Don't just seek it for yourself, but give it away. Love is the only debt you should owe. (Romans 13:8) But unfortunately, you might be behind on the payments, which is causing despair. **Today**, whether you are battling mild cases of depression or not, purposefully *give away* love. Love is rooted in sacrifice. So, make plans today to sacrifice for someone else by going out of the norm to help that person in need. Do this with regularity and watch how this attention to others will bring healing to your soul. (If necessary, seek guidance from a biblical counselor.)

August 8

Choose How God Will Respond to You

Nahum 1:2-3 & 7

In the first chapter of Nahum, God's fair justice is revealed. If you are an adversary of God, you will bring His vengeance upon yourself. God is jealous to avenge His name when it is disrespected. He desires that all His creation worships Him and follows His way. So if anyone chooses not to revere Him, that individual will face the penalty of His wrath. This also implies He is jealous for *our* protection. He knows what is best for us, so when we do not follow Him, danger lurks. Full respect and worship of God is best for us!

In contrast, if you trust God and do not turn away from His teachings, His goodness will follow you. For He is a refuge for believers in times of trouble. (Psalm 28:8) The Christian life is not difficult to understand. If you trust Him, you will receive the blessing of His favor. This doesn't mean you'll receive all you desire nor can you avoid tests of faith, but you can live confidently knowing God has His *final* good in mind for you. (Romans 8:28) Ultimately, at the end of this life, you will receive His everlasting delight in heaven. Yet, if you do not trust Him, you will face His wrath. (John 3:36) Though His full wrath is delayed until the time of death, it will come. Don't be deceived by the postponement of judgment, choose *each* day to follow God.

<u>Closer Challenge</u>: Have you considered the consequences of not following God? You cannot live off of yesterday's obedience. Today is a fresh day to obey Him. We all must stand before the judgement of God to give account of how we lived. (2 Corinthians 5:10) **Today**, in every minor or major decision you face, consider the consequences before you act. Determine if that decision will honor or dishonor God. Examine both possible outcomes and make the wiser choice. Then, urgently run in His direction. Each decision draws you closer to God or further away from Him. What will you choose to follow?

August 9

Looking Forward

---

2 Peter 3:11-14

Three times in this passage, Peter reminds the church to *look forward*. (Some Bible translations convey the meaning as eagerly *waiting*.) *Look forward* to the speedy return of our Lord and live with urgency because your time on earth is short. (2 Peter 3:12) *Look forward* to the new heaven and new earth with the holy expectation of full righteousness. (2 Peter 3:13) *Look forward* to the Lord finding you, His servant, spotless and blameless due to the sacrificial blood of Jesus. (2 Peter 3:14) What a sight it will be for Jesus to look at you and say, "Welcome home, my forgiven child." (Romans 15:7) There is much to look forward to; our Lord has wiped out our past and has prepared a wonderful place for us!

Do not get caught up in looking backwards. (Philippians 3:13) That is how you lose momentum in life as you mature in godliness. The only reason you should look back is to remember God's teachings and to gain understanding from your mishaps. But do not dwell on your mistakes. Learn from them and progress. God instructs you to look forward at what is to come. He granted you freedom from your past with a future worth celebrating!

Closer Challenge: Have you been guilty of eyeing the past instead of looking forward to what is ahead with Jesus? Even your present situation can distract you. So, practice looking forward. **Today**, for a few moments before you start your day, push everything aside and simply meditate on your future reality of being with Jesus in heaven. No more pain, suffering, or tears. (Revelation 21:4) An eternal bliss awaits you! What current or past experience is clouding your mind today? Look forward, because your future is bright!

August 10

The Importance of Followship

―――――•―――――

John 8:12

Our culture typically gives greater attention to *leadership* rather than *followship*. Everyone wants to be a leader! And though it is noble to lead, *everyone* must be a follower, and whom you follow is of utmost importance. You have one of two options. You can either follow the dark ways of Satan and his influence, or you can follow the light and truth of Jesus. If you were to trace the life of every leader, you would see they are either swayed by Satan or Jesus. There is no other way; we all follow one or the other.

Most people believe everything rises and falls with leadership. Though there is merit to this belief, if leaders don't have faithful followers, they cannot achieve much. A godly follower carries out the vision of a leader. Followship takes *sacrifice* of personal agendas, *faith* to move forward even without full understanding, and *discipline* to dependably execute your leader's orders. When you follow like this, you will accomplish much *together*! (John 12:26).

Closer Challenge: No matter what position or title you carry, have you realized you are a follower? Even with the loftiest title, you still follow Jesus. **Today**, list all whom you follow. Start with Jesus, and then recognize all others. Now, honestly evaluate *how* you follow. Are you a complaining, wavering, doubting follower, or are you a loyal, encouraging, servant follower? Strive to be the latter by purposefully displaying the traits of a good follower. Don't be a burden on your leader. (Hebrews 13:17) Go out of your way to show your support. Write a message, give a phone call, or display your loyalty by assisting in a task out of the norm. *Delight* in your role as a godly follower of Jesus and those whom He has entrusted over you.

August 11

The Gospel in Three Verses

Colossians 2:13-15

It's important that we're able to summarize the gospel so that we can explain it to others at any given moment. Flipping from page to page in the Bible can be beneficial as long as you know where you are heading, and you can keep your explanation in context. But there are three verses in Colossians that abbreviate the gospel without compromising any elements of Jesus' work. In Colossians 2:13-15, you can explain the gospel.

This is the gospel according to Paul in Colossians 2:13-15: First, Paul avows that we have a sinful nature, leading to death. And due to our sin, we cannot be made alive by our own might. (2:13a) Secondly, Paul gloriously testifies that even though all are dead due to sin, we can be made alive in Jesus because He has *forgiven* our trespasses. (2:13b) The price for sin has been paid through Jesus! Thirdly, by Jesus' death on the cross, He became our substitute of death by cancelling the debt we owed for breaking the law. (2:14) For those who believe, He has *freely* taken our penalty! Finally, Jesus destroyed the powers of evil by His triumph on the cross, and for those who *believe* in Him (John 3:36), they will triumph with Him! (2:15; 2 Timothy 2:12) That is the beautiful story of the gospel in three verses!

Closer Challenge: Do you have difficulty sharing the gospel? If so, further study this passage of Scripture so you can be better prepared. **Today,** find someone who needs to hear Paul's version of the gospel story. Tell it to an unbeliever if possible, but at the very least, practice this story with your devotional partner. As needed, supplement other verses from the New Testament so you can expound on Paul's points and further clarify the message. You must be prepared to share the gospel (1 Peter 3:15), so do your part to be ready! As you do, you and others will draw closer to Him.

August 12

Transformed Inside-Out

John 3:1-6

When speaking to the Pharisee, Nicodemus, Jesus described what it takes to enter the kingdom of heaven. It commences with being born again. Just as this confused Nicodemus, people today are baffled by this instruction. Being born into the physical world doesn't warrant eternal life with God. Spiritually, all people are separated from God due to sin. (Psalm 14:2-3) As a result, when the Spirit draws you, you must choose to believe in the One who erased sin through His death. Belief in Jesus yields a changed life through repentance and followship. (1 John 3:5-6) This is being born again.

Christian transformation is from inside-out, not outside-in. It starts with belief and results in action. Attempting to transform outside-in through works (such as going to church, being kind, or serving the poor) cannot produce eternal life because it is your sin that separates you from God. Sin has always been the issue. Even if you were sinless starting today for the rest of your life (which is impossible!), any previous sin separates you, and that leads to death. (Romans 6:23) To escape death, something must die in your place! Jesus did that by taking your sin in His body and nailing it to the cross. (Colossians 2:14) Only belief in Jesus can cleanse you and bring you eternal life. And your *belief* in the Son will produce an outward transformation.

Closer Challenge: Are you certain you have been born again? Have you been transformed from the inside-out? **Today**, evaluate your life to determine if your belief in Jesus has led to genuine change. (1 Thessalonians 5:21) If you claim to be a Christ-follower, there must be evidence of transformation. In your journal, create a list of ten evidences of change since being born again. Make a life "before Jesus" column and a life "after Jesus" column. Is there evidence of transformation into a new creation? (2 Corinthians 5:17) If not, be born again! *Believe* in the power of Jesus to change you from the inside-out.

August 13

Who is Your Neighbor?

Luke 10:29-37

An expert in the law sought to trap Jesus with a question. He asked Jesus, "Who is my neighbor?" Instead of Jesus giving a straightforward answer that everyone would expect, He told a parable to explain not only *who* your neighbor is but how you should *love* your neighbor. The expert in the law was attempting to snare Jesus in racial discrimination, but instead, Jesus clarified the law by broadening the call of loving your neighbor to *all* people, not just those who you *want* to help.

In the parable, a man was beaten and abused by robbers. Both the priest and Levite saw the man but walked by without assisting this helpless individual. But a Samaritan, scorned by the Jews because of spiritual and racial matters, not only stopped to assist him, but he went above and beyond the call of duty to bandage his wounds, transport him to shelter, and pay for his stay. In a similar way, Jesus is instructing you to "love your neighbor as yourself," extending assistance to anyone you see in need; and when you do, you are actually displaying love to Jesus. (Matthew 25:35-36)

<u>Closer Challenge</u>: Who is *your* neighbor? **Today**, it's highly likely you will cross paths with someone in need. The need could range from assisting a person with a broken down car to delivering a hot meal to a hungry individual. Keep your eyes open and when the need arises, extend God's love to that person. Use wisdom as you act so you don't place yourself in danger or condone sinful activity. But do your best to help even if there is a little risk and sacrifice involved. Be like the Samaritan who went the extra mile to love this man as himself.

August 14

Defining Your Name

Isaiah 42:8

Names carry meanings, no matter how great or insignificant. When you hear the name Hitler, you immediately associate his name with World War II, dictatorship, and incomprehensible human cruelty. When you hear the name Mother Teresa, you think of compassion and love for the poor. A character judgment typically follows the saying of a name. The name of the LORD is the greatest name in the universe. Every person on earth has an opinion about God's name. The sheer mention of His name sends comfort or conviction to the listeners. God's name is full of righteous character, but only those who believe in Him can begin to understand it.

Whether you know it or not, your name carries perceptions too. Those who know you have created character associations with your name. When they hear or speak your name, immediately they associate you with particular character traits. Some of your character traits may be worthy of repeating, but others may need modification. Overall, you have the freedom of building up your name or tearing it down. Carefully watch how you develop your name, so you can rightfully craft it to please the Father.

Closer Challenge: What do people think of you when your name is mentioned? Is it a legacy worth leaving or does it need improvement? **Today**, ask three good friends what they think of when they hear your name. Tell them to be brutally honest. Prepare your heart for whatever they say. Do not become angry with them if they say something unflattering! (Proverbs 27:5-6) It is up to you to change your ways, not your friends. After your examination, begin to work on developing your name into a reputation that pleases God. Only you can create the definition of your name, so develop it according to God's ways.

August 15

Your Place of Strength

―――――⋅❖⋅―――――

Daniel 10:19

Daniel had an extremely stirring experience with the Lord. On the bank of the Tigris River, Daniel encountered the glory of God. (Daniel 10:5-6) The presence of God resulted in him being helpless and pale, leaving him too weak to do anything but gaze at this great vision. (Daniel 10:8) Yet when the Lord opened His mouth and spoke to Daniel, He calmed his fears and restored his strength. Daniel was refreshed due to God's Word, and it left him wanting more! (Daniel 10:19)

The power of God's Word brings unfathomable strength to all who humble themselves and listen intently to Him. In God's Word, we find our place of strength. At times, you will become so weak and helpless that it is hard to function. Whether it is due to a humbling encounter with God or personal struggle due to an unfortunate circumstance, you may feel too drained to take your next step. The best way to regain your strength is to receive the words of God! Listening intently to God will bring you peace and hope unlike anything else. If you want strength, persistently draw close to God by receiving doses of His Word.

<u>Closer Challenge</u>: Are you weary and helpless today? Are you left unable to move forward due to a burden? If so, seek to regain your strength by humbly listening to God. **Today**, simply *pause*. Block out of your mind all cares and worries. Block out *everything* but the voice of God. Grab your Bible and find a quiet place to rest your soul. Echo the words of Daniel by voicing his prayer, "Let my lord speak, for you have strengthened me." Now open your Bible and just listen. Do not move until the Spirit has given you enough strength to move forward in this day.

August 16

Quiet Hero

2 Timothy 1:16-18

Quietly, some people do more work for the Lord than the preacher proclaiming God's Word before a congregation. Onesiphorus was never recorded preaching a sermon to the masses. He was never known for healing the blind. It is not even known if he held a title in his local church. But what we do know about Onesiphorus is that he is a hero to Paul. Paul was lonely while imprisoned in Rome. He was placed in a dungeon and chained as a criminal. Yet while in his place of confinement, Paul was refreshed, sought out, and helped by Onesiphorus.

Onesiphorus applied a basic principle to his life that we should all model, which is to reach out to the afflicted even if there is no recognition outside of the one being helped. Onesiphorus truly cared for Paul, and you can hear Paul's deep appreciation. Even Paul, an esteemed apostle, was in need of a quiet hero to seek him out and bring him encouragement. Take notice of Onesiphorus' example because there will be times when you will need to be like him for someone burdened by life's struggles.

<u>Closer Challenge</u>: Have you sought to be a quiet hero? **Today**, examine your sphere of influence. Who is in need of spiritual refreshing and selfless help? As Onesiphorus sought to help Paul, do likewise for the person you know who is in need. Without seeking any sort of recognition, selflessly assist this person. Don't delay! This person might be hanging on by a thread. Be a quiet hero as Onesiphorus was for Paul, and you will be displaying love to Jesus. (Matthew 25:40)

August 17

Treating Idol Worship with Disgust

2 Kings 10:18-27

Jehu was on a mission to destroy the prophets of Baal. His plan to bring judgment on these pagan worshippers was to deceive them into thinking they were to perform a great sacrifice in the temple of Baal. When all of them were in the temple, he sent his soldiers inside to slay every one of these false prophets. Not one of them survived. After this mass execution, he expressed his great abhorrence for pagan worship by converting the temple of Baal into a latrine. (2 Kings 10:27) By making this once highly admired temple into a latrine, it signified the disgust he had toward the worship of Baal.

Far too often, Christians are not disgusted by idol worship. Even though they may go to church, read their Bibles, and pray, many believers do not take seriously the need to totally eliminate idols. Consequently, this apathy can leave a portion of their hearts exposed to the influence of foreign gods. God hates worship that is devoted to anything other than Himself. If you have any object of affection that has taken the place of your sovereign, jealous God, eradicate it and allow the Spirit of God to reside fully in your life. Stay purely devoted to Jesus, and He will bring you more than enough satisfaction, diminishing the craving for worthless idols.

Closer Challenge: Is there an idol influencing you away from God? It could be subtle, so closely examine what is diverting your attention and affection away from God. **Today**, if there is something stealing from Jesus your time, talents and treasure, ask for forgiveness, and then totally eliminate it from your life. Confess this idol with your prayer partner; and together, pray for the strength to refrain from it. View your personal idol as a disgusting latrine. God hates idols; you should too!

August 18

A Battle of the Mind

Romans 8:5-8

Your mind is a battlefield. Perpetually you are faced with choices to pursue either good or evil, and depending on what you decide, it can create peace or chaos. And though the choice is ultimately up to you, your environment greatly influences how you choose. If you place yourself in an environment where temptation flourishes, then the likelihood to stumble increases. But if you position yourself in environments of righteousness, your mind will be more likely to follow its ways. Positioning yourself in healthy environments will assist you in making good decisions.

However, you will encounter situations when you will not able to control your environment. Sometimes you are involuntarily forced into unfavorable surroundings. These moments become some of your greatest tests of faith. But it's important to consider that the battle starts long before this moment. Like preparing for a test in school, being proactive to study the course work *before* the test is essential for passing. Likewise, to win spiritual battles, you must allow God to work His righteousness in you *before* the test so you will make wise decisions in the midst of the conflict. Preparing your mind for battle is critical in regard to surviving these imposed tests of life.

<u>Closer Challenge</u>: Is your mind set on things of the flesh or of the spirit? Whatever you are thinking, eventually you will act upon it. **Today**, win the battle of the mind by setting your thoughts on things of the spirit. As Paul writes in Philippians 4:8, set your mind on good, true, lovely, and praiseworthy things. In your journal (or on the back of your hand!), write down at least *three* good, noble, true and pure things you can set your mind on today. At the beginning of each hour on *this* day, remind yourself of these praiseworthy things. This will help you keep every thought captive. (2 Corinthians 10:5) If you discover this to be a good training exercise, practice this on a regular basis so you can win the battle of the mind each day and remain close to God.

August 19

Awakening Romance

Song of Solomon 5:1-16

After reading just one chapter of Song of Solomon, you can easily see the strong attraction the beloved has for her lover. When he is with her, her heart melts. When he is gone, she sinks into disappointment, passionately seeking to find him. (Song of Solomon 5:6) As you read more, you will discover the love is mutual. The romance between the two is quite astounding, and it's an example for lovers today.

In the context of a biblical marriage, God desires that you enjoy your mate, not withholding pleasure from your spouse. (1 Corinthians 7:5) When you become united in one flesh, you are *wholly* bonded, seeking to bring out and provide the best for the other. It's God's plan. But for some people, the romance recorded between these two lovers might seem unnecessary or even embarrassing, because individualism and shame have warped our biblical worldview. There is nothing sinful or wrong about two lovers merged in marriage enjoying each other in physical, emotional, and spiritual bliss. It is what God has intended for marriage. So enjoy your lover, and discover healthy ways to stir up the romance.

<u>Closer Challenge</u>: Has your marriage become dull or maybe even unstable? **Today**, seek to discover ways in which you can escalate the romance. This week, plan a romantic date with your spouse. Without seeking a return and placing undo pressure on the other to perform, do something special for the other that expresses love in a way he/she will feel it. Before you go to bed together tonight, read out loud a few chapters of Song of Solomon. It is likely to increase the romance. If you are not married but desire this kind of union, pray today for a Spirit-filled spouse and settle for nothing less. Enjoy the wife (husband) of your youth and be an enjoyment for the other. (Proverbs 5:18) Not only will it draw you closer together, but you will also experience closeness with God.

August 20

Poor in Spirit

Matthew 5:3

All people desire happiness. We want to experience circumstantial goodness while living on this side of heaven. So in the opening of the Sermon on the Mount, Jesus outlines the characteristics of a *blessed* (happy or fortunate) person. Jesus begins by directing us to be *poor in spirit*. To be *poor in spirit* simply implies that you admit you are in great spiritual need. The one who is poor in spirit is happy because this recognition of need releases the strength of God. When you are weak, He is strong! (2 Corinthians 12:9) Admitting your need for God actually places you in a position of power. If you want to be *happy*, humbly declare your need for God.

Many people believe admitting a need is a sign of weakness, leading to unhappiness, but that could not be further from the truth! Once you recognize your need for God, you receive a supernatural understanding that gives you vision beyond your circumstances. Being *poor in spirit* yields happiness because you no longer trust in your limited strength and understanding but in the powerful, endless wisdom and strength of God. How can you not be *happy* when you have that kind of power leading your life? Seek the happy life by releasing control over to God.

<u>Closer Challenge</u>: Are you hopelessly trying to control your life without God? Control is challenging to release, but blessed is the one who can humbly let go and depend on Jesus. **Today**, identify at least one area your life where you struggle to release control. Typically it's the place where you are most unhappy! Drop to your knees right now and admit your need for God! As you open up yourself to God, watch how He will lift you up and bring you strength like never before. (James 4:10) If you are not a Christ-follower, being poor in spirit is the first step in inheriting eternal life. You cannot come to God until you admit your need for Jesus and place your belief in Him! Be poor in spirit; for it will leave you rich with happiness and close to God.

August 21

Mourning over Sin

Matthew 5:4

Following Jesus' call to be poor in spirit, He directs His followers to *mourn* so that they can be happy. At first, this doesn't seem sensible, since mourning is typically associated with grief. But, as we look closer at Jesus' intention in relation to being poor in spirit, we can begin to understand what Jesus means. The type of mourning inferred here is not a weeping due to bereavement or physical suffering. It is mourning generated from *brokenness* over personal sin. Only after you have been contrite over your sins can you find happiness and peace with God.

When you sin, guilt lingers; and where guilt resides, happiness ceases to exist. So to find happiness after you sin, you must purge guilt with godly sorrow over your disobedience. (2 Corinthians 7:10) God already knows you are imperfect, so it is better to admit your imperfection and lament before God in humility. For when you do, God will not despise your contrite heart. (Psalm 51:17) As a result, mourn over your sins, and as you do, you will find happiness in the comfort of the Father's merciful and loving arms.

<u>Closer Challenge</u>: Is there a sin currently reigning in you? Has the accumulated guilt of that sin left you unhappy? **Today**, somberly confess any lingering sin you have to God. (1 John 1:9) As David mournfully went before God in Psalm 51 after committing adultery with Bathsheba, write in your journal a personal psalm to the Lord, expressing your brokenness. Explain your wrong within the letter and plead for God's mercy. When you do this, God will not refuse to forgive you. Genuinely mourn over your sins, so you can experience the tender mercy of God, and happiness will once again flood your life.

August 22

Being Meek

Matthew 5:5

People often misinterpret what it means to be meek. Meekness has been often paralleled with weakness. Being *meek as a mouse* is a commonly used phrase when describing soft individuals. However, this is not the proper interpretation of Jesus' intent for the word. It would be better to associate meekness to a wild horse that has been tamed so it can be ridden calmly. The horse does not lose its great strength, but its strength is now controlled by its rider to accomplish his will.

When Jesus reveals that the meek shall inherit the earth, He is inferring that those who have allowed their wild flesh to be tamed by the Spirit are now heirs of the Heavenly Father. Being meek does not mean you lose your strength and become a doormat to the world; it simply means you have yielded control to the Spirit so your actions can rightly reflect Jesus and accomplish His will. Jesus is the chief example of biblical meekness. Though He had all power necessary to defend Himself from the torture of the cross, He surrendered to the Father's will by restraining His superior strength. With this in mind, meekness is not weakness; it is a picture of true strength!

<u>Closer Challenge</u>: Are you reflecting the biblical model of meekness or are you selfishly living out of control? **Today**, examine your life to see if anything you have been doing is out of control. Maybe your tongue is untamed. Maybe you have an uncontrolled substance abuse problem. Maybe your eating is unrestrained. Maybe your anger runs wild. If you are not reflecting meekness in any particular area, confess it to God in repentance. Share your struggle with a close friend. Ask this friend to hold you accountable so you can rectify this problem of uncontrolled living. Pray together, asking the Spirit to tame your fleshly, wild behavior. As you apply this challenge, keep in mind that as you accept a meekness-filled life, you will find happiness!

August 23

Righteousness Brings Happiness

Matthew 5:6

The fourth beatitude contains an outstanding promise. If you hunger and thirst for righteousness, you will be filled. As you simply *do right* according to God's Word, you will experience happiness because the shame of sin will be absent from your life. Doing wrong stirs up feelings of emptiness and guilt, but when you seek righteousness and do it, you are left fully satisfied in Jesus. Sometimes it's not easy to do what's right, but after you do it, you are blessed.

The world offers many tempting pleasures that have the appearance of satisfying your emotions, but it only brings temporary gratification. Pursing worldly cravings not only leaves you empty, but you'll also be confused, wondering why this pleasure left you disappointed. It is heartbreaking to watch large numbers of people believe that worldly pleasures can please them greater than God can. And in this endless cycle of disappointment, happiness is unfound. Stop letting the culture attempt to fill your deepest longing of the soul; instead, *do right* and let the Lord satisfy you.

<u>Closer Challenge</u>: Does pleasure tend to escape you as you slip into patterns of the world? If so, simply do right! ***Today,*** take this test. Do at least one *righteous* act you typically would not do in a day. After this test, evaluate to see if there is a greater inward reward in this act than when you selfishly feed your flesh. Here are some examples: buy someone else's lunch unexpectedly; give a surprise visit to someone hurting; physically help someone in need of assistance; shock your pastor by assisting him; relieve a church staff person of a duty; willingly serve at a community food bank or other organization; patiently listen to someone else's dreams and encourage that person; volunteer at a local school; refuse to participate in a sinful act that others are practicing. Put yourself to this test! Discover that as you do right, God will fill you, and you will be happy! Most importantly, as you operate with the right motives, you'll glorify God and draw closer to Him.

August 24

Extending Mercy Produces Happiness

Matthew 5:7

Even with the best intentions in mind, you will disappoint people, and others will disappoint you. Though it's not desired or sought, offending and being offended is unavoidable. In fact, there is a good chance you have been offended by someone this past week. Yet instead of seeking revenge, Jesus reverses the desire of the flesh and directs us to grant mercy when offended. Since extending mercy does not come naturally to the flesh, it takes a supernatural reliance upon the Spirit to obey this command of Jesus.

Extending mercy is actually for *your* good. For when you give it generously, you free yourself from additional harm produced by bitterness and anger. Most importantly, extending mercy is evidence that you have *received* mercy from Jesus. Only after you have experienced divine mercy can you graciously extend loving mercy to another. (Luke 7:47) Out of the overflow of receiving God's mercy, you can give it to others when they don't deserve it. You will also discover it becomes less challenging to grant mercy when you recall Jesus' mercy given to you. Be merciful, for you will receive the unexpected, amazing gift of *happiness*.

<u>Closer Challenge</u>: Consider the many ways in which you have offended God. Has He mercifully forgiven you? Use His forgiveness for you as motivation to grant mercy to others. (Matthew 6:15; Colossians 3:13) **Today**, no matter how major or minor the offense, extend mercy to someone who has caused you grief, pain, or disappointment. First, pray to the Lord, asking for forgiveness since you have harbored bitterness and anger. Now, extend a comforting hand to that person by attempting to restore the relationship. (2 Corinthians 2:5-8) Even if you never become good friends, bury your bitterness by giving mercy to this person. It might be difficult at first, but as you wisely choose to be merciful, you will be blessed.

August 25

The Heart of the Matter

Matthew 5:8

Every evil action and foul word spoken originates in the heart. Jesus said that from the heart come all evil thoughts, murder, adultery, sexual immorality, theft, false testimony and slander. (Matthew 15:19) He also clearly affirms that from the overflow of the heart the mouth speaks. (Matthew 12:34) The heart must be cleaned and controlled by the Spirit if we are to reflect holy living. It's not enough to change our exterior behaviors, for the heart is the engine of all actions. When the heart is Spirit-led, your actions will yield righteousness. When it's not, the flesh will rule and you cannot please God. (Romans 8:8)

Since the heart is extremely vulnerable, it must be given strict boundaries. If your heart is continually set in environments conditioned to condone sin, eventually you will stumble into wickedness. But if you set your heart on things above (Colossians 3:1) and position yourself in righteous environments, goodness is the likely outcome. God continually tests your heart so He knows you are devoted to Him. (1 Thessalonians 2:4) So as each test appears, choose right and you draw closer to God.

<u>Closer Challenge</u>: Whether a pattern of sin is controlling you or you're living righteously, your heart is in need of continual maintenance. Even the slightest evil desire can turn vile and create chaos. **Today**, allow God to do some spiritual surgery on your heart. Each time you are confronted with the opportunity to sin, immediately set your heart and mind on heavenly things. Think and act as directed by the Spirit. You must continually surrender to the Spirit if you are to remain pure. Dedicate your heart to God, and consciously look to Him to clean you from the inside out. And when you do, you will find happiness.

August 26

Seeking Peace

―――――•―――――

Matthew 5:9

Few things are worse in life than residing in continual animosity with others. Relational conflict can slowly deteriorate you from the inside out. Jesus understood the devastating nature of relational hostility, so He challenged His follower to pursue peace. A peacemaker is much different than a peacekeeper. A peace*keeper* seeks to obtain a false reality of peace by avoiding the confrontational situations. Sure, a peacekeeper might shun external conflict but internal conflict remains. This is not being a peacemaker. A peace*maker* courageously and lovingly faces conflict with the full intention of resolving the issue through biblical compromise.

The chief threat against being a peacemaker is selfishness. Acting selfishly enables relational conflict without a course of resolution. When selfish, you fail to act with the greater good in mind. Instead of seeking what is best for others, a person driven by selfishness avoids conflict and allows bitterness to fester. Seek to be a peacemaker by ridding selfishness, and when you do, you will discover lasting happiness as a true child of God.

<u>Closer Challenge</u>: Are you in a relational conflict? Is the cause of your conflict due to your selfishness? **Today**, pinpoint any relationship you have that is lacking peace. Stop waiting for peace; start taking action to create it! Humbly ask God to search your heart and find any wrong in you. (Psalm 139:23) After a short time of internal reflection and repentance, seek peace with that other individual. Drop your selfishness at once and consider the needs of that person more than your own. (Philippians 2:3) Whatever that person wishes from you (within Biblical boundaries), do your best to present it as a peace offering gift. When you humbly act in this manner, you will rediscover happiness in that relationship.

August 27

Suffering for God

Matthew 5:10-12

Jesus verifies that as we live worthy of His name by following His teachings, we will face resistance from those not willing to submit to Him. Yet in a strange twist, Jesus declares we are blessed (happy!) when we are persecuted. This may not make sense at first, but that is exactly what Jesus intended. You are *happy* because it demonstrates you are living rightly before God. Paul proclaimed that everyone who wants to live a godly life in Christ Jesus will be persecuted. (2 Timothy 3:12) As you unashamedly follow Christ, it's not a probability of being persecuted; it's a certainty.

Conversely, if you are *not* persecuted, it's likely you are living more like the world than Jesus. Gliding through your day without a hint of persecution is often a sign you're not making the most of every opportunity. The world will not take offense at your life if they see no difference in you. Even though you should never aim to be persecuted, if you live a normal Christian life in speech and deed, you will inherit at least some level of opposition. And when you do, *rejoice* because great is your reward in heaven!

Closer Challenge: Honestly answer these questions: Have I been persecuted lately? Have I *ever* been persecuted? If not, it's likely you don't have faith in Jesus or you're fearfully hiding it. **Today,** without being obnoxious, when you hesitate to say or do something for Christ in fear of offending someone, press forward in faith. In an attitude of love, say the name of Jesus in a conversation with an outsider and express your dependence upon Him. Let the butterflies in your stomach be a sign that you should talk. If that individual engages deeper into the discussion, praise God that the Spirit has opened a door for you to share the gospel. If that person rejects your message, inwardly rejoice that your reward awaits you. Happy are the persecuted, for theirs is the kingdom of heaven.

August 28

Simply Believe

―――――・―――――

John 6:28-29

Most of the world supposes that if they work hard enough, live rightly, and stay out of serious trouble, they will make it to heaven. This certainly fulfills their moral responsibility as citizens of their country, but it is far from the message of the gospel. Entering heaven has nothing to do with your goodness; it has everything to do with the work of Jesus on the cross. (Galatians 2:16) There is nothing you can do to receive eternal life except believe! (John 6:29)

Since Jesus did all the external work for salvation, all that is left to be done comes from within you. You must *believe* in Him who the Father sent. To believe in Jesus means to put your *trust* in Him. It is not simply acknowledging He exists. Even demons believe in the existence of Jesus, but they do not trust Him nor place dependence upon Him. (James 2:19) Many people say they believe in Christ, but the evidence of their dependence is lacking. If you possess true belief in the full work of Christ, an overwhelming rush of gratitude will spill over from your life, and you'll be seen as a new creation!

<u>Closer Challenge</u>: Have you fully trusted in the work of Jesus on the cross, or are you still trying to achieve your salvation? **Today**, concede to the reality that there is nothing left for you to do concerning salvation except *believe* in Jesus. To serve as a reminder of this amazing truth, write on the top of your hand with an ink pen, "Just Believe." Each time you take a glance at these words written on your hand, thank Jesus for His sacrificial work on the cross for you. Rejoice that your work is to believe. And as a result, let your belief transform you from the inside out!

August 29

Be Zealous for God

Galatians 4:18

All of us have a unique purpose ordained by God to accomplish good. (1 Corinthians 3:8-9) Some callings *seem* more important than others, but *nothing* is insignificant. No day is wasted. Everyone has an opportunity to glorify God. With each new day, God specifically calls *all* His children to impact their culture; so it is zeal, not calling, that separates the faithful from the rest. The zealous believer sees every event as an opportunity to leave an eternal mark. Every breath has meaning. Every second matters. (Romans 12:11)

It is tempting to believe much of your day is meaningless. If you fail to focus on God, it can certainly feel that way. (Ecclesiastes 1:2-3) But even a seemingly meaningless task can have eternal value if you zealously use it as a platform to advance the gospel. Something as trivial as walking your dog can have eternal impact if it is used to strike up a conversation with an oncoming pedestrian. Everything you do can have purpose, but you must be aware of your surroundings and be willing to take advantage of every opportunity. You have no idea when the Spirit will turn a simple conversation into a splendid display of His glory!

Closer Challenge: Do you have a seemingly meaningless task you must accomplish today? You might need to fill up your gas tank. You may need to pick up a few items at the store. You might have a doctor's appointment. What is it in your day you must do that seems quite routine? **Today**, be zealous to advance the gospel when you perform that task. Keep your eyes aware of those around you. Invite someone to church, share your testimony, or provide a helping hand to someone in need. You can make a difference even when things appear to be routine. Be zealous with a purpose!

August 30

Rejecting Laziness

Proverbs 10:4

God instructs you to labor hard in all you do. When at work, don't cut corners. When at home, offer full strength to your family. When you are volunteering, give it your best. Do not slack off, for you are reflecting more than just yourself. As a Christ-follower, you are created to reflect the Lord in your actions and attitudes as you serve Him well with purpose. (Ephesians 2:10) With this in mind, dedicate yourself fully to God in everything you do, and you will be rewarded justly. (Proverbs 10:4)

Slackers will not receive rewards. Laziness is a seemingly harmless sin that can dangerously misdirect a person's life. In fact, many laugh at it as a cute personality trait. But when you are lazy, you decrease your chances of impacting this world for Christ. Furthermore, slothful people often lead themselves to poverty. (Proverbs 13:4) It is no laughing matter. You've only been given a short amount of time on earth. If you are lazy, you'll find yourself looking back at your life with a large amount of regret due to missed opportunities.

<u>Closer Challenge</u>: Which label do you most resemble: hard worker or lazy slob? If it's the latter, the good news is you can change! **Today**, repent and then fully give yourself to complete a task that has been lingering. Is there an assignment you need to complete at work? Do you have an incomplete project at home? Have you been lazy in strengthening a close relationship? Remember, procrastination is a form of laziness. Don't put off this task any longer! Disallow laziness to creep into your life. Habitually give your best each day so you can review your time and think, "Well done." Ultimately, as you draw closer to God in this manner, He will reward you with increased responsibility and reward. Be diligent in all that you do.

August 31

Associating with Underprivileged

Romans 12:16

Much of our time is spent focusing upon people in higher positions of power and social classes, wondering what it would be like to live in their shoes. Even though it can be healthy to learn from these individuals and set high goals for yourself, never lose sight of those who are less fortunate than you. Paul urged Christ-followers to associate with the underprivileged. It can be uncomfortable to humble yourself by associating with such people, but as you apply this instruction, your efforts will be recognized by God. (Matthew 25:40; Proverbs 14:31)

You probably know someone beneath you socially and economically. Even if you feel as if you haven't accomplished much in life, someone is trying to achieve your level of success. Pray for the compassion to connect with this person. Those with less renown are often avoided because they have less to offer in return. Yet, seeking return from such an individual should not be your motivation. Never allow vanity to control your life! Thinking too highly of yourself will drive you away from the ones you can most significantly impact. So instead, turn to associate with those of a lower status. After all, Jesus humbled Himself to relate to us in our lowly state. (Philippians 2:4-8)

<u>*Closer Challenge*</u>: Do you associate with those who are underprivileged? **Today**, initiate contact with someone *less* fortunate than you. (Keep in mind this person isn't any less important to God than you are!) This person could be a co-worker employed beneath you, a socially awkward acquaintance, or a beggar you often pass by on the streets. You are not called to fix all this person's problems, but merely associate with this person. Take this person out for a cup of coffee. Share a hobby together. Invite this individual to your house as a sign of acceptance. Sit with this person at church. Drop your smugness, and you'll reflect the compassion of Jesus.

September 1

Aim for Perfection

———◆———

2 Corinthians 13:11

In some of Paul's final words to the Corinthians, he urges the church to be fully restored. Being complete in this manner is a passive idea of being made perfect or being made fully mature in the faith. His plea was not a gentle request to keep striving in our attempt to live good lives, but a high expectation of God making us excellent in all areas of life, including our relationship with others. Paul understood that anything less than our best was not good enough for the Lord. And even our best falls short of His flawlessness. However, we are called to reflect His perfection with righteous works.

As a Christ-follower, you should always trust and rely upon grace. It is God's grace that saves you, and it is His grace that sustains you. (Ephesians 2:8-9) However, grace does not remove your call to aim for perfection. (Matthew 5:48; Romans 6:1-2) In all walks of your life, you should desire to better yourself and constantly surrender your life to the Spirit to resemble Jesus in the best possible manner. Though perfection is unattainable while in this life, that doesn't mean you should stop striving for it. Aim for perfection, and when you fail in your attempt, rely on grace to redeem you.

<u>Closer Challenge</u>: Are you still aiming for perfection in all areas of your life or have you given up in some ways? **Today**, locate an area of your life where you have settled for less than striving for perfection. Write down in your journal five different ways you can improve that area to better reflect Jesus. Today and over the next several days, attempt to perfect that area of your life by embracing those values you wrote down. Do not quit until you have made strides in working toward perfecting it. Never give up. Your call is to aim for perfection, so keep progressing.

September 2

Don't Waste Your Abilities

Matthew 25:14-30

We all have been uniquely created by God to strategically build up God's Kingdom on earth. Some have been given a greater amount of responsibility with their giftedness, so God expects a greater return from those individuals. (Matthew 25:15) Yet the measure God uses to evaluate faithfulness deals more with effort than the amount of return. As illustrated in the parable of the talents, one servant was given five talents, and he invested it and had a return of five additional talents. The second servant was given two talents, but his return of two additional talents was less than the first servant's gain. However, regardless of the size of return, God considered both of them good and faithful servants. The amount of the return was not the issue; it was the effort not to waste what was given.

But the third servant greatly displeased his master. He was given a talent, but merely hid it. He wasted his responsibility. There was no *attempt* to gain more. Therefore, his master considered him a wicked and lazy servant, and he was cast into darkness. God has given you abilities to serve Him. There is no question you will vary in your abilities and return compared to other believers. However, whatever you have, you must not waste it! Whatever gifts, talents, skills, abilities, and resources God has given you, do not hide them but use them for His glory.

<u>Closer Challenge</u>: How has God equipped you to serve Him in this world? What is your special or unique talent? **Today**, determine if you are wasting that talent. If you are, discover new and fresh ways in which you can serve God with your abilities. If you need ideas, talk with your pastor or another church leader today to help you discover possibilities for using your abilities. Once you have an idea, do not hide it! Make your Father proud by investing your life into His work. What a beautiful sound it will be when you hear your Father say, "Well done, good and faithful servant."

September 3

Remember, Repent, and Return!

Revelation 2:4-5

The church in Ephesus was a good church. They faithfully served God, worked hard, persevered, stood against wickedness, and even endured hardships in the name of Jesus without growing weary. Outwardly they were doing as instructed, but inwardly they had lost something. They lost the passion and love they had at the beginning. Sure, they were doing the work of the Lord, but they had forgotten why they were serving God in the first place. They were not motivated by love.

Many believers are in this same trap. They are doing the work of the Lord, but they are not driven by the love that captured them from the beginning. If you view Christian service this way, you will eventually become numb to the reason why you served God in the first place. Furthermore, you will begin to view your calling as a meaningless chore instead of a privilege inspired by gratitude. You might still do the work, even until death, but the joy will be erased if you keep viewing your service this way. If you have gotten to this point, Jesus calls you to remember from where you had fallen, repent of your loss of focus, and return to your first love. Once again, stir up the love you had for Jesus!

Closer Challenge: Are you still doing the work of the Lord, but you have lost your love for Him? **Today**, first spend some time remembering where you were without Jesus. If that is difficult, take a walk in the park or at a mall and observe so many living without Him. Be reminded of where you would be without Jesus. Then, repent of your first love abandonment. Ask Jesus to forgive you; return to Him. In your next service opportunity, serve Him with joy, not as a chore. Remember the first time you experienced God's love and the inexpressible joy that gushed through your soul. Let that be your motivation to serve.

September 4

A Dreadful Place

―――――•―――――

Jeremiah 8:12

The most dreadful place on earth is not a physical location. It is a condition of the heart when you are unable to feel shame after doing, seeing, or thinking wrong. Initially, when Adam and Eve experienced sin for the first time, they were filled with shame, so they hid. (Genesis 3:8) Though repentance would have been a better response, hiding at least displayed an *awareness* of their guilt. However, if sin reigns in or around you for an extended amount of time, you can become so desensitized to it that awareness will fade and the hardness of your heart will block out conviction induced by the Holy Spirit. When you have reached this ghastly state, you have lost the ability to blush. (Jeremiah 8:12) You are no longer embarrassed when you are caught in sin or hear of it. Shame no longer draws you to repentance. This is a dreadful place!

Unfortunately, many Christians reside in this place. Their hearts are numb to the working of the Holy Spirit, due to patterns of widespread sinful activities in the culture and in themselves. Sins that once made God's children blush with shame no longer have that effect. These sins are now accepted as cultural norms, and disoriented believers look at them with indifference instead of disgust. What a wretched state! You must stand for righteousness by asking the Holy Spirit to reveal sin and make you uncomfortable when you see it in your life and the culture. If not, you will lose the ability to blush, and drift further away from God!

Closer Challenge: Are you desensitized to the work of the Holy Spirit? Are you numb to the sins of the culture? **Today**, check your ability to blush. When you see or experience sin in or around you throughout the day, examine your heart to see if you become uncomfortable. From the smallest sin to the greatest, you should blush with embarrassment if you are allowing the Holy Spirit to work through you. Before you do anything today, drop to your knees and ask the Holy Spirit to open your eyes to the immorality around you and be repulsed by it. Only then can change begin to occur.

September 5

Confronting Leadership

---

1 Timothy 5:17-20

In the life of the church, it's likely you will be at odds with decisions made by church leadership. It is impossible for leadership to please each church member due to diverse personalities, different passions, and various levels of spiritual maturity. That is why your leadership must focus on the heart of God. It is a formidable task for leadership to move the church in the direction God desires and maintain unity in the body of Christ. As a result, Paul enlightens young Timothy and his church that elders are worthy of double honor. Leadership should be given more respect and appreciation than criticism and complaints. Positive support should always outweigh negative retorts.

However, when criticism is warranted, Paul explains the mode in which it should be delivered. (1 Timothy 5:19) If there is an accusation of false doctrine or immorality against your leadership, it should *not* be delivered by a well-meaning, solo, third-party messenger speaking on behave of other anonymous, disgruntled church members. A well-articulated, thorough reproach should be prepared. Then, after a time of concentrated prayer and self-evaluation (Matthew 7:3-5), it should be delivered with love in person, along with two or three other witnesses. Confronting your leadership in this manner is respectful and will offer the best possible environment for a healthy conversation and change.

<u>Closer Challenge</u>: Do you have a charge against a church leader? If so, follow God's directions. **Today**, if you have an ethical rebuke to offer an elder, cautiously gather two or three witnesses and approach this person in love. Be careful that you are not stirring up unwarranted conflict. If you have a legitimate issue with leadership, others will have witnessed it without speculation. If the witnesses do not agree with you, repent immediately and drop the issue. You must be cautious not to crush the spirit of your leader by creating more problems in reporting gossip or promoting preferences. More importantly, you are called to extend double honor to your leaders. Also **today**, kindly honor your leadership. If you are a pastor, staff member, or fellow elder, affirm those who serve with you. Constant support is needed for those who carry the burden of leading.

September 6

What Is Your Reputation?

Acts 17:6

When Paul and his missionary crew arrived in Thessalonica on his second missionary journey, his reputation arrived before him. After Paul reasoned with Jews in the synagogue for three days (Acts 17:2-3), many of them became jealous of his influence, and they rounded up some bad characters to destroy the movement in their town. It was believed by many Thessalonians that Paul had come to shake up their town and cause trouble. They were correct in that he was causing a stir everywhere he went, but they failed to understand that the disturbance was for their good.

Though this kind of negative attention is not desired when spreading the gospel, it is unavoidable if you simply live out your faith as intended. Those who came in contact with Paul knew his worldview was different. His reputation had become universal for spreading the life, death, and resurrection of Jesus. Even though many did not welcome him because of his reputation, Paul did not alter his mission to acquire approval from people. He simply obeyed God, regardless of their opinion of him.

Closer Challenge: What is your reputation? Does your reputation for being a Christ-follower precede you? If people don't already know your stance in Christ, they ought to know fairly quickly after meeting you. **Today,** tell at least one person, whom you have never told, that you follow Jesus. See if your reputation preceded you. And yes, voicing this might cause some disturbance, even if it's only inward. But since eternity might be at stake for this individual, find the courage to share who you are. You may not be called to go on missionary journeys like Paul, but you have been given a sphere of influence to infiltrate the gospel. May your reputation of Jesus precede you!

September 7

Facing Opposition

Ezra 4:1-5

While in exile, the Jews received a decree from the Persian King Cyrus to return to Jerusalem and rebuild the Temple, as prophesied by Jeremiah. (Ezra 1:1-3; Jeremiah 29:10-14) God's plan for Israel was to bring them back from captivity and make them into a great nation once again. So when they returned and began to rebuild the Temple, some of their enemies offered to help with false motives. Israel's leadership sensed they were being disingenuous, so they declined their offer. (Ezra 4:3) This created a disturbance with their enemies. Through intimidation and fear, Israel's enemies frustrated their plans and attempted to thwart their work. (Ezra 4:4-5) The Jews faced more opposition later and even had to stop work for a period of time. (Ezra 4:24) But in the end, they were resilient and eventually finished the reconstruction under the rule of King Darius.

When God's people seek to perform a task for His glory, it's likely they will face resistance. But as seen throughout history, when God's people display resilience, they will prevail even if they experience a few scars and delays along the way. God has given you a plan for your life. Yet it's foolish to believe that plan will be executed smoothly. The evil one has a plan for you, too. It's to destroy. (John 10:10) Furthermore, sometimes God will allow hardships to test your faith. (Job 1:9-12) So even if you are staunchly committed to Jesus, you will face challenges but persevere to complete it.

Closer Challenge: Is God's plan for your life delayed or interrupted due to resistance? Name that plan and identify any areas of opposition. Is it an exterior opposition from others? Or is it an internal opposition, such as struggling against your flesh? It could be a combination of both. If you know God's plan for your life, show some resilience to keep going! **Today**, pray with your partner to overcome this opposition. Only through prayer, strategic planning, and perseverance can you overcome the schemes of the enemy.

September 8

Seeking an Undivided Heart

Psalm 86:11

Our heart's devotion is never idle. It is constantly pursing something. And if it is left unattended and undisciplined in its natural state, it is perfectly content gravitating toward exalting self and seeking idols of this world. But when the heart is introduced to Jesus, being exposed to the knowledge and goodness of God, the heart wages battle. It becomes divided. The sweet mercies of Jesus and divine clarity of the gospel satisfy its longing. But darkness doesn't give up easily. The evil schemes of the devil lurk around your heart, seeking to mislead and divide your affections away from God.

Possessing an undivided heart doesn't happen by accident. It's a daily choice. David pursued an undivided heart by beseeching God for the teachings of His truth. The constant pursuit of saturating yourself in divine teachings brings you a heart fully devoted to God. You must surround yourself with godly conversations, Bible studies, good preaching, and personal devotions. Satan isn't concerned with taking your *whole* heart; he just wants a *piece* of it to divide it. God wants the whole thing. God is jealous for your devotion, because He knows what you need. So, perpetually pursue and obey His teachings, and you will unite your heart with His.

<u>Closer Challenge</u>: Do you have an undivided heart that seeks God? If not, follow David's example to acquire it by receiving the teachings of God. **Today**, think of new ways in which you can be taught the Word of God. Even if it's just for a short season, commit to a Bible study you have not experienced. Follow a solid, renowned teacher through an online resource. Read a book from a respected author you have never read. Study a portion of the Bible that you often overlook. If you want an undivided heart, you must constantly be taught the ways of God. Choose an undivided heart by asking God to inject His teachings in you.

September 9

Remaining Consistent in Your Faith

Joshua 23:6

In Joshua's final days on earth, he repeated what was entrusted to him when he took over as leader after Moses. Earlier in Joshua's life, the Lord exhorted him to be strong and courageous and never let the Book of the Law depart from him. (Joshua 1:6-8) And through his reign as the leader of the Israelites, he fulfilled this mandate as he fought battles in faith, followed God's law, and led this new nation to obtain God's Promised Land. Then, at the end of his life, he simply repeated these words of faith to the ones who would follow him. Joshua remained consistent in his life, and it paid off in the end.

A consistent, steady life is a great virtue. (1 Corinthians 15:58) But on the contrary, a spiritually inconsistent life reveals a certain level of doubt. Doubt does not honor God. For the one who is double-minded should not think he will deserve anything from God. (James 1:6-8) God desires that you attach to His Word in faith and never sway from it. When you do, you will gain victory and peace. (Isaiah 26:3) Regardless of your circumstances, aim to be consistent in your journey with Jesus, and you will be rewarded like Joshua.

<u>*Closer Challenge*</u>: Is your faith consistent, or do you tend to fluctuate depending on your circumstances? **Today**, begin to place some consistency in your life by creating a routine of praise and prayer. Possibly, listen to worshipful music in the morning on the way to work; read a Psalm during breakfast; or take a prayer walk during the day. Some days it may not appear to make a difference, but when life presents a challenge, you are in position to remain steady with God. Practice consistency, and you'll be able to wrestle through tough times.

September 10

Live or Die for Jesus

Romans 14:8

Your life as a Christ-follower is marked by the answer to this one question: Did you live for Jesus? All other matters are frivolous. Whether you rose to the top of this world with success galore or sank to the bottom with numerous hardships, when it is all over, all that matters is how you responded to Jesus. In this statement, Paul makes it clear that what matters most is if you are the Lord's in life and death. In your strengths and weaknesses, use them both to exalt Jesus while you walk this earth.

Each day, people are faced with death. Some deaths are tragic accidents while others are prolonged sufferings. Either way, death is coming to us all. But death is not the final chapter. How you decide to live on earth will determine your destination and rewards in the afterlife. If you choose to believe Jesus by faith through His grace, the overflow of your life will be to live for Him. You belong to Him. Your life is sealed with His mission. There is one call for your life: whether you live or die, you belong to Him, so live it for His honor. (2 Corinthians 5:14-15)

<u>Closer Challenge</u>: Is Jesus your Lord? If so, every breath should reflect that truth. **Today**, think about the life you have been given. You were not brought into this world by your own efforts. You were created uniquely with a purpose to serve and honor God. Therefore, no matter what you do through your occupation, relationships, hobbies or other means to fill your time while you live, do it for Jesus. (1 Corinthians 10:31) Reset your life to *think* differently today. Be mindful of what you have been given, and glorify the Lord with it.

September 11

Life-Altering Events

Genesis 50:20

Joseph was a man who arrived at great influence, but it wasn't without a great deal of pain. He was hated, beaten, and sold into slavery by his brothers. He was wrongly accused of sexual abuse and adultery and then locked behind bars for two years. But in spite of such tragedy, God raised him to great power and influence, being second only to Pharaoh. And when finally confronted by his brothers in his new leadership position, he ultimately granted them mercy. Joseph realized that his unexpected hardships allowed a way for him to save many lives, including his family. Instead of harboring hate, he chose to view life from God's perspective.

It is likely you have experienced inordinate adversity in life. Evil lurks around every corner. Often, it comes in the most unexpected ways, such as Joseph being mistreated by his own family. September 11, 2001 will always be a tragic, memorable event that changed the course of history. However, though tragedy defines much of this day, God can make good out of it for those who love Him. (Romans 8:28) And in your personal times of tribulation, He can turn the most dreadful situation into a beautiful expression of His glory if you just trust and love Him.

<u>Closer Challenge</u>: Have you recently faced an event that has altered your life? **Today**, use that event as faith fuel for your future. God has allowed certain events to occur to shape you uniquely for His purposes. Instead of focusing on the evil that is associated with this life-changing event, write down in your journal three ways this event can bring meaning in your life and glorify God. Seek to begin accomplishing these objectives today. As you maintain a godly perspective, you will be able to draw closer to God and see the good in even the foulest circumstances.

September 12

Judging the Family

1 Corinthians 5:12-13

Paul asks a question that many believers answer incorrectly. He asks, "Is it not those inside the church whom you are to judge?" It is commonly assumed the answer is no. After all, what right do we have to judge when we ourselves are sinners? Isn't that Jesus' role? (John 5:22; Revelation 19:11) It is true that we are sinners and Jesus is the ultimate Judge, but you are not completely eliminated from the role of righteous judging. God's desire is that we correct other Christians so that we do not display a poor witness of Jesus or His Bride, the church. Outsiders (unbelievers) are not to be judged by Christians. That is God's role. (1 Corinthians 5:13) We are simply to speak truth to them pertaining to salvation so that the Spirit will change them.

But there is a proper way to judge those within the Body of Christ, as explained in Matthew 7:3-5. Before you are to say a word to another Christian about his or her lifestyle choices that are resulting in sin, you must first make sure your life is as clean as possible so you are not a faulty messenger of truth. Furthermore, your approach should not be smug or arrogant, but gentle and meek, filled with love, to see your brother or sister restored. As a Christian you are called to keep other believers accountable, so do your part in love, aiming for restoration. (2 Thessalonians 3:14-15)

Closer Challenge: Are you aware of another Christian's sin? Have you kept quiet in fear of being labeled as judging? **Today**, find the courage to confront that individual. First, examine your life and rid any sin that may block your credibility. You may even need to confess your sin to that individual to minimize the resistance. Then, motivated by love, speak of the other person's wrongdoing with a heart that aims for healing. This course of action will be difficult, but believers commune with one another for the sake of building up each other. (1 Thessalonians 5:11) Remember, if you really love someone, you will speak truth regardless of the pain it may inflict on both of you. (Proverbs 27:6) In the end, proper judging will draw you closer to God and each other.

September 13

The Voice of Correction

2 Samuel 12:1-13

David was the anointed king of Israel. He was God's chosen man to be the earthy ruler of His nation. Yet, David was still a normal man with the capacity to sin like anyone else. During a time he should have gone off to war, he stayed home and fell into sin by committing adultery with another man's wife. (2 Samuel 11:1-5) The Lord sent Samuel, the prophet, to approach David and speak the truth to David about his wrong. After Samuel had opened these wounds of sin in David's life, David realized his wrong and confessed his sin. (2 Samuel 12:13) However, the damage had been done and he had to face the consequences of his transgressions. (2 Samuel 12:15-18)

At some point in your distant or recent past, it's likely you have sinned without getting caught. David probably had thought he would be able to slide by and keep his little dirty sin a secret. But this story is evidence that God sees everything, and He punishes sin accordingly. Your sin does not go unnoticed by God; so it is better for you not to hold it but expose it before your Maker. When you face correction, heed it before you face greater consequences.

<u>Closer Challenge</u>: Have you committed a hurtful sin but have kept it a secret? **Today**, consider this devotional entry as your voice of correction. Though you may not have a prophet look you in the eyes and say, "You are that man," believe God is using this entry and David's example as your wake-up call. As David did, fall to your knees and repent by crying out, "I have sinned against the Lord." (Psalm 51) Though this will be difficult, confide your rebellious act with your partner or a close friend. This will be helpful to you as you release it from secrecy. If restitution is necessary, do not delay. Make things right so you can be clean from the guilt that troubles you.

September 14

The Search for Truth

———◆———

Colossians 2:8

The world is full of lies, false doctrines, and carnal lifestyles that attempt to steer you in the direction opposite of your Savior. All it takes is one applied erroneous teaching to make you fall into the trap of Satan. Paul understood the danger of falling away from truth. He wrote that you should be aware of the hollow and deceptive philosophies that await your acceptance. These teachings have an appearance of something good, but they are void of true substance. They root themselves on manmade traditions instead of the rich truth of Christ.

Examples of these kinds of hollow teachings are all around you, and they penetrate your heart and mind on a daily basis. Some of the worldly philosophies you encounter regularly include debauchery, sexual freedom, selfish gain, and covetousness. You can follow the ways of the world or you can turn to the truth you find in Christ. But the only way you can stay true to Christ's teaching is to be immersed in it. Take the time to learn something new about your Lord, and you will be less likely to stumble into the empty teachings of the world.

<u>Closer Challenge</u>: Do you find yourself struggling to resist vain teachings of the world? **Today**, try something a bit more challenging. Begin to slowly read through a theology book written by a reputable, conservative biblical scholar. Allow this book to sharpen your mind in biblical truths as you read it. Ask your pastor or a spiritual leader for guidance in regard to which book would be appropriate for you. As you search for truth, the ways of the world will become less influential in your life.

September 15

Running to Mercy

Isaiah 30:18

Israel had been rebellious toward God. And in their uprising, they had refused the loving comfort of the Holy One by running in the opposite direction. (Isaiah 30:15) Yet God did not turn His back on them. In fact, He yearned to receive them back into His arms. Scripture teaches that God rises to show you compassion. (Isaiah 30:18) The picture denotes a seated King standing to His feet to embrace His wayward child. That is the unconditional love your Father has for you.

Why run from God when He longs to show you compassion? It is tempting to suppose that God would refrain from showing you mercy after you betrayed His kindness. But that is far from the truth! Whatever you have done to turn your back on God and embrace the things of this world, God longs to be gracious to you. He deeply desires to be brought back into union with you. But you are the one who must turn around. He is already waiting with open arms. Stop fleeing God, and start running to mercy!

Closer Challenge: Are you longing for mercy but fear God would reject you? Reread Isaiah 30:18. Now, **today**, run into the arms of your caring Father by dropping your sin and reaching out for His mercy. At some point throughout the day, give at least fifteen minutes of uninterrupted time to God just to reflect on His mercy. Take a walk outside; sit in a quiet place where you can observe His creation; relax on a swing. Do what is pleasing to you, but when you do this, *think* about God's love for you. It will help you run from your sin and sprint to God. Do not make yourself a prisoner of your own pride. Drop your pride and be embraced by your Father who loves you deeply.

September 16

Your Trust Is Your Strength

———•———

Isaiah 30:15

We often believe our strength comes from our physicality, talents, gifts, experiences, personality, or looks. But this is far from the truth. Those are God-given qualities that allow and enable you to glorify God and find purpose in this world, but they are not the source of your strength. Your strength comes from your *trust* in God. When you are facing challenges, you demonstrate strength by remaining calm and quiet as you wait for God to work through your situation. And whether or not He does what you request is irrelevant; what is relevant is fully trusting that He will do what is best for His glory and your eternal benefit.

If you desire to become strong, you must regularly exercise your trust. As you would walk to gain a good cardiovascular workout for your heart or lift weights to strengthen your muscles, you must exercise your faith. You will never grow stronger if you continue to worry and complain about your trials. Calmly, trust that God is in control and begin to build strength from the inside out. You can be strong, but you must trust in God's strength, not your own.

Closer Challenge: Are you consciously exercising your faith in God so you can build up a strong inner core? **Today**, train your spiritual strength. Name one thing that has been burdening you. This affliction could pertain to an illness, a relational conflict, or some other constant burden. Bring this challenge to God by praying for strength to live by faith throughout the struggle. (Galatians 2:20) Without considering the outcome of the situation, simply focus on God and *trust* in His ability to do His will. If you do this with regularity, you will allow your trust to be your strength.

September 17

Changing Plans

---•---

Acts 16:16-40

When Paul and Silas were on their way to pray, their day morphed into a Spirit-filled adventure. They probably didn't expect beforehand that on their way to pray they would be redirected to cast out an evil spirit from a little girl, which set them before the town authorities. This created a riot, resulting in them being stripped, flogged, beaten, imprisoned and chained. While in prison, they conducted a worship service and experienced an earthquake to release them (but chose not to escape), resulting in them leading a jailer and his whole family to Jesus. What a day! And none of it was planned. This is what can happen when you choose to follow the Spirit on a daily basis.

Most of your days are probably already filled with scheduled events. (If not, it is time to find some purpose in life!) But just because you have planned your day, it does not mean God can't interrupt it and completely change it as part of His will. The events that preceded the jailer's conversion didn't appear to be Paul and Silas' plan for the day, but when it was all said and done, they did their part in that day to glorify God. You must open your eyes to situations around you and respond as God directs. As you do, you may have a Spirit-filled adventure awaiting you.

<u>Closer Challenge</u>: Do you live by the Spirit, following His lead? **Today**, even as you leave your house, open your eyes to God-ordained opportunities. Keep your commitments as best as possible for today, but if you sense God is moving you in a different direction, do not miss out on what He may have in store for you and His kingdom. He may lead you off the planned path in a slight way or He may drastically alter your day. However He leads, be adventurous by living according to the Spirit. Whatever happens, be sure to write down your experience in your journal. Make a habit of being led by the Spirit each day of your life.

September 18

Avoid Godless Chatter

2 Timothy 2:16-17

Speaking and listening to godless chatter has a destructive impact on your wellbeing. It may seem harmless to say a few crude words or listen to ungodly remarks, but you are damaging your soul and others when you participate in such conversations. As Paul implies in these verses, if you welcome godless chatter, it will spread feverishly, creating unhealthy environments. (2 Timothy 2:16-17) The godless chatter Paul is referring to deals more with false teachings, but godless chatter is any form of speech that contaminates your life with evil babbling.

Godless chatter can arise in many different forms throughout your day. You may speak it to a co-worker or neighbor. You may hear it on a television show or movie. You may read it online. You may casually overhear someone speaking negatively about another. You could be confronted with false teachings. No matter what the vehicle of godless chatter, it will slowly but surely hinder your spiritual growth if you continue to embrace it. As best as you can, avoid such conversations; but when it's unavoidable, intentionally direct the conversation in an uplifting manner.

<u>Closer Challenge</u>: Do you find yourself regularly engaged in or surrounded by godless chatter? **Today**, if you encounter a situation where you are confronted with godless chatter, ask if you could pray out loud for that person or situation. Praying often squelches godless chatter quicker than anything else. It may seem awkward to pause and pray in this moment, but it is the healthy thing to do. Steer away from godless chatter with the simple act of praying.

September 19

Prayers for Missionaries

2 Thessalonians 3:1-3

Near the end of Paul's second letter to the Thessalonians, he asked Christ-followers to pray for him and his missionary team. His request was not for money or power, but it was a specific twofold prayer. First, Paul asked that they would pray for him to be able to spread the gospel. Paul's ultimate call was to deliver the gospel to those who did not know the Lord in foreign lands, so he asked for prayer to continue this effort. Secondly, he asked them to pray for safety against those who resisted the gospel. He knew he would face fierce danger, but he firmly believed the prayers of the saints would protect him.

You may never cross the border into a foreign country in an attempt to spread the gospel. But it does not remove your responsibility to be a part of the global gospel movement. You have the call as a saint to pray for those who venture into cultures unaware of the way to salvation. Paul's request to the Thessalonians should remind you to pray for those who are on the field right now. And if you are not aware of anyone on the mission field now, take time to learn about a few by name and pray for them.

Closer Challenge: When is the last time you prayed for a missionary? Do you even know any missionaries by name on the field right now? If not, seek out a couple you can pray for. **Today**, as Paul requested, spend some quality time on your knees, interceding for these individuals. Pray Paul's twofold prayer request over these missionaries. Also, in an effort to bring them encouragement, send them a letter, email, or some other form of communication to let them know they are being prayed for. It is very likely they need your personal touch today. Do your part to extend the Kingdom of God through specific prayers over God's missionaries.

September 20

Attracting Others to Godliness

Zechariah 8:23

Godliness is contagious. As in Zechariah 8:23, people from all walks of life and languages are attracted to someone who has the Spirit of God resting over him or her. It does not take a translator to see the Spirit working through an individual when the Spirit of God is controlling that person. When others see the power of God over someone's life, they are compelled to live likewise.

There is a key element to attracting others to godliness. It is visibility. You must be in the path of others as you live, reflecting the wonderful attributes of God. Jesus went so far as to say that no one hides a lamp, but instead sets it on a stand for all to see. (Luke 8:16) He is not talking about being showy and ostentatious, but courageous and open to lead others to the Light. When you allow the Light of Jesus to shine through you, you are allowing the Spirit of God to be multiplied in those around you. You, yes YOU, can be the one the Spirit uses to draw people to Jesus as you live to honor Him!

Closer Challenge: Are others drawn to Jesus through your life? If not, maybe you are living too much like the world and not like Jesus. **Today**, use this day as an opportunity to put the light of Jesus on a stand through the actions of your life. Not in a legalistic or boastful way, but in a caring, loving manner, go above and beyond to attract others to Jesus. Do a random act of kindness, speak a caring word, or listen to someone hurting. Be the person God uses today to draw someone to the Light!

September 21

Giving That Pleases the Father

———◦———

Matthew 6:1-4

Giving is the first of three acts of righteousness within the context of the Sermon on the Mount. (Matthew 6:1-18) These three acts of righteousness are somewhat of a sermon within the sermon. In Jesus' day, He rebuked men who gave ostentatiously. In fact, He called them hypocrites. A hypocrite is someone who sees the world as his stage and attempts to put on a show for everyone else. A hypocrite acts to impress others, but his heart is far from virtue. This kind of giving repulses the heart of God.

So instead of giving like a hypocrite, Jesus instructs His followers to give quietly, not in a showy, self-righteous manner. Furthermore, He states that you should not let your left hand know what your right hand is doing. In other words, make giving so routine and natural that it is not something you need to consider doing or do to seek approval from others. You just regularly give as an ordinary response to God's love for you, not to impress others. When you provide secretly and affectionately to please God, He will reward you accordingly when you enter eternity.

<u>Closer Challenge</u>: Do you have a habit of giving to those in need? If so, wonderful! (And by the way, Jesus did not say "*if* you give" but "*when* you give.") But do you give humbly as Jesus instructs? **Today**, practice giving privately, only to please God. Extend your spiritual antennas and watch for a need to arise. When you see it, immediately meet that need without recognition from anyone. If you already have a need in mind, meet it without gaining attention. When you do this, you will prove your heart is in the right place, and you will please God.

September 22

Praying That Pleases the Father

―――――•―――――

Matthew 6:5-15

Prayer is the second act of righteousness Jesus addresses in the Sermon on the Mount. As Jesus did with giving, He rebuked those who prayed in a showy manner. Often, the religious leaders would pray loud, long, elegant prayers on street corners to impress others. Though it caught the attention of man, it surely did not impress the Father. Instead, Jesus gave His followers a simple prayer to model in their prayer lives.

There are five elements of Jesus' modeled prayer. Jesus began the prayer with *praise*. (Matthew 6:9) *Hallowed* means to revere or treat as holy. Open your prayer by bidding God to revere His holy name, as you do the same. Next, Jesus revealed you are to recognize your *position*. (Matthew 6:10) This life is about God's will, not yours. Therefore, in your prayers you should submit to Him. Then, ask God for His *provision*. (Matthew 6:11) You obviously have needs, so come to your Father with your requests. Next, since you are a sinner, you must plead for *pity*. (Matthew 6:12) You are in need of forgiveness, so turn to the one who can forgive and restore peace. Finally, close out your prayer with a request for *protection*. (Matthew 6:13) Satan is out to destroy your life, so you need your Father's shield to surround you. Use this five-fold modeled prayer, and you will please the heart of your Father in heaven.

Closer Challenge: Do you aimlessly pray? **Today**, begin to use Jesus' prayer as your guide. At least for the next week, any time you pray, follow this five-fold model. Make this prayer model a habit in your life. Whether you are praying privately or publicly, pray as Jesus instructed, and you please your Father.

September 23

Fasting That Pleases the Father

———————◆———————

Matthew 6:16-18

Fasting is often a neglected practice of the Christian faith. Yet as it is with giving and praying, fasting is expected. Jesus taught it was not *if* you fast but *when* you fast. But, why should we fast? Fasting is a discipline that causes you to fully concentrate on God. When you remove a desire from your life for a season of time (such as food) and replace it with a craving for God, you extend your spiritual antennas to hear God in a greater capacity.

Biblical saints fasted for various reasons. In Judges 20:26, Israel fasted for God's guidance and favor before they entered war. In 1 Samuel 7:6, Israel fasted again when they repented over their sin. In Nehemiah 1:4-11, Nehemiah fasted as he wept over Israel's sin and prayed for success to return to Jerusalem. In Matthew 4:2, Jesus fasted to prepare Himself for His public ministry. In Acts 14:23, Paul and Barnabas fasted and prayed for the newly appointed leaders in Lystra, Iconium, and Antioch. As documented in Scripture, there are many reasons why you should fast. It's just a matter of you submitting to the challenge.

<u>Closer Challenge</u>: Do you have a big decision to make or a significant event approaching? Is there a sin you need to overcome? Do you need to intercede for a loved one in bondage? If so, maybe it's time you fast. **Today**, do some additional studying on fasting so you can better prepare yourself. There are several great resources available, such as Bill Bright's *Seven Basic Steps for Successful Fasting and Praying*. After you investigate more, choose an appropriate time this week to fast. Whether it is a short fast or a more extended one, practice this wonderful discipline to draw closer to God. Remember, fasting is between you and the Lord, so do your best to keep it private. (Though, don't lie when asked.) When you practice this discipline, you will experience God in a fresh, deeper way.

September 24

Being Reminded of Old Teachings

2 John 1:5-6

When John wrote this short letter to the chosen lady and her children, it was designed to readdress an issue of truth they needed to hear again. Apparently, John believed it was necessary to remind them to love one another. Maybe there was a quarrel or at least tension between them and other individuals, so they needed to be reminded that love is needed to saturate the situation. John was not telling them something new, but he was attempting to keep this truth in the forefront of the mind. These small reminders gather our thoughts and place us back on track with the Lord.

After you have been a follower of Christ for a long period of time, your knowledge of His ways increase. So your walk going forward is more about being prompted by His teachings, rather than learning something new. Since the flesh constantly seeks to mislead us, we often slip away from doing what we know is right. That is why we can never hear the simple truths of God enough. Even if you know doctrine, you must be reminded of it frequently so you don't forbid the Spirit's control over your life. When you are retold simple truths, take action to apply them immediately so that you do not forget them.

Closer Challenge: What truth have you recently been reminded of but you've ignored? ***Today***, name that truth and study it in Scripture. Use a concordance or some other online word search tool to look up that truth by topic. Study several passages of Scripture pertaining to that teaching. Now, take action immediately. When you are reminded of an old teaching, it is essential that you persist in practicing it. Do not fall away from what God has taught you, and you'll remain close to Him.

September 25

Overcoming Disbelief

Mark 9:23-24

Among a crowd of people, Jesus encountered a seemingly helpless situation. A boy had been demon-possessed since birth, and the disciples could not expel this demon from him. So, the boy's father cried out to Jesus that *if* He could do anything, take pity on them. The father's lack of confidence, requesting *if* He could help, disappointed Jesus. So Jesus gently rebuked him by stating that all things are possible for those who believe. (Mark 9:23) The father then made a plea to help him overcome his disbelief.

Many Christians are like the father in this story. They have observed Jesus' miracles, but simply do not believe He can help in *their* situation. You may be like this. You might be dealing with a health crisis, relational conflict, or stressful situation that is out of your control. If so, your faith is what must carry you. You must move beyond your disbelief to absolute trust. Anything is *possible* for God, not certain, but possible. His will comes first. But He can do anything, so believe God can turn your situation around at any given moment.

<u>Closer Challenge</u>: Are you struggling to overcome disbelief? What is causing you to lose hope? **Today**, write in your journal at least one thing you're struggling to believe God can overcome. Spend some time in concentrated prayer to erase your doubt and replace it with a simple trust in Jesus. Do not come to Jesus with your "ifs." Come to Him with the possibility of Him completely changing the course of this situation. Now, it may not be in His will for things to turn out as you wish, but that simple trust will give you the peace you need even when circumstances appear unfavorable.

September 26

Do Not Lose Heart

2 Corinthians 4:16-17

Paul faced many ministerial challenges. He was persecuted to some degree in most every city he visited. But Paul saw himself as a jar of clay with the marvelous treasure of Jesus inside him. (2 Corinthians 4:7, 10) Though he was scorned and hard-pressed, he knew the treasure within him would set him free one day to experience the glorious riches of heaven. Like Paul, there is no reason for you to lose heart. For you are being renewed daily by the power of the Spirit. Furthermore, your light and momentary troubles of the day grossly fail in comparison to the wondrous eternal glory to be received in heaven!

It is very likely you are facing a passing trial. It may feel incredibly intense and unbearable, but as Paul modeled, do not lose heart. Your trouble is light and momentary. It is not eternal. It is temporal. Though it may seem heavy and torturous now, it will seem insignificant compared to the treasure you have in Christ Jesus. Lift your face toward heaven, for that is where your hope rests.

<u>Closer Challenge</u>: Are you discouraged due to a current burden in your life? **Today**, allow your spirit to be lifted by the power of Him who raised Jesus from the grave. As a blood-bought child of God, there is no reason to be crushed by the cares of this world. Change your perspective today by speaking about heaven to all who you encounter. Intentionally abstain from speaking about your light and momentary trouble. Instead, talk about the glorious treasure you have in Jesus and the hope you have in heaven. This life is full of hardships, but the next life is filled with glory! Which life do you choose to focus on?

September 27

Deception Is Never Right

Joshua 9:1-27

The Gibeonites had heard of Israel's great success in battle, so they were afraid they would be the next to fall at the hands of God's people. So they approached Israel in peace. But instead of just stating the truth of their location, they deceived Joshua and the other leaders into believing they were from a distant country even though they were from a nearby town. They even saddled worn-out sacks and old wineskins on their donkeys and wore patched-up sandals to create a more convincing cover-up for their lie. Israel did not inquire of the Lord and accepted the lie, forming a treaty with Gibeon. (Joshua 9:14) Three days later, Israel realized they were deceived and made Gibeon woodcutters and water carriers as a punishment.

It never fails: deception will not help you in the long run. It is possible Gibeon could have humbly stated the truth, and in submission, they may have been able to form a peace treaty. But their foolish mistake of deception caused them to become lowly servants the rest of their lives. Deception does not produce long-term gain. At some point, your lie will be revealed, and it will cause more destruction on you later. (Proverbs 20:17) When you are tempted to deceive, think through the possible consequences before you act foolishly. It is much wiser to state truth plainly.

<u>Closer Challenge</u>: Are you deceiving anyone right now, but have not been caught? If so, **today**, humbly approach the victim of your deceit and reveal the truth. In addition to your confession, supply some sort of restitution to verify your admission of wrong. This is not easy. But you would rather limit the damage now than potentially ruin the relationship later. Most importantly, from here going forward, rid deception from your life by being a man or woman of righteousness and truth. It will bring you peace and keep you close to God. (Proverbs 12:20)

September 28

Lose Pride Before It Destroys You

Obadiah 1:1-4

Edom was a nation that had a strong sense of pride over their security. They believed they were safe from all harm. Furthermore, they even reveled over the devastation of Israel. However, this pride would soon bring them down. God was not pleased with their arrogance, so in this small oracle of the Lord from Obadiah, God expressed Edom's certain demise. Edom's collapse was a direct result of their failure to realize the kingdom was the Lord's. (Obadiah 1:21).

Our Lord is not pleased when pride rules. (Proverbs 8:13) Pride does nothing but place trust in self. And when this occurs, you remove your confidence in the Lord. That is not a desirable position. The only pride you should have is in God. Paul said he would only boast in the cross of our Lord Jesus. (Galatians 6:14) So, if you must boast, boast only in the great God you serve, never in yourself or the accomplishments of your life.

Closer Challenge: Are you full of pride due to your accomplishments or position? If so, be aware that a fall is coming if you do not humble yourself! **Today**, release your pride before it destroys you. When flattery is offered, direct all success to God. After all, God created you, gifted you, and gives you breath for the next moment. You cannot live apart from God, and you cannot function without His hand on your life. How can you dare place pride in self? View your life in that regard, and humility will begin to creep in as you gaze at God's greatness.

September 29

The Berean Way

―――――•―――――

Acts 17:11

Scripture teaches that the Jews in Berea had noble character, but they did not have knowledge of Jesus. When Paul came to them and preached the gospel, they received it with open arms. So by *faith*, they accepted the message and received Christ, but their quest for truth did not end. After they received the free gift of salvation, they continued to *examine* and *reason* together the teachings of Paul to see if they were true. Faith began their journey with Jesus, but the quest for truth inspired them to dig deeper each day.

Genuine faith in Jesus always leads to deeper examination. Our method for understanding more about God is *faith seeking truth*. It's not by accident that faith comes first. Faith is needed to drive the quest for truth, because at times it is very difficult to explain the mysteries and greatness of God. So by faith, you accept Him. But don't allow blind faith to discourage you from increasing your knowledge. Fervently seek to understand God better! The Berean way is this: Believe God in faith and let faith be the basis of your relationship, but continue studying Scripture so you can know God more intimately.

Closer Challenge: Do you come to Jesus like the Bereans? Do you believe by faith but also quest for more knowledge? It's quite possible you have heard many Christian doctrines and have believed them by faith, but you are not sure *why* you accept them as creedal. (Such as, doctrines of Soteriology, Eschatology, Ecclesiology, and more). **Today**, follow the Berean way. Never remove faith as your foundation, but seek to know more. Study a doctrine of the faith that you struggle to understand so you can acquire greater knowledge. By doing so, you will adopt the Berean way and you'll draw closer to God by sharpening your mind.

September 30

An Honorable Trait

2 Chronicles 27:6

Jotham became King of Judah at the age of twenty-five. Like his father, he was remembered for doing what was right in the eyes of the Lord. Jotham rebuilt towns, forts, and towers and was successful in war, but he was best known for his steadfastness. Due to his firm consistency to follow God, Jotham was rewarded with great influence. Regardless of his circumstance, he remained faithful to the calling of God. He was steadfast.

Often we want the miraculous to occur in our lives. We desire wondrous stories and great achievements to consume our days to feel God is looking upon us with favor. But greatness is not measured by achievements; it's measured by your relentless quest to know and follow God's will. He longs to esteem you as you remain faithful to Him. In light of this, do not concern yourself with seeking greatness but only the face of God on a *steady* basis. And as you do, He will raise you up in His time and bestow on you favor as He did with Jotham.

<u>Closer Challenge</u>: Is your walk steady with the Lord? Are you firm in your commitment to Him and unwavering when it comes to seeking Him? If you have remained faithful to this book and its challenges, you present the quality of steadfastness. **Today**, drop to your knees in prayer and reaffirm your commitment to seek Him on a daily basis. Periodically, you must recommit yourself to stay the course so you do not lose focus. And as you remain steadfast, you will be rewarded with the closeness to God.

October 1

Who Knows?

Joel 2:11-14

Judgment was coming to Israel in the prophetic book of Joel. The Day of the Lord was upon Israel, due to their disobedience. (Joel 2:11) Yet even in the coming days of this treacherous occurrence, there was still a sliver of hope if Israel would return to God. The prophet so eloquently wrote, "Who knows? He may turn and have pity." This ray of hope is a reminder that you do not know the broad coverage of the mercy that lies within the heart of God. Even an outright defiant rebel against the ways of God has an opportunity to experience His marvelous blessings if he just turns!

Often you can become overwhelmed with the depravity you see within yourself on a daily basis. This can lead you in two directions. It can cause you to dive deeper into your state of sin because you fear there is no hope. Or, you can be led into the loving arms of grace. No one knows the full extent of God's mercy. But He has proven in Scripture that He shows great pity to even the worst of sinners. (1 Timothy 1:13-16) So why not test His mercy? If you feel enormous guilt from sin, test His loving kindness. Who knows? He might turn your unfaithful situation into a testimony of grace.

Closer Challenge: Is there disobedience in your life that has slightly or greatly severed your relationship with God? Has it left you doubting God's mercy while living in a state of pity? **Today**, turn back to God. From memory, write down in your journal as many people as you can remember in the Bible who were forgiven by God. Try not to think too long on their failures; but instead, focus on the true character of God as He poured His mercy over them. Now, let that loving kindness rain over you. Release your guilt and strive to obey Him. Only God knows the extent of His love; and certainly, you have not reached the end of it.

October 2

Leading Family to Believe

John 7:1-9

Though some are blessed with a rich ancestry of Christ-followers, most of us have family members who have not believed in Jesus. Often, this can cause great distress, because you desperately want the confidence of reuniting with them in heaven. Many Christians have gone to great lengths to ensure or provide opportunities for their loved one to encounter Jesus and turn to Him. Yet after several attempts, they have refused to put their trust in Him. This can seem like a hopeless battle, but don't give up.

In this passage, we receive rare insight into the earthly family of Jesus. Though His family had the privilege of observing Jesus up close, they still did not understand His ways nor believe in Him. (John 7:5) It was not until after His death and resurrection when James, the half-brother of Jesus, became sold out for his brother's cause. If Jesus Himself did not immediately lead His family into belief, don't be alarmed if you do not succeed after several attempts. It's comforting to know that in God's time, He will do the drawing! So, find rest in that word.

<u>Closer Challenge</u>: This is not a call to become lazy in regard to exposing your family to Jesus. Continue to provide opportunities for your family to know Jesus, but receive a peace of mind from this passage that God is in control. **Today**, intentionally reach out to an unbelieving family member. Make a phone call. Write a letter or an encouraging email or text message. Take one out to grab a bite to eat and demonstrate God's love. Bring one to church with you if that individual is willing. Do your part to expose them to the gospel and explain it when given the chance, but let God do the work of saving. It's not easy to lead family to Jesus; but by the power of the Spirit, it can be done.

October 3

Specially Crafted

Psalm 139

There are some marvelous truths in Psalm 139. Nothing escapes the mind and touch of God. From the tiniest cell at conception to the greatest mass form within the universe, God knows it and has specifically placed His hand upon it in creation. He has taken who you are and specially crafted you to be exactly who He wants you to be. No one is like you. No one looks exactly like you. No one talks like you. No one thinks like you. You are just how God intended you to be, apart from the sin you do.

He created your inmost being (Psalm 139:13); He knit you together in your mother's womb (Psalm 139:13); He made you wonderfully (Psalm 139:14); He knew your frame before you were formed (Psalm 139:15-16); He ordained all your days (Psalm 139:17). You are not by chance! In fact, no life is by chance and all life is sacred. From the vilest person to the greatest leader and from the wisest to the one who is mentally challenged, God formed each person sacred because He created them all. Never devalue life. Each of us is specially crafted, including you!

<u>Closer Challenge</u>: Have you devalued your life or someone else's? **Today**, celebrate life! Find a way to be grateful for the life God has granted you. Do something wholesome that you really enjoy. It may not be what everyone else likes to do, but it symbolizes who you are. And who you are is exactly who God created you to be, so celebrate the life you have.

October 4

God in the Minor Details

2 Kings 6:1-7

When Elisha traveled with a company of prophets, a seemingly minor story was written down. As the prophets were building a new place of meeting, a man who was cutting down a tree dropped a borrowed ax head into the Jordan River. It seemed to be lost for good, but Elisha, through the power of the Spirit, tossed a stick into the water, which caused the ax head to float upon the surface. At that point, the ax head could be retrieved.

There wasn't an army defeated with this miracle, nor was there a life preserved, but God displayed His power in a small detail of life. Now granted, an ax head was an expensive tool to replace, but the miracle of an ax head floating was relatively small in comparison to some of the other great acts of God. So you see that God is not just concerned when you have a major crisis; He also wants to be engaged in the seemingly minor issues of your life. You may not feel like bothering God when you lose a small possession or need a bill paid, but if it's important to you, turn to the Lord. (Matthew 7:7-11) He longs to be in all of your affairs. Nothing is too minor for God to interact in your life, so turn to your Lord.

Closer Challenge: Is there something seemingly minor in your life in which you have refused to turn to God for help? Stop thinking that God is too busy for that matter! **Today**, in an attitude of prayer, talk to God about this issue. It's the small touches of God throughout the day that remind you He's watching over you. So don't negate coming to Him with any request. After all, He is your Father, and He desires to display His love to you. Furthermore, bringing minor requests keeps you in constant communion with Him, drawing you closer to Him in relationship.

October 5

Eating God's Word

Ezekiel 2:7-3:3

Ezekiel had many strange sensory experiences with the Lord. And in this particular experience, God commanded that he literally eat the scroll provided to him. So Ezekiel did, and he discovered the taste of the scroll to be as sweet as honey. Metaphorically, God displayed to Ezekiel that His Words are delicious to the human spirit when consumed, even though the content of this scroll was bitter judgment. Regardless of the subject matter, God's pure and holy Word is sweet to the soul.

You are in desperate need to hear from your Father in heaven. And God knows this. That is why He makes even the most difficult words taste sweet to the soul. Whether you need a *comforting* word in the midst of a trying time or a *convicting* word while in the middle of a sinful activity, when you receive the words of God, it tastes delightful. It's hard to believe a rebuke could be delightful, but once consumed, you discover its necessity for spiritual nourishment. So consume *all* of the Lord's words; you need it.

<u>Closer Challenge</u>: How do you position yourself to eat God's Word each and every day? (If you are consistently using this book as a tool, you are on the right track. But make sure you are reading the *Bible*, not just this book!) **Today**, restructure your priorities to receive a daily intake of God's delicious words. Set a time of day in which you can do this and keep a steady dosage of it for at least a week. Observe and take note of the difference His Word makes in your life. You are in constant need of feeding your soul. So taste and see that the Lord is good! (Psalm 34:8)

October 6

Rebuking Postmodernity

John 7:14-18

Today's culture generally views morality in opposition to absolute truth. Since each person sees and experiences life differently, truth is relative to the eye of the beholder. Our world has accepted this perspective as a norm; and sadly, truth has become personalized to situations instead of the Bible. But there is only one source of Truth, and Jesus brought it with Him when He came to earth. When Jesus speaks, He does it only on behalf of the One who sent Him. (John 7:16) All He can do is speak truth.

To turn the tide on the culture's lack of truth caused by postmodernity influence, those who claim to be followers of Jesus must speak as He did. Your voice should not be based on assumptions but direct teachings of Jesus. The world does not need more opinions; it needs Christ-followers boldly articulating the Bible accurately! Yet so often, we have cowardly Christians who refuse to rebuke scandalous teachings in fear of being rejected. If you believe the Bible as truth, live it and speak it with love and confidence!

<u>Closer Challenge</u>: Do you boldly speak truth when you hear something false? It's quite possible you will be tested today. So, **today**, when you overhear someone speaking against God's truth, gently direct that person to a biblical stance. Share with love, but be firm. In addition, at the end of the day, journal at least five false teachings you heard throughout the day. Do this because it will help you become more aware of the false teachings subtly seeking to persuade you. This world desperately needs truth. Be the one to bring it in your area of influence.

October 7

The Value of Having Hope

---

1 John 3:3

Why should you place your hope in Jesus? Many have struggled to answer this question affirmatively, especially while facing hardships. But John provides a good reason for it. As he wrote, when you place your hope in Christ, you position yourself on the path to purification. By leaning on hope, you shun ungodly influences, such as worry, impatience, and fear. These negative alternatives lead to other ungodly characteristics, such as frustration, anger, and hate. But when you have hope, you disentangle yourself from the snarls of sin and position yourself on the path of purification.

Purification is never an easy process. When silver is purified, it must be heated up to a certain temperature so it can be molded into the desired form of its craftsman. Likewise, purification of the soul is a demanding process. God will often heat up your circumstances to shape you into what He desires to accomplish His purposes. But as you remain hopeful in Jesus, regardless of your current sufferings, you can experience inner peace, knowing the end result will be beautiful. Therefore, the value of hope in difficult circumstances is the purity you gain from it. (James 1:2-4)

Closer Challenge: Is a current trial of life tempting you to lose hope in God? Have you failed to see how God is refining you? **Today**, identify at least one personal situation that is troubling you. In this situation, do you see worry and impatience rather than faith and hope? If so, you will lose a great opportunity to be purified by your Craftsman. Instead of focusing on the pain of your hardships, place your mind's attention on the hope you have in Christ as He develops you into a well-refined instrument for His glory. Set your focus on the end result, not your current sufferings. If you do, you'll find the strength to battle through your troubling times.

October 8

Your Biblical Purpose

---

2 Corinthians 5:1-5, 9-11, 20

When it comes to discovering God's purpose for our lives, many Christians make it too complicated. They attempt to uncover the specifics of His will before they understand with clarity the *general* purpose God has for every believer. In 2 Corinthians 5, Paul outlines the biblical purpose for every believer. First, our ultimate end in life is to dwell with God in heaven. (2 Corinthians 5:1-5) Scripture teaches that we *groan* to be clothed in our heavenly dwelling. We long to worship God in heaven because that's why we were created. But sin entered the picture and disrupted our calling to fulfill this now. Through Christ, this relationship is restored, but we must wait until He returns or we face physical death.

In the meantime, since we can't be in heaven now, we have a mission on earth to fulfill. It's to please God. (2 Corinthians 5:9) No matter what your vocation, gifts, or abilities are, your aim is to make Him happy. And the most prolific way to please God comes with our ultimate purpose on earth, which is to persuade mankind to follow Jesus. (2 Corinthians 5:11) You are not beamed up to heaven when you accept Jesus because you have a task of convincing others to follow Him. You are an ambassador for Christ. (2 Corinthians 5:20) You represent Jesus on earth, though your home is in heaven. That's your biblical purpose. Are you fulfilling it?

Closer Challenge: Do you now understand your biblical purpose? Has this been your aim? You have a great mission while on earth: to please God by persuading others to trust in Jesus. That's it! So, what are you doing to accomplish this mission? **Today**, intentionally speak to someone about Christ. Be bold; be courageous; fulfill your purpose. Don't be confused any longer. Use all your resources to reach people for Jesus! You are an ambassador for your homeland and Master!

October 9

The Key Ingredient to Peace
―――――•―――――

Isaiah 32:17

We all cherish the thought of having consistent peace in our lives. Everyone longs for serenity, but how can we attain it? The prophet Isaiah explains in this simple verse logged in the middle of his prophecy. He wrote that the fruit of righteousness is peace. It is righteousness that brings a person the everlasting peace that is greatly desired. By doing what is right according to God, you acquire peace because you know you have honored God. Even if the result isn't personally desirable after you have done right, you are at peace because you have accomplished what was necessary for God to say to you, "Well done." (Matthew 25:21) Those words will bring inexpressible peace!

Doing right isn't always the easiest thing, but it supplies you the freedom of peace. In addition to peace, Isaiah also wrote that righteousness will instill in you quietness and confidence. You'll have *quietness* in that there will be no confusion concerning a decision, which leads to a calm spirit. And your *confidence* will be elevated because you know you have done well to please God. If you want a boost in peace, quietness, and confidence, strive to *do right* in all your endeavors.

<u>Closer Challenge</u>: Do you lack peace? If so, it would be wise to evaluate if you have been making unrighteous decisions. **Today**, don't hesitate to do right. If there is a decision lingering in your mind, discover what lines up with God's Word and fully commit to it. That decision may immediately cause a little grief; but over time, you'll discover the peace, quietness, and confidence that follow righteousness. Seek peace by doing right!

October 10

Being Refreshed

Acts 3:19-20

Being refreshed is a daily desire. We all long to have the Spirit shower us with His blessings, mercy, and love. And God longs to supply His children with those things. However, the road to refreshing leads down a path of brutal honesty. If you long to be refreshed, you must seriously look at your life and remove those beliefs and habits that do not align with Him. As Peter preached to the onlookers near the Temple in Jerusalem, he strongly urged them to repent by turning to God. Then he added something that will make your repentance worth it. When you repent, times of refreshing and renewal will follow. (Acts 3:20)

Repentance comes from realizing you are in disobedience to God, resulting in a deep sorrow for displeasing Him. And this sorrow compels you to change directions by removing yourself from sinful patterns and advancing towards righteousness. Many reject repentance because they are addicted to their current lifestyles. They fail to see that refreshing comes from God, not sinful patterns of this life. A sinful lifestyle can never refresh like the River washing away your impurities.

Closer Challenge: Do you feel unclean spiritually due to a sinful pattern? Would you like to be refreshed again? ***Today***, repent! Name a sin you have recently committed and take aggressive measures to remove it. Don't hesitate to purge yourself of certain objects or acquaintances that tempt you into sin! It might be difficult at first to change directions, so share your repentance with a trusted godly friend to bring you encouragement and support. Cling to the promise that times of refreshing will come. Plunge into repentance and experience His cleansing powers today!

October 11

Respecting the Elderly

Proverbs 16:31 & 20:29

In biblical times, old age was respected and honored. It was understood that someone of age had a wealth of experience and wisdom that could greatly benefit those who were younger. The heads of clans were typically older individuals because they were the ones able to distinguish between what was right and wrong due to personal experiences throughout life. Gray hair was never mocked; but instead, it was revered by all.

In today's culture, many younger people have allowed their views of the elderly to become skewed. Instead of seeing the value of experience with those who have gray hair, they often see the aged as irrelevant, dead weight in society. What a tragedy! There is no reason why any society should lose respect for the elderly, for they still have much to offer. (1 Peter 5:5) Remember, Moses led the Israelites out of Egypt when he was around eighty years old! (Exodus 7:7) Never lose sight of the value an elderly man or woman can offer you.

Closer Challenge: Have you overlooked the value of the elderly? Do you respect them or mock them? **Today**, take a step toward respecting an elderly person by setting up a meeting with one for a cup of coffee, lunch or dinner. Ask many questions about life and spiritual matters. Listen to what that person has to say. Their words can be more precious than jewels. And if you are elderly, don't give up on life! You have so much to offer. Entrust what you have been given by intentionally instructing the younger. (Titus 2:1-8) Many younger people may not approach you because they may think you are uninterested in them. Show them your desire to pass along what has been given to you. Let's all do our part to learn from and encourage one another.

October 12

A Sacrifice Must Cost Something

---

2 Samuel 24:24

Can a sacrifice cost nothing? Not according to King David. When David insulted the Lord's power by conducting a census of able-bodied fighting men, God's discipline came upon the whole nation due to his self-reliance. David's discipline resulted in choosing one of three punishments. (2 Samuel 24:12-23) David chose the third option, which was three days of plague over Israel. Seventy thousand people died. To stop the plague, David was instructed by the prophet Gad to offer a live sacrifice on the threshing floor of Araunah the Jebusite. When David arrived, Araunah offered to give away *freely* the supplies needed for the sacrifice, but David refused. (2 Samuel 24:22-24) David would not conduct a sacrifice that cost him nothing! Due to David's repentant heart, the Lord was pleased and stopped the plague.

David made a foolish mistake of trusting in his own power, and it cost him and his people dearly. And when it came time to mend the situation, David would not take the shortcut by receiving charity from Araunah. His sacrifice had to cost him. Many Christians *talk* about sacrifice, but they want it to be comfortable. The sacrifice that honors God is one that stings when offered. If it costs you nothing, how can it be a sacrifice? Think about this next time you make a *sacrifice* to please God.

Closer Challenge: When was the last time you truly *sacrificed* something of worth? **Today**, give a costly sacrifice. Maybe a coworker is behind on a project. Consider sacrificing your time to help. Maybe a friend or relative cannot make a payment, and though it may stretch you financially, assist that person. Maybe it's time for you to abandon a cherished hobby so you can spend more time with God or family. Whatever sacrifice you feel led to offer, do it unselfishly without any thought of repayment. God is honored by a sacrifice that is motivated by serving Him regardless of the cost. Keep this attitude as you serve Him.

October 13

Tell of His Wonders!

Psalm 9:1-2

When you receive wonderful news, normally you have this burning desire to tell someone. If you have been hired for a new job, you announce it. If you are applying for college and you are accepted, you share the news. When you win something, you are not shy to shout a word of excitement. But, why do we often remain silent when God answers a prayer or performs a miracle in our lives? Psalm 9:1 reminds us to tell of God's wonders! From ancient times to the present, God has done marvelous things, and we must continually speak of these wonders so we can bring fame to His Name.

Several things happen when you tell of His wonders. First, you identify yourself as a Christ-follower. Others will know where you stand spiritually and will likely turn to your guidance when they are in need of supernatural intervention. Secondly, when you share His wonders, He receives attention. You remove the focus off yourself and onto the One who gives victory. And thirdly, your witness of His wonders is a form of praise! God longs to be thanked and adored for what He has done in your life. So, create a habit of telling of His good works to all you encounter!

<u>Closer Challenge</u>: Has God done something wonderful in your life recently, but you have failed to mention it to anyone? Don't be shy; let people know of His greatness. **Today**, tell someone of God's wonder. It may be a recent miracle or one from the past but speak to someone about a divine encounter that has changed your life. If you can't think of a personal one, tell of a wonder He performed in Scripture. Be a constant voice of praise for all who you encounter. After all, He deserves it!

October 14

Being a Role Player

Psalm 47:7-9

In this delightful portion of Psalm 47, we are reminded of the Lord's role in our lives. It's quite simple. He is the Ruler, and we are not! Even the highest of titles on earth, such as kings and nobles, *belong* to the Lord. These royalty are nothing more than role players to the King of King Himself. He sits on the throne; He rules with authority. He supplies all power to gain victory; He proves His wisdom over and over again. And if we dethrone Him from our lives, we miss out on the greatest teammate possible!

If life were a basketball game, you would be considered a role player, not the star player. A role player does his best to assist the star player because the role player knows the star's giftedness can elevate the whole team. Jesus is the ultimate star in the game of life. When He has control, good things will happen. But when you selfishly start to take control and not allow Him to be the top player, you will eventually see your life change for the worse. A role player does all the little things well to set the stage for the star. That's what you should do in life for Jesus. If you can view yourself as a role player and allow Jesus to shine, you'll experience victory. Let Him be the eternal, all-knowing, all-powerful King He is!

<u>Closer Challenge</u>: Who calls the shots in your life? Do you really seek God's wisdom and power or do you rely on self? ***Today***, shift control to the King. Be a role player. Name one thing in which you tried to control but have failed. It could be a relationship, an unfortunate situation, or a faith test. Do all you can to be a great role player by doing right, working hard and living holy (Micah 6:8), but release control of the *results* to God. Let Him be the Sovereign King who will shine when you let Him.

October 15

Soothing Anger

———•———

Proverbs 21:14

It will happen. Someone will say something, do something, or imply something that will awaken rage within you. You live with sinful people, so it is just a matter of *when* (not *if*) you will be stirred to anger. But since anger is often associated with bad things, it's not good to keep it and allow it to control you. (Ephesians 4:26) Proverbs 21:14 reveals a secret to soothing anger so you will not be led down the path of sin. It wisely avows that giving a *gift in secret* soothes anger.

Giving has a mystical quality to it. When you practice delivering something of value to someone, even when you are upset, you will discover a power many have neglected. Giving a gift in secret allows your soul to be settled. Furthermore, the person you blessed will be astonished because it is not natural to receive a gift when you have failed another. This is the example of our Lord. Though we did not deserve salvation at the cross (and He should have been angry with us), He sacrificially gave us something we could never attain on our own. (Ephesians 2:8) His gift daily leaves us amazed and grateful. (2 Corinthians 9:15) That's the power that giving has to reconcile!

<u>Closer Challenge</u>: Are you angry at someone right now? Has it left a void in your relationship? ***Today***, attempt to soothe your anger with a gift given in secret. Whoever offended you, give that person something that will yield amazement. Discover something that person likes and give it freely. Do this quickly while the Spirit is controlling you. If you wait, your anger may hinder you from acting! As you obey this proverb, observe how your anger will begin to vanish. You may need to repeat this again until your anger disappears. From now on, prevent anger with selfless, secret giving. It will produce sweet harmony in your life!

October 16

Never Shaken

Psalm 15

We all desire to be calm and collected when trials and painful situations head our way. It should be our aim to have a faith that is never shaken due to circumstances. (Psalm 15:5) So how can we have this kind of faith? David writes a short psalm that reminds us to be stable even when the world attempts to rattle us. He wrote that to remain unshaken by the world, pursue righteousness, speak truth, live honestly, despise the vile man, honor the God-fearer, and be a good steward of money.

When you live this way, Scripture teaches you will not be shaken. When the world hurls pain in your direction, if you're walking in these ways, you'll experience peace because you know God is pleased with you. And when you're at peace with God, you can be calm in the midst of a storm. Maybe you're having a hard time finding peace today. Be mindful that it can only be found by following God's moral will for your life. Strive to implement these qualities, and when a challenge comes your way, you will not be shaken!

<u>Closer Challenge</u>: Are you being shaken by the world right now? Have you been shaken in the past, and you are still feeling its affects? **Today**, wiggle away from the clutches of the world and pursue God's peace. If your struggle is due to unrighteousness, stop sinning and chase after God's holiness. Is your tongue deceitful or are you hiding something? Start speaking truth today! Have you cheated a friend or neighbor? Make your wrongs right. Are you being a bad steward of money? Correct the way you use your resources. When you do these things, peace will enter and you will *never be shaken*!

October 17

Identifying Bitterness

―――――♦―――――

Ephesians 4:31

Many live with it, but few admit it. Many hold on to it, but few realize its effects. What is *it*? It's bitterness. Bitterness is a nasty tool of Satan that hinders joy in a Christ-follower's soul. A little bit of bitterness can disrupt one's perspective to see all the good God has provided. Bitterness can arise in many different ways. Most often it originates from some sort of disappointment or unmet expectation. Though the pain is real, holding on to it does *nothing* for you. It's like peddling a stationary bike. You exert a lot of energy, but you go nowhere.

Solomon wrote that each heart knows its own bitterness. (Proverbs 14:10) Everyone has experienced letdowns that can result in resentment. However, here's the lonely part of bitterness. Only *you* share in its perceived joy. (Proverbs 14:10) As a result, no one else can carry the weight of your bitterness except you. So, why do you hang on to it? It doesn't help you, and it doesn't protect you from future disappointments. It is time to break the bitterness cycle in your heart. Release it so you can enjoy life once again.

Closer Challenge: What's going on in your heart? Only you know if there is bitterness taking up residence there. And only you can share in its false joy. **Today**, release any bitterness. There are two ways to rid it. First, if someone has disappointed you, *forgive* that person. (Matthew 18:21-35) Find the motivation to pardon that person by remembering Jesus forgave you. (Colossians 3:13) Secondly, be an intentional encourager daily. (Hebrews 3:13) When you are oozing with encouragement, it is hard to be bitter. So, if there is bitterness festering in your soul, purposely apply these disciplines by the end of today. Make them both a pattern in your life.

October 18

Real Faith

―――――•―――――

Mark 11:22

There may not be a more relevant verse in all Scripture than this one. There is not one second in life when you can refrain from applying this verse. Each step, each word, and each thought should be saturated in faith. You cannot move without full trust in the Lord or you should not move at all! When Jesus was speaking to His dismayed disciples about the wilted fig tree, He spoke four simple words of truth, "Have faith in God." These four words resonate with every Christian, every day. But often, we do not live by faith.

Often, when we encounter difficult situations and major decisions, we place our trust in *our* knowledge and abilities instead of God. Then, when we reach the end of the rope, we finally sense our need for Him. When this happens, you are right where Jesus wanted you from the beginning of the circumstance. He wants you to come to Him in faith! When you refuse to trust Him, you forfeit one of the greatest teachings and blessings of Jesus. More than likely, you are facing a situation that needs God. Will you trust yourself, or will you do as Jesus said, "Have faith in God"?

<u>Closer Challenge</u>: When was the last time you dropped to your knees and said, "Oh God, I have faith in You"? ***Today***, if at all possible, symbolically find a place of spiritual significance (such as a church building or other sacred place) and enter this holy refuge. God does not dwell in buildings alone, but for the sake of creating a spiritual marker, go to this place to help create a sacred memory. Whatever is creating worry and consuming your thoughts, drop to your knees and spend quality time in prayer with God. Throughout the prayer, frequently repeat these simple words, "I have faith in You." When you leave this special time with God, walk away refreshed, with a renewed sense of faith. Release your worry and simply trust God to deliver His will in your life.

October 19

A Tale of Two Church Members

―――――•―――――

3 John 1:1-11

The two men addressed in John's third letter had two very different reputations. Gaius was well-respected by John. He was faithful to the truth, and he practiced hospitality to strangers. (3 John 1:3, 5-8) He did his part to further the gospel. But Diotrephes, on the other hand, damaged the church. He placed himself before others. (3 John 1:9) He disrespected John and his mission team's authority. He refused to welcome other Christians with kind hospitality and also thwarted faithful Christians from doing good to others. (3 John 1:10) He was a pest to the church due to his selfish heart.

None of us want to be viewed as Diotrephes within our church. You hope to be remembered as Gaius. But unfortunately, there are many who act like Diotrephes and don't even realize it. If you impede positive change, hamper caring ministries for frivolous reasons, or disallow inclusion of outsiders, you are like Diotrephes! Receive this letter as your warning and change before you are held accountable for it. (2 Corinthians 5:10) God is not pleased with the evil of Diotrephes. It takes away from Kingdom growth.

Closer Challenge: In an honest evaluation, which man's actions do you most resemble? Is it the faithful actions of Gaius or the damaging actions of Diotrephes? **Today**, examine closely the vision and ministries of your church. How are you *contributing* to these causes? How are you *hindering* forward progress? If you are hindering forward progress, turn it around immediately by supporting your church in word and deed. Do something today that will express your loyalty so others will see your support. It's not worth being a pest to your church like Diotrephes. Gain the respect of your fellow partners in ministry by faithfully backing the mission.

October 20

Using Stories

―――――•―――――

Mark 4:33-34

Jesus knows the way our minds function. After all, He was there at the beginning when man was created. (Revelation 22:13) So Jesus keenly understood how He should converse with us for us to understand the Kingdom of God. As a result, He used the method of storytelling, or in biblical terms, parables. He told stories of preparedness (Matthew 25:1-13), responsibility (Matthew 25:14-30), service (Matthew 25:31-46), evangelism (Matthew 20:1-16), heaven (Luke 14:15-24), salvation (Luke 15:1-7), hell (Matthew 13:36-43), forgiveness (Luke 15:11-32) and much more to convey His message. He spoke of heavenly things in story form for us to understand better the knowledge of the Holy.

In fact, the full gospel of Jesus itself is a dynamic story! It involves deep love, a courageous hero, horrific tragedy, and a glorious victory. It is a story that draws us in and leaves us wanting more. And so, this marvelous story starts with Jesus and continues through each of us! God knows the language of the human heart is story. So He shows us the truth of Himself and the Kingdom of Heaven through narratives. We need to recognize this daily and tell His stories to others.

Closer Challenge: Do you understand you are part of a magnificent story that is much bigger than your small world? Do you realize you play a significant part in this story? **Today**, take a look at the big picture of life. You are not here by chance. God has made you part of *His* story to have impact in it! When it comes to explaining the gospel and biblical truths, don't forget to tell stories. Use personal stories and experiences to give people His truth. God did it for you; you do it for others. Tell a powerful faith story to someone in need today. It might be the catalyst for pulling that person through a difficult experience or lead someone a step closer to submitting control to Jesus. Speak stories of faith!

October 21

Persistence Pays Off

Luke 18:1-8

Prayer can be quite frustrating if you are impatient. Often, many people compare God to a magic genie. They think He should make our "wishes come true" as soon as we ask for them. But that is not how God works. He is the Sovereign God, and He knows what is best for us at the right time. Therefore, it is paramount for you to *wait* on Him even when you believe your situation is desperate. Yet, your waiting is not idle.

Jesus shared a story about a ruthless, godless judge refusing justice to a helpless widow. In her weakness, she continued pleading with the judge. And after repeated attempts of asking for fairness, he finally succumbed to her wishes. Jesus' point was that if a godless judge will supply pity, how much more will our loving Father grant mercy! The message of the parable is quite simple. When petitioning God, keep asking! However, don't overlook the final sentence in this parable. God responds to prayers cast in faith. If faith is not present, the prayer is rubbish. God honors the believer who approaches Him in faith. (Hebrews 11:6) As a result, genuine faith constantly lifts prayers to God but ultimately waits upon Him to deliver.

Closer Challenge: Have you stopped coming to God concerning a particular request? Be encouraged by this story. **Today**, take the approach of this helpless widow. Name one thing in your life God has *seemed* to overlook. Commit that one petition to prayer for at *least* a week. Drop to your knees and spend quality time communing with God over this issue. In *faith*, keep tugging on the cloak of your Father in heaven, asking Him for what you need. Ultimately yield to God's will, but never stop coming to Him in faith!

October 22

What Did Jesus Really Bring?

Matthew 10:34-39

After you read the words of Jesus in this passage (Matthew 10:34-39), confusion might set in because most people think He only came to bring peace. After all, He did say that if you come to Me, I will give you rest. (Matthew 11:28-30) So what is it? Did He come for peace or chaos? Clarity comes when you look at the world from two perspectives. It is a case of inward and outward realities. As a result, He actually came to bring *both* serenity and pandemonium.

Inwardly, Jesus came to bring peace. He offers a tranquil mindset that can be found nowhere else. Whatever you are facing, He provides a sweet, surreal calm. But outwardly, He came to disturb your world. When you became a *new creation*, you had to leave behind your old ways. You joined forces with God, and all the darkness of the world is trying to sway you back. Once you were a friend to the world, but now you are an enemy to it. Your mission is to rescue those perishing, which leads to resistance and suffering. So you can see you will have both peace and pain. Your world will consist of a peace that surpasses all understanding (Philippians 4:7) and a suffering that will make you yearn for heaven. (Philippians 1:29)

<u>Closer Challenge</u>: Can you see these two realties at work in your life right now? It's important you understand both so you will know what to expect as you follow Jesus. **Today**, take the next ten minutes to consider your life from both perspectives. First, know that if you abide in the teachings of Jesus, you will face chaos. But also remember that on the inside, you can have the calmness of a sheep protected by its shepherd. Meditate on the loving arms of Jesus. It will bring you peace in the midst of any storm.

October 23

Bringing the Needy to Jesus

———————✥———————

Mark 2:1-12

In an amazingly compelling story of faith for another, four men would not stop at anything to intersect their paralytic friend with Jesus. They had their reasons not to proceed. Jesus was preaching a sermon (Mark 2:2); the crowd prevented them from carrying him to Jesus (Mark 2:4); they had to lift this man on a roof, dig a hole, and use their strength to lower him on a mat. (Mark 2:4) If that was not enough, stingy, critical religious leaders were observing all that was happening. (Mark 2:6) Yet in all this, these men did their part to facilitate the environment for a miracle. As a result, Jesus was pleased with their faith, and He responded favorably, both to forgive sins and heal the body.

Imagine if you were one of these four men. What if Jesus saw *your* faith and changed the life of someone else? Wouldn't that be satisfying? You can be that person! You just need to care for someone with a supernatural love. This is a type of love that doesn't think of self but genuinely recognizes another's need and does everything possible to have that person touched by the Spirit of God. When you display this kind of caring faith, you clear the way for a miracle. So, with all your might, muster up the faith and courage needed to intersect people with Jesus. It can be a blessing for all!

Closer Challenge: Who in your life needs a touch from God, somewhat like this paralytic man? Do you have the audacity to do something outrageous to intersect that person with Jesus? **Today**, attempt to link that person with Jesus. Maybe bring that person to a prayer meeting. Escort that person to a worship service. Talk to your elders, deacons, or pastor about conducting a prayer visit. (James 5:14) In faith, bring this person to Jesus! Trust that He is the same today as He was when He healed the paralytic man. Your faith might be the catalyst for spiritual, emotional or physical healing!

October 24

Roles in the Church

Ephesians 4:11-13

Paul addressed a much-needed topic when he wrote about the different roles between church leadership and the rest of the Body of Christ. There are specific standards that should be followed by a church. First, Paul mentions that church leaders (the apostles, prophets, evangelists, pastors, and teachers) are to *prepare* God's people for ministry. The word *prepare* means to equip. It is not leadership's role to do everything, but to equip and set the church on a mission to accomplish God's purposes. God's people (the church body) are to do the works of service prepared in advance for them by God. (Ephesians 2:10) The church body should receive training from leadership to faithfully carry out their works of service. (Ephesians 4:11-12)

When roles are clearly defined and executed, great harmony will exist and the church will flourish. But too often there are church leaders overextending and church members underachieving. This is not a recipe for success within the Body of Christ! It is vitally important to understand your role and do everything humanly possible to accomplish it. When all parts are doing their role, great success will occur within the church, and God will be glorified!

<u>Closer Challenge</u>: What is your role within the body of Christ? Are you doing everything possible to accomplish it? **Today**, decide which role you are to execute. If your role is to lead, routinely discover ways in which you can pour yourself into others so they can be equipped and built up. You are in a role of mentoring and training, so execute it. If you are not called to church leadership, you still have a role in completing God's mission. Discover God's work for you and continue to be equipped through teaching and training. But never stop serving! Every Christian should be on mission for God. Find your role and fervently accomplish it.

October 25

A Hosting Decree

Luke 14:12-14

When Jesus was invited into a home for a feast, He noticed other guests seeking seats of honor, and He gave them humbling instructions. (Luke 14:7-11) Then, He had some instructions for the host. (Luke 14:12-14) Instead of entertaining financially stable friends and acquaintances who can easily pay back the favor, invite those who have nothing to give in return. For that will please the heart of God, and you will be rightly rewarded in heaven.

God is deeply concerned that the affluent help the poor. (Proverbs 14:31; Matthew 25:35) But it's not just for the obvious reasons of meeting needs of the unfortunate. A great heavenly blessing awaits the giver. When you host those who are able to return the favor, the motive of your heart could be to receive a repayment. There's danger in expecting a return, for it can lead to bitterness if the favor is not duplicated! Furthermore, you only receive earthy reward. But when you give to someone who cannot repay you, you will be honored in heaven, pleasing the Father.

<u>Closer Challenge</u>: Are you routinely giving to those who can repay you? If you want a reward in heaven, host those who cannot return the favor. **Today**, look for those near you who you often overlook to invite to your house because of their social standing. Seek to please your Father by hosting this person or family. Invite them to your home, knowing they will not be able to return the favor. (Or at the very least, take them out for a nice meal at a restaurant.) Treat them as well as your most honored guest. As you humble yourself in this manner, you will be rewarded in heaven. But it's likely you will also be blessed by their smiles.

October 26

Be Careful Who You Support

Proverbs 18:5

In Proverbs 18:5, we encounter a warning to curb our enthusiasm for those who repeatedly shun the ways of God. When you become aligned with someone who does not follow God, you condone that person's ways, failing to administer justice. Though you might not actively participate in that person's dealings, your association can be viewed as passive support. To make matters worse, it is often the case that the immoral person you support is depriving the innocent of justice.

As a result, do not closely associate with wicked people. Yet on the contrary, also be careful not to develop self-righteous patterns of behavior. That can also be damaging. It is a delicate balance. The solution rests in swaying the rebellious from evil practices without condoning their efforts, nor looking haughty. An example of this is the woman caught in the act of adultery. (John 8:3-11) Jesus defended her in the public's eye when He refused to stone her, but He didn't condone her evil ways. Instead, He urged her to go and sin no more. He became a loving, positive influence in her life without accepting her actions. We should seek this same balance.

Closer Challenge: Have you been guilty of enabling poor behaviors in others? It will not lead them to Jesus. **Today**, determine if you are actively or passively condoning another person's poor ethical behaviors. Name that person. Without totally disengaging from that relationship, stand firm on things you will not support but find ways to challenge that person to move from their rebellious ways toward Jesus. If needed, share a personal struggle to soften a self-righteous accusation. Remember, the goal is to support the individual without supporting the action. As you do this, you will be a catalyst for change in that person's life.

October 27

Tending to Strangers

Luke 9:1-6

When going on a trip, you typically gather the things you need before you depart. You make sure you have in your possession all articles necessary for the journey. After all, in our modern culture, it is abnormal for us to assume we can depend upon strangers for survival. But in first-century Jewish culture, Jesus actually encouraged His disciples to leave their belongings and trust the generosity of people they did not know. For their generosity would be a sign of their acceptance of the gospel.

Placing yourself on either side of this scenario in our culture is a great test. If you were one of the disciples, it would take extreme faith to trust a stranger for your basic needs. And as a homeowner, you would need to set aside your selfishness and fear as you care for an outsider, tending to that stranger's needs as you would a family member. This practice is a foreign concept to us today, but Jesus puts great value on the action of caring for strangers. After all, everyone is your neighbor. (Luke 10:25-37)

<u>Closer Challenge</u>: How extreme is your faith? Could you be like the disciples, trusting strangers to care for you? Could you be like the homeowner, tending to the needs of a stranger in your home? **Today**, though it is not a typical practice in our culture, decide how you could care for the needs of a stranger. (Matthew 25:35) Or without being a freeloader, possibly allow a stranger to care for you. Either way put your faith to the test and watch how the gospel can be expanded. Certainly, be wise and use caution, for some will seek to take advantage of you. But as the Lord leads, display great faith! And as you do, watch the power of the gospel at work.

October 28

Practicing What You Already Know

Philippians 3:16

True believers are compelled to draw closer to God. And with that drive, there is a desire to learn something *new* spiritually. Though gaining new knowledge of God is a noble aspiration, it is equally important to practice what you already know. Paul wrote that we are to live up to what we have already attained. (Philippians 3:16) This means you are to take the knowledge you have and live it! The Christian life is not merely about acquiring knowledge. You are to put that knowledge into practice.

It is likely there are Christ-centered values you have learned but are not practicing right now. You know you are to feed the poor, share your faith, trust God with your finances, love your family, be content, refrain from anger, and so much more. There are many principles in Scripture you have already acquired. But, are you practicing them? If not, take Paul's advice and begin to work on the truths you have already attained. Typically, only after you begin to implement known truths will God bestow upon you *new* truths to experience. Obey Him now to experience Him deeper each day.

Closer Challenge: What truth have you learned from Scriptures that you are struggling to apply? Maybe it was unintentional, but nonetheless, you have overlooked it. **Today**, one by one, begin to practice truths you have been neglecting. Start with one truth you have failed to apply. Confess your neglect of that truth by discussing it with your accountability partner. Give permission to your trusted friend to ask you about it later. After you begin to apply that truth, select another truth you need to execute. Do not become overly focused on learning new truths until you have lived up to what you know. The Spirit will add understanding as He sees you mature. For now, aim to live up to what you already know!

October 29

How Do You Know Jesus?

Matthew 7:21-23

In the original New Testament language, there is a distinction between two similar words that can be difficult to convey in English. First, *pistueo* means you *know* something exists, but you are not trusting in that object. It is a distant knowledge. Secondly, *ginosko* means you *know* something in a personal way due to an intimate experience. *Ginosko* conveys not only knowledge of facts but a personal encounter with the object. Therefore, it is a more intimate and unique understanding.

In Matthew 7:21-23, when Jesus expressed that He never knew (*ginosko*) these imposters, He is implying that He never knew these shallow followers personally and intimately. Sure, Jesus knows (*pistueo*) them because He knows everything, but because they never took time to have an intimate relationship with Him, He never knew (*ginosko*) them. Therefore, these false followers are cast away from Him at death. In James 2:19, the demons know (*pistueo*) Jesus, but they do not trust in Him personally. In Matthew 1:25, Scripture teaches that Joseph had *no union* with Mary. *Ginosko* is used here. It could be translated, "Joseph did not know her intimately." Again, this conveys a close, personal relationship. It is important that you strive to know (*ginosko*) Jesus closely, or you too will be cast out like the false followers.

<u>Closer Challenge</u>: How do you know Jesus? Do you only know (*pistueo*) He exists or do you know (*ginosko*) Him in a personal, intimate way? **Today**, make it your aim to *ginosko* Jesus. This takes daily sacrifice and submission to His Word and will. It takes an attitude of complete surrender of your life like Paul. Paul declares that he wants to know (*ginosko*) Christ and the power of His resurrection and the fellowship of His suffering. (Philippians 3:10) This entails a close relationship. Likewise, in suffering, joy or steadiness, seek to *ginosko* Jesus. Don't just know about Jesus, know who He is personally! And this starts with submitting to His Lordship in your life.

October 30

Finishing Strong

Matthew 21:28-32

In this parable, there is a father and two sons. The father asked the first son to work in a vineyard, yet the son refused. Later, however, he came to his senses and obeyed his father. The father also asked the second son to labor for him, and this son promised he would work but never did. Though the first son started poorly, he was honored because he finished strong. The second son was not honored, for he not only disobeyed his father, but he also lied. Many of us stumble early in life, failing God greatly. But thankfully, our God is full of mercy and is ready to provide us with fresh starts. Though starting well is commendable, finishing strong brings great pleasure to God.

This parable was shared in the context of Jesus informing the religious leaders that tax collectors and prostitutes will enter the kingdom of God before them because these *sinners* finished strong. (Matthew 21:31) Sure, they started poorly, but their repentant hearts and changed lives yielded pleasure to God. Paul also started poorly, for he was an avid follower of the law and even authorized the killing of Stephen. (Acts 8:1) Yet after his conversion experience, he turned his life around and followed Christ fully. It is possible you have started your life poorly. Or you might have started well but faded of late. Either way, you have an opportunity like these individuals to start over and follow Christ faithfully going forward. It's not a matter of how you start but how you finish!

Closer Challenge: Are past failures holding you back from serving God? If so, you can start over. There is no reason for you to allow your past to dictate your future with Christ. **Today**, determine if you have slipped in your commitment to the Lord. Is it church attendance? Serving? Giving? Caring? Communing? Make a concentrated effort to correct that today. Whatever God has asked of you, aim to finish it. Do not let Satan dissuade you from spiritual obedience! Seek to honor your Father in heaven, and you will be rewarded with His blessed presence.

October 31

Evil Among Us

Romans 12:21

In our culture, this is a day that celebrates darkness and evil. There can be some good, clean fun associated with it, but the day itself is something dishonorable to God because God hates evil. Does evil bother you? If it does, you might wonder why God does not annihilate all evil now. Why does He permit evil to roam on earth? Well, instead of removing evil or charging us to purge evil from our midst, He allows it to remain until the end of time. (Matthew 13:24-30) Now, this may not sound fair until you understand the true heart of our Lord.

God desires that none should perish. (2 Peter 3:9) He longs for *every* sinner to be rescued by the blood of Christ. If we aggressively attempted to rid all evil on earth, we would remove physically the very people Jesus came to save. Furthermore, before you believed in Christ, you would have been eliminated too! Our Lord withholds judgment until the end to allow all of mankind the opportunity to hear His word and repent. So, victory over evil is not obtained by rooting it out; rather, it is achieved by God when an evil person turns over his life to Jesus. As a child of God, your calling is not to retaliate against evil, but to overcome evil with good. (Romans 12:21) And in the meantime, *wait*! God will judge evil in His time (1 Corinthians 5:12-13), but not before He allows ample time for all to repent.

Closer Challenge: Are you sick of evil? Most believers are. We hate the evil around us and in us! (James 1:13-14) But your role is to share the mercy of God; after all, it was His mercy that saved you! **Today**, instead of aggressively rebuking evil or simply ignoring it, attempt to overcome evil with good. Decide how you can offer a good deed to a stranger. Use this day as an opportunity to show others the complete opposite of evil, which is the love and mercy of Jesus. By extending mercy and light, you will provide someone a fresh look at the Savior.

November 1

Regretting a Decision

Matthew 27:1-10

Judas' decision to betray Jesus resulted in his demise. At the time of his betrayal, it may have seemed like a good idea to hand Jesus over to the authorities. After all, more people were increasingly turning against Jesus, and he would receive a wage for his actions. However, that one decision haunted him shortly after making it. At the moment he understood what he had done, he rushed to the religious leaders to return his wage, but they didn't receive it back. Feeling unaccepted and lost in his own shame, Judas took his life.

Even if you make a poor decision, it doesn't have to end like this. Though Judas fell into the trap of the flesh, he could have been bailed out by the mercy of God. Yet he focused on the guilt and shame of his decision. It is quite possible you have made a decision or two that has paralyzed you from pursing a freedom-filled life. Like Judas, it is quite possible you are living in the past more than experiencing the liberties you can acquire through the sacrifice and forgiveness of Jesus. For the sake of God's mission, it is time to disallow a poor decision to handcuff you from impacting this world for Him. Though the memory of that poor decision is painful, use it as motivation to serve your Lord who loves you in spite of that action.

Closer Challenge: Is a poor decision crippling you from serving God? Are you too ashamed to admit your failure? ***Today***, at this very moment, drop to your knees, ask for forgiveness, and allow the Father's mercy to overcome you. God the Father does not want you suffering from this decision, even if you think it's dreadful. He has plenty of love flowing from the cross that can wipe out your wrong. Don't allow a poor decision to dictate your future. It is time to move forward in sweet fellowship with God.

November 2

Hurting with Others

―――――•―――――

Proverbs 25:20

It is likely you will encounter a hurting person today. Maybe someone is struggling with marital strife. Maybe an illness has entered a family. Maybe a friend has lost a job. Maybe an acquaintance is just lonely. No matter where you turn, if your eyes are open, you will encounter someone who has a need for another to share in the pain. Yet more often than not, we minimize the pain by trying to cheer up that person before dealing with the issue at hand.

This proverb reminds us to be sensitive to those who are hurting. When we are not, it is like stealing a garment from someone on a cold day. You would not yank away a blanket from someone who is cold. Likewise, you shouldn't sing a cheerful song to someone who is mourning. The wise option is to sit with that person, listen closely, and allow some time for healing. At the appropriate time, rejoicing will come but not until the person is ready. As you apply the wisdom of this proverb, you will exemplify the very nature of Jesus. Jesus, who had all the power in the universe, first listened to Mary when Lazarus died. Then He wept with her. (John 11:32-36) It proved His love for her. In a similar manner, hurt with the one who is suffering. It will mean the world to that person.

Closer Challenge: Are you willing to hurt with someone who is in pain? You may already know of someone needing you. **Today**, stay alert and notice someone requiring emotional and spiritual care. When you encounter that person, follow the example of Jesus and share in that person's pain. Simply do your best to listen and practice the principle of presence. You will be an extension of the Heavenly Father to that person. Not to mention, you will gain a friend for life.

November 3

Relentless Praying

Luke 18:1-8

By studying the Lord's Prayer (Luke 11:2-4), you can learn *what* to pray, but your attitude concerning *how* you should prayer is taught in a parable like the persistent widow. Jesus told this parable to display to His disciples the determination and aggressiveness they should have when they pray. A widow, who is often neglected since her husband is not present to defend her, was being mistreated by an adversary. So she turned to an unjust judge to protect her. She was not successful in the first plea, but she consistently returned to him, begging for justice. Finally, after he had wearied, he granted her request.

In a similar manner, God the Father wants you to interact like this when you pray. It may sound *pushy* to come continually to God in this way, but this kind of faith pleases God. He desires to see you determined in faith. For when you approach Him like this, your focus is on Him instead of your concern. And that is where He wants you! In addition, as you pray perpetually, you position yourself to commune with your Father. After all, God seeks to acquire time with you, and persistent prayer will lead to that. So, come to the Lord with persistence and aggressiveness when you pray.

<u>*Closer Challenge*</u>: Have you abandoned the Lord in a particular request? If so, change your attitude and return to the Great Gift Giver. **Today**, lift up your burden to God. Write it down in your journal and revisit it daily for *at least* the next week. If possible, use each time you eat as a reminder to pray for this matter. Be persistent like this lady and wait upon your Lord to answer in His time. And as you wait, be grateful that you are communing with your Heavenly Father. That in itself is victory regardless of the results.

November 4

Traveling Alone

———◆———

Habakkuk 3:19

Due to our selfish, prideful nature, we have a tendency to wrestle through life on our own. Individualism is a disease that plagues each of us. Often we refuse the advice of another, shy away from help or sneak off from the pack to handle situations by ourselves. And even more disturbing, we have this same attitude with Jesus. When we are in need, turning to Jesus is often the last place we look. Traveling alone in life is foolishness, considering you have an able, affectionate God longing to walk with you.

The prophet Habakkuk symbolically sends a clear message of God's divine interest in your affairs. Your Sovereign Lord can make your feet as a deer on steep cliffs. What a beautiful picture! When life seems to present extreme challenges, God can help you climb further than you could ever dream. He can carry you to great heights if you just trust in His ways. It really does not make sense to experience life alone when you can have the Rock of Ages bring you shelter and strength. If you desire to go further in life, travel with your Maker.

<u>Closer Challenge</u>: Are you attempting to undertake a feat, project or struggle in your own strength? If so, be aware that a crash might be coming. **Today**, release control of that issue to the Lord. Take a step back and realign your priorities. Instead of striving to climb this mountain on your own, allow God to guide you. Set aside special time to be with God. Maybe you should experience a retreat or conference to reestablish your walk with Jesus. At the very least, the next time you corporately worship with other believers at church, leave your cares at the door and just *be* with God. Stop traveling alone and acknowledge your Companion for life!

November 5

Caring for Your Parents

John 19:25-27

As Jesus was hanging on the cross, His compassion is still noticed. His mother was devastated as He was clinging to life, so Jesus turned to John and commissioned him to care for her. He knew He would not be able to tend to her needs as a son would for his mother due to His eminent death. As a result, He charged John to be the one to love her and care for her as if she were his mother.

There is a principle behind this conversation that we should all embrace. Even though Jesus was not the one who could care for her in person, He arranged a plan for her needs to be met. As a child needs care, so do the elderly among us. Parents will eventually rely on their children. Yet, we often surrender their care to medical facilities even when we are capable. What a travesty! As a child of God, you have a calling to care for those in your immediate family, especially your parents and grandparents. (1 Timothy 5:4) To be fair, some situations demand specialized care, but most do not. Inconvenience is not a reason to shift your responsibility. And for some, it might be more complicated due to a strained relationship. Therefore, you must attempt to mend any broken relationship through forgiveness so you can care for the ones who brought you into this world.

<u>*Closer Challenge*</u>: Do you have a plan to care for your parents as they age? **Today**, think about how you can extend compassion to your parents in the latter years of their lives. Instead of waiting for the time to arrive, begin to discuss how this can be done. In addition to communicating with your parents, if you have other siblings, talk with them about it too. As Jesus arranged care for His mother after His death, look ahead and create a plan for your parents.

November 6

Gladly Cooperating

2 Chronicles 24:1-12

For a short period (during the time of Jehoiada the priest), Joash was a king who did right in the eyes of the Lord. When he saw there was a need to restore the Temple, he commissioned the priests and Levites to go throughout the towns of Judah and collect annual dues. But they failed to respond. So, Joash ordered a large chest to be placed outside the Temple and issued a proclamation to restore the Temple. At this decree, all the officials and people brought their contributions *gladly*. (2 Chronicles 24:10) The chest was filled many times, and they collected a large sum of money. They hired masons and carpenters to finish the work.

A tax does not typically bring glad givers. However, in this case, the people of Judah saw its importance. There was a cause worth supporting, so they gladly supplied a portion of their wages to the restoration of the Temple. It is a glorious sight to behold God's people joining together for a cause in cooperation. There is strength in numbers. More than likely, your church has a purpose and mission it is seeking to accomplish. Whether the cause is your passion or not, do your best to fully support it. As long as it does not contradict God's Word, there is room for agreement. As you do this, you will honor God and strengthen your church.

<u>Closer Challenge</u>: Are you cooperating with the mission of your church? Are you intensely against the mission or are you passively watching from a distance? Either way, you are not cooperating. **Today**, take time to revisit the mission of your church. If you find the mission is unclear or nonexistent, humbly help lead the charge to reevaluate its mission. But if your church does have a clear purpose, do your part to *gladly* cooperate. Do not be a naysayer that destroys the spirit of agreement and movement. The church is needed to be a light in this world, so unite together and make a difference for Christ.

November 7

Recognizing Quiet Heroes

---

1 Corinthians 16:15-18

Near the end of Paul's first letter to the Corinthians, he reminds the church to do something we often overlook. He admonishes them to recognize those who have served the Lord faithfully. Three men, Stephanas, Fortunatus, and Achaicus, were recognized by Paul for their service directed to the saints. Even Paul was personally touched by their labor of love. For we see these men provided for Paul what was lacking, and they refreshed his spirit, along with others too.

These kinds of individuals often do not seek recognition, for they understand their role is to serve God quietly. However, as Paul knew then and we know now, a little encouragement can add fuel to a person's drive to serve. There are some humble individuals within your church who are often taken for granted. Yet, if their service was removed, it would have a tremendous impact on the flow of your church. Therefore, as an act of grace from the Lord, thank these individuals. The church could not function without them.

Closer Challenge: Who is a quiet laborer in your church, constantly impacting lives and refreshing the spirits of the saints? **Today**, select at least one individual in your church who has had a profound impact on your life behind the scenes. Provide this person some much-deserved recognition. Meet this person for lunch or coffee just to shower this individual with admiration. At the very least, write an encouraging letter or extend a well-deserved gift to this individual. Let this person know the Lord has been glorified through him or her. Most importantly, be inspired to be like this person. We need more *quiet heroes* in the church who refresh the spirits of the saints.

November 8

The Folly of Clutching This World

―――――•―――――

Luke 12:13-21

One day Jesus was asked to interfere with a family estate affair. But He refused to become this man's ally because Jesus knew the man's heart was greedy. Then, as a warning, Jesus told a parable of a rich fool. A farmer had good ground to grow crops. It yielded so much abundance he did not know what to do with it. So, he decided to waste it on himself and build bigger barns, living lavishly. In the end, God called this man a fool because he missed the point of life. Life is not about acquiring wealth for selfish gain, it is about using your resources and gifts to impact eternity and fill the heavenly storehouse with everlasting treasures.

This parable is a strong warning to those who have much. Being rich is not inherently wrong, for God blesses people. But, when wealth is used for personal gain and not eternal purposes, you are deemed a fool because you have missed the point of life. The core problem is much deeper. It is that you are hanging on to this world too tightly. This world is fleeting, and for those living solely for it generate great waste. Living on this side of heaven is just a portal to our eternal destination. For how we live here will impact eternity. Do not be a fool with what God has given you. Loosen your grip on this world by fervently storing up heavenly treasures!

Closer Challenge: Are you hanging on to this world too tightly? Is your heart controlled by the lusts of the world? Does fear keep you from being generous? **Today**, examine your life to determine if a faulty heart condition is keeping you from fully serving and trusting God with your resources. Is it attaining wealth? Is it wanting more? Is it hoarding resources? Decide now a practical way you can loosen your grip on that mindset. Remember, you are only a mist, and soon, you will vanish. (James 4:14) But how you impact eternity will last forever. Do not be a fool. Be wise and release whatever is holding you back from fully trusting God and impacting eternity.

November 9

A Home for the Lonely

Psalm 68:6

Even with all our technology and multiple modes of communication, it has been said that we live in the greatest time of loneliness. There is a lack of deep, personal connections that we desperately need. For the most part, this string of loneliness occurs in our generation because people are too busy. In fact, they are so busy they disallow time for close-knit fellowship. Busyness keeps people longing for the thing they need most, meaningful relationships.

If you are lonely today, think of the words David wrote in Psalm 68:6. He shared that God sets the lonely in a family/home. Family might be a major component you are lacking; though, some of it may be out of your control. If you have lost family members or you have never had blood family, you might think this is not fair. But your blood family is not necessarily what David is speaking of here. The family he speaks of is the family of God, which is the family you were adopted into by the heavenly Father! God places the lonely in a community that has Jesus as the common denominator. If you are lonely, surrender time and effort to be with the family of God, your church.

Closer Challenge: Are you lonely today? How much time have you spent with your church family? **Today**, whether you are lonely or not, make sure you are spending quality time with your church family. When you separate from your spiritual family, you miss some of the greatest moments you can have on earth. Spend time studying your church calendar and commit to as many events as possible to help ease your loneliness. It will help immensely. And when that is not enough, remember your heavenly Father is with you at all times. (Matthew 28:20) Turn to Him through His Word and experience His closeness. You do not have to feel lonely.

November 10

Those Who Happen to Be There

Acts 17:16-18

Paul had a wonderful philosophy when it came to sharing the gospel. He simply traveled around looking for people to whom he could speak God's message. When he traveled to Athens, he reasoned with Jews, God-fearing Greeks, and anyone in the marketplace. Whoever *happened to be there* was his target. He had a ministry that did not see race or social standing or religious preference. Whoever was on his path, he presented the redeeming message of the Savior.

As you go about your day, more than likely you will encounter many individuals. Some might be believers, while others might not know Jesus. If you adopt Paul's attitude of speaking *as* you go, you would see each person you pass as a target for the gospel. All those who *happen to be there* are not around you by chance. God ordains every day as an opportunity to spread His love to others. So be alert to those who you can touch with God's love today.

<u>Closer Challenge</u>: Are you aware of those who *happen to be there* on your path? Casual conversations are polite, but do you regularly go beneath the surface and talk about your Savior? **Today**, as you go about your business, notice who happens to be there with you. This person might be at work with you, in the grocery store, or just anywhere in the community. As the Spirit leads, initiate a spiritual conversation with one of these individuals. Speak about your church family or ask that person if he or she needs prayer right then. There are several opportunities each day for you to share the love of God. Simply focus upon those who are already there with you.

November 11

The River

Psalm 46:4

Rivers are sources of life for many major cities. A river provides food, trade, transportation, and much more. So a river is seen as a blessing to those who live along it. Jerusalem has no physical river near it. It almost seems foolish to build a major city there, but when the Creator of the Universe is the source of provision, an actual river seems insignificant. The Psalmist used a river as a metaphor describing God's provision. Just as the river brings forth blessings to a city near it, God is the blessing giver to Jerusalem. He is the sustainer and giver of resources to His people!

God is your river of blessings. If you look around at your life, even during the darkest hours of the soul, you can find where God has been a river of blessings to you. The key issue is to focus on the blessings, not the troubles. Focusing on your troubles can limit your vision to walk through it, but as you focus on the River, you will have a sense of peace and hope to get through any struggle. Take a look at what the River has brought you, and you will be reminded of His great and glorious ability to deliver you once again.

<u>Closer Challenge</u>: Have you taken time to remember the blessings God has brought you? **Today**, make a list in your journal of the blessings you have received in the past year. Jot down at least ten Godsends in which you can be thankful to God. Let this be the conversation piece for your day. As you journey along throughout the day, tell at least five people a few of these blessings. Give God the glory today for being the Great River in your life! Be grateful for the life-giving provisions God has brought you. He is your river giver, so thank Him.

November 12

Serve As You Are Expected to Serve

Luke 17:7-10

In this often overlooked parable of Jesus, you discover a powerful lesson on being a servant. After a long day in the field, a servant came into his master's house. Instead of the servant receiving a break, the master ordered him to prepare dinner. And only after the servant was finished serving his master's dinner was he able to eat. This sounds so insensitive if you do not understand the nature of a servant. The servant's role is to serve. It is normal to him. It is what he is supposed to do. It is what he lives to do! So, when the servant is asked to serve, no matter what the assignment is, he simply does it.

In Mark 10:45, Jesus said He came to serve, not to be served. The very nature of Jesus, though He was King, was a serve. So, if you claim you are *in Christ* and you desire to be *like Jesus*, you are destined to be a servant. In fact, being a servant is part of your identity. And when you are not serving, you are in an identity crisis. It is strange to think like this, but you do not serve because you even want to help others. You serve because being a servant is who you are! It is your image, the image of God. Like the servant in this passage, you are expected to serve because it is your normal role. This does not make you a *super* Christian; it just makes you a *normal* Christian.

<u>Closer Challenge</u>: Do you find it hard to serve? If so, you are in an identity crisis. **Today**, find a place of service that will help build up your church. Do it without complaining, quitting, or seeking praise. Just do it because it is who you are. *How* you serve may vary by your giftedness, but if you are not serving, you are missing out. Christ's example of a servant is our model and His sacrifice is our motivation, so serve as an unworthy recipient of His grace!

November 13

Mercy for the Doubter

———————•———————

Jude 1:22

Let's face it. Believing in someone being raised from the dead is not easy if your eyes have not been opened by the Holy Spirit. Sure, you believe it because you have seen resurrection power work in your life. But for those who have not experienced Jesus for themselves, doubt floods their minds. When Paul wrote the letter to Jude, he reminded us to be merciful to those who doubt. He knows it may take some time before the Spirit draws them into a knowing faith. Our role is to present to them the love that was placed within us when we believed so they will be able to see His love is for real!

There are many things an unbeliever may doubt. They may doubt the existence of heaven and hell. They may doubt Jesus is the only way to heaven since there are so many other religions. They may even doubt Jesus ever existed. For some, faith is not something they want to turn to when their eyes are revealing to them something different. We must instruct them to walk by faith, not by sight. (2 Corinthians 5:7) Be patient to the ones doubting, but do not allow your patience to become idleness. Keep persuading them to adopt a faith seeking to understand; and as you do continue to display to them the love and mercy of your Heavenly Father.

Closer Challenge: Do you know someone who doubts God? Name that person right now. **Today**, write a prayer in your journal featuring that person. Ask God to break the chains of unbelief in that person's life. Pray that God would reveal Himself to this person in a special way today. Also, do something in that person's life that will exemplify the love of Christ. Let that person see a love they cannot deny and remind him or her this love comes from knowing Jesus. Have mercy for doubters and lead them to faith!

November 14

What a Day It Will Be!

Isaiah 65:17-20

Pain. Suffering. Senseless murders. Family feuds. Greed. Selfishness. Lust. Unforgiveness. The list is quite lengthy concerning the depravity of this world. It makes us sick to think of such corruption. The human heart yearns for a day to escape this evil. Yet it is hard to envision the end while we are stuck in the midst of it. How can we attain hope when all we can see is wickedness? We turn to Scripture and trust that the Lord's return will be swift.

In Isaiah 65, we see a glimpse of what we can expect in the afterlife for those who trust in the Lord. Scripture teaches that the former things will not be remembered. Hallelujah! It teaches that the sounds of weeping and crying will be no more. Glory be to God! Also, tragic, heartbreaking occurrences of infants passing away will no longer be a reality! Thank You, Lord! The new heaven and the new earth will be something special to behold. We will finally be able to escape this wretched place! It's hard to grasp our future reality from this side of eternity. But as you encounter the struggles of this life, knowing the truth of what is to come can carry you through any difficult circumstance.

Closer Challenge: Do you struggle with the pains of the present? Is it impeding you from serving God? Change your perspective about your present circumstance by clinging to the future reality of heaven. **Today**, in your journal, write down ten things you look forward to when you get to heaven. Meditate on these things and allow them to fuel your day. As you change your perspective, you can overcome the hardships of this world. Nothing in this world can shake you with heaven on your mind! It does not mean you will escape all pain, but viewing life from heaven can help cope with it better. So, think of your future and know that all things will be good!

November 15

Prepared Just for You

Luke 22:7-13

Near the time of Jesus' death, Peter and John had a fascinating encounter. Jesus ordered them to go ahead of Him to meet a man carrying a jar of water. This man would lead them to his house where preparations for the Passover would be waiting for them. At this point, Peter and John had experienced great wonders in the midst of Jesus, so it should not have shocked them that everything was just as Jesus said. But once again, it is a reminder that Jesus always seemed to have a calculated plan waiting for them to accomplish. This day was no different.

Each day is another opportunity for Jesus to align you with His mission. Each day, there is something prepared for you to accomplish for Him if you just believe His word. There are plenty of "men carrying jugs of water" opportunities on your path, but you must be willing to probe each situation and determine if you have a divine appointment with that individual. Jesus has your day prepared, filled with glory and wonder if you just open your eyes to His work. Your problem is not having opportunities; it is focus and execution. So, look to what Jesus has prepared.

<u>Closer Challenge</u>: Do you realize God has something specially prepared for you on *this* day? There is something He has planned just for you if you give attention to your surroundings. **Today**, be keenly aware of those who cross your path. More than likely, there is a person who God has divinely prepared for you to encounter. Maybe the person is in need of your help; or quite possibly, this person is to help you! Be sensitive to the Spirit of God, and allow Him to direct your actions and words. If you are not attentive, you may miss a great or subtle miracle. God has a plan for you today. Find out what it is!

November 16

Hold Your Tongue!

Proverbs 10:19

Words are fickle. They can be used to edify a person by lifting the spirit, or they can be used improperly to cause pain. (Proverbs 12:18) One wise use of the tongue can heal a broken heart, stand in the gap for a loved one, or lead a charge. Yet one slip of the tongue can cause you to lose a job, damage a relationship, or vow carelessly. Unfortunately, it seems many of us often error on the side of slipups because we speak when it is not wise.

Knowing this, Solomon provided some much-needed advice...*hold your tongue!* The less you use words, the more likely you will not cause problems. For when your words are abundant, sin will be present with you. (Proverbs 10:19) Many words leave room for misinterpretation or carelessness, which often leads to sin. Furthermore, with many words, you will water down the meaning of what you are trying to convey. (Ecclesiastes 6:11) So with God as your witness, it is better to speak less, but appropriately. (Ecclesiastes 5:2) Use your words on a limited basis, and you will prove to be wise.

<u>Closer Challenge</u>: Is it hard for you to control your tongue and only say what is needed? If so, you need to heed Solomon's advice! **Today**, try to limit your words as you engage in conversation with others. Only say what is needed. You can control this by thinking before you speak and provide quality instead of quantity of words. If someone needs encouragement, do it kindly but with few words. (Proverbs 16:24) If you are in a disagreement, listen, listen, and listen some more! And if you must talk, do very little of it. (James 1:19) As you control your tongue, you will find yourself steering more and more away from sin.

November 17

Refining Your Passion

―――――•―――――

Acts 9:28-30

Once Paul began his relationship with Jesus, he wasn't immediately tasked with an incredible mission. Instead, he was taken to Tarsus, so God could spiritually groom him before he was commissioned. (Acts 9:30) During those years, God prodded and poked at his heart and mind, teaching him and refining him until his passion was focused. And once Paul's passion was defined to bring the gospel to Gentiles, God then matched his passion with a perfect opportunity. (Acts 13:1-3) But this process does not happen overnight. It took several years of precious training to shape Paul for his specific calling. During his time of preparation, Paul needed to remain faithful in the little and patient for his time to come.

Many new believers desire to hurry up and plunge into an influential position in ministry. But often, God delays you until you are ready for a larger task. He needs to refine your passions until you are equipped to accomplish His plan for you. As a result, do not neglect the Lord's training. It may take years of small faith steps before you actually understand your calling. Receive the responsibility God has given you *now* with cheer because you can be confident your role *now* is shaping you for something else later.

<u>Closer Challenge</u>: Are you requesting a greater task but none are coming your way? If so, it could be you are in a time of training. Every good leader has needed instruction. **Today**, look at your life right now. No matter how small or great, where do you have responsibility? Whatever that responsibility is, do it faithfully. Do not give up! God might be shaping you through that task so you will be prepared for something greater. Pray for a renewed vigor to finish your current assignment strongly. The training you are receiving now is important if you are to rise to the next level in the future. Do not underestimate the value of your training now!

November 18

Not Sure of Your Next Move?

Acts 16:6-10

Living today brings an immense amount of pressure in regard to knowing your next move. For example, in business, you are expected to know the next big deal or else it could cost you your job. We are obsessed with planning out everything perfectly. Unfortunately, this is not how God often works. It even appears the greatest missionary and biblical scholar did not have everything figured out either! Though the Apostle Paul understood his general calling to the Gentile world, there were times when he was uncertain about what God wanted next of him.

In Acts 16:6-10, we read Paul and his team traveled throughout the province of Asia. Their intent was to preach the gospel to those not knowing Jesus in this region. This sounds like an extremely worthy mission that God should allow, but they were denied by the Holy Spirit. This happened several times on the trip until they spent the night in Troas. Then, during the night, Paul had a vision that led him to Macedonia. He may have thought, "Finally!" So why would God not let him know earlier? If Paul were a businessman seeking the next big deal, He might have been fired due to wasted time! This is what we learn from Paul's experience. You do not have it all figured out! Only God does, so keep trusting Him. If you are in a place of utter confusion or uncertainty about what's next, do not panic! Just keep seeking God and things will work out.

Closer Challenge: Have you been frustrated at not knowing your next move? Are you just as confused as Paul and his team were when God sent them on a wild goose chase of closed doors? If so, you are in good company. **Today**, simply take a step back and receive the Holy Spirit's closed doors as Him gently guiding you. In due time, you will have your Macedonia calling. In the meantime, be observant about your next move, but also patiently worship Him as you wait.

November 19

Remember What You Have Heard

Hebrews 2:1

Drifting. It is appropriate when your intent is to float down a river in a canoe or gently fly a kite in the sky. But often the word is used to express a negative movement. Drifting can define what happens in a marriage when two are not spending time together. Drifting can describe the slow moving torture of substance abuse as a person gradually is taken over by it. Drifting can also define your relationship with God when your attention becomes focused on the world.

Drifting away from God has plagued mankind since Adam and Eve *drifted* to the Tree of the Knowledge of Good and Evil and took a bite of the fruit. Drifting even harms those who are most respected. Famous pastors have *drifted* away from God when they have allowed immoral thoughts to move them to action. Drifting is a temptation for us. So, how can we stop this slow-draining madness that leads us away from God? The author of Hebrews reminds us to "pay much closer attention to what we have heard." Most drifting occurs when we *forget* what we have been told. Forgetting always leads to drifting. That is why God called the Israelites to write His law on their doorframes so they would not forget them. (Deuteronomy 6:4-9) It is paramount you remember what you have been told to be true about God before you too drift away.

<u>Closer Challenge</u>: Are you slowly seeing yourself slipping away from God? If so, **today**, return to the truths you know! Do not merely recall them but *obey* them. Soon you will find yourself resting once again in the arms of God. This may take you joining a Bible study or accountability group. And if your guilt of drifting away is controlling you, remember that God has not moved! He still longs to be close to you. God does not drift; we do! He is our firm foundation. So set your feet back on what you have heard to be true in His Word, and do not allow our culture's influence drift away from Truth again!

November 20

The Fakes Among Us

Matthew 13:24-30

When reading this passage, you might feel betrayed. As you strive to live a passionate life following Jesus believing those around you are doing the same, this passage is a reminder of our gullibility. People aren't what they always claim! They may have the appearance of following Jesus, but in their hearts and private lives, some are far from it. So, how do the weeds enter our midst? Jesus explains it occurs while we are sleeping. (Matthew 13:25) Since sleep is natural and we cannot go without it, how can we protect ourselves? What should we do?! Scripture teaches that we leave them alone. (Matthew 13:28-29) Yes, we are to let the spiritually unregenerate grow with true wheat. Even though they might cause problems, we are to leave them alone.

This passage is frustrating because it goes against the conventional wisdom of pulling out weeds like we would in our yards. It seems natural in the flesh to seek removal. However, as Jesus clearly points out, the sifting of the weeds among us is not our job; it's His role! After all, since we can't see the heart, we might root up or damage someone with genuine faith. (Matthew 13:29) Thus, our responsibility is to love all and seek to persuade them with the redeeming message of the gospel.

<u>Closer Challenge</u>: Is there someone near to you claiming to be a Christ-follower, but the spiritual fruit is lacking? Who is that person you believe could possibly be a weed? **Today**, show that person the mercy and love of Jesus. Invite that person to lunch or spend some time with him or her over a cup of coffee. Do something to begin building a spiritual relationship, knowing the ultimate goal is leading that individual to Jesus. Stop looking at this person as a liability and start seeing him or her as a potential asset for the Kingdom of God.

November 21

Enter His Gates with Thanksgiving

Psalm 100:4

Quite often when we wake up on Sunday mornings, we're expecting the music leader or preacher to challenge us in a way that will stir us to praise and thanksgiving. Maybe you've had a tough week, and so you're longing for a word that will revive your heart and lips to praise. It's a common routine for many Christ-followers today. But it's really a shallow approach to worship.

According to the Psalmist, he didn't wait for an external force to stir him to praise when he arrived for worship. Instead, he *entered* the gates with thanksgiving. Before anyone sang a song or spoke a word, praise was already in the Psalmist's heart. He was able to look back at how the Lord had already blessed him and be filled with thanksgiving. You might have had a tough week, but even with the challenges of the week, there are enough blessings in your life to praise God.

<u>Closer Challenge</u>: Do you enter worship settings with thanksgiving? **Today**, identify a recent blessing. Now, next time you attend a worship experience, enter through the doors with praise on your lips because of this blessing on your mind. You will need sharp discipline because so many matters can distract you from entering in this manner. But before you step foot in the door, think upon this blessing. If you make it a pattern to be attentive to His blessings before you enter His gates, you will experience great freedom as you worship!

November 22

Repent and Follow Me

───◈───

Matthew 4:17-19

The first words out of a leader's mouth when he starts a mission are very important. Followers should pay close attention to that moment. When Jesus began His ministry after being tempted (Matthew 4:1-11), His first two mandates were memorable and direct. In fact, they set the stage for the rest of His ministry. All other teachings flow from these two directives, and when a person submits to these commands, closeness is experienced.

What were His first two directives? "Repent, for the kingdom of heaven is at hand.", and "Follow me, and I will make you fishers of men." He gave two mandates, *repent* and *follow Me*. Coming under the reign of Jesus can be simplified to those two commands. To *repent* means to sorrowfully acknowledge your rebellion against God and make a decision of the will to turn away from your former life. To *follow Me* denotes that after repentance, you aggressively pursue the ways of Christ in all things. If everything else was stripped away from your walk with Jesus, these two directives must remain to be called a Christ-follower. It's important that we daily measure our walk in light of these two commands.

<u>Closer Challenge</u>: Many people today think they are Christians because they attend church or occasionally read their Bibles. Even though those are healthy habits that stir Christian growth, they do not make you a Christian. What makes you a Christian is wrapped up in whether or not you have genuinely repented, and as a result, you are following Him. **Today**, if you cannot honestly say you have done that, kneel down and in a prayer, repent of your ways and commit to follow Christ. By doing this, you will have secured a place in heaven and started your pursuit of drawing closer to God. If you just did this today, talk to a pastor or a Christian friend immediately. They will help you take the next step.

November 23

Replacing the Sun

Revelation 22:1-5

Can you imagine living in a world without the sun? We need the sun for the essentials of life. The sun is necessary for light, warmth, growth, and health. The earth is so reliant upon the sun that it even needs the sun just to stay in orbit. We and our planet cannot survive without the sun. Yet in an unfathomable way, Scripture teaches that we will no long have or need the sun when we transition into eternity with Jesus.

It's hard to grasp that in the next life, there will be no need for the sun. But that day will come when the Lord is revealed in His magnificent glory. Built within His own being exists all the light and warmth we need to survive. There will be no need for us to depend upon creation to thrive in eternity. There is no need for flashlights, headlights or street lights. We won't need furnaces, space heaters or pocket warmers. All we need for light and warmth exists in God. As we are dependent upon the sun on earth, we are even more dependent upon God. What an amazingly all-powerful God we serve!

<u>Closer Challenge</u>: Truthfully, we're just as dependent upon God now as we will be in eternity, but we're often misled to think we can survive without Him due to the incredible, created provisions He has given us while living in the flesh. In a very practical sense, are you relying upon God as the earth is in need of the sun? **Today**, consider the great need you have for God. In your journal, jot down a list of reasons why you need God in your life. Now, as the moon reflects the glory of the sun, it's time for you to reflect the glory of the Son by displaying His character and will through your life.

November 24

Hope Fuels Praise

Psalm 42:5-11

Each of us has moments when praise doesn't roll off the tongue as well as we'd like. Sometimes, the stresses of life divert our attention away from the Savior, and we end up complaining, moping or hating instead of praising. When in a season of discouragement like this, it's impossible to return to praise if you're only focused upon your hardships. Thankfully, the Psalmist gives us clear direction on how to return to a life of praise.

When the Psalmist's soul was downcast, he didn't deny his pain or suffering to God. He openly declared his grief. (Psalm 42:3) However, he didn't end his conversation with a complaint, worry or objection to God's will. He concluded it by vowing that his *hope* was in God and he would again praise Him. (Psalm 42:11) The psalmist understood that when he was able to hope even in the darkest of circumstances, praise would return to his mouth. He didn't state *when* praise would return, but he was certain it would. So even in the midst of his grief, he declared his hope in God's salvation for those who trust in Him.

<u>Closer Challenge</u>: Are you struggling to praise God? If so, it's time to return to a heart of hope instead of harboring a heart of doubt. **Today**, name and own the struggle causing you grief. Now, replace the corrupted thinking due to this struggle with biblical thinking. (Philippians 4:8) For every destructive thought, substitute it with a hopeful belief based upon the Word of God. Jot down these phrases of hope in your journal so you can accurately exchange the bad with the good. Again, the goal isn't necessarily to change your situation (because it may not change), but the goal is praise. And in a strange way, praise can return to your mouth again if you place your sights on hoping in God.

November 25

One Small Act of Obedience

―――――•:•―――――

John 2:1-11

When Jesus performed His first miracle, He tested the obedience of a few unsuspecting, unknown servants. As they were attending to their job of taking care of the party needs, a strange order came to them from the mother of Jesus when the wine was gone. She simply said, "Do whatever he tells you." (John 2:5) At this moment, they had a decision to make. Would they execute the requests or would they disobey? Thankfully, instead of balking at these seemingly senseless acts, they filled the jars and delivered the beverage to their master. And to their amazement, they were a part of Jesus' first miracle.

Often, one simple act of obedience is all it takes to witness God's glory. Your next small move, after being instructed by the Holy Spirit, can ignite a chain reaction of events that can astound everyone around you. God doesn't ask you to heal the blind or walk on water; instead, He often asks you to be faithful in His small orders. And then as you obey, He'll work the wonder and draw people to Himself! All these servants did was fill jars and deliver a beverage. You could've done that! It was a small task, but God can stun the masses when we obey like this.

Closer Challenge: What has God been asking of you over and over again? If you can't remember, what is He asking of you *now*? **Today**, no matter how senseless it may sound, simply obey. Do you need to simply ask for help? Do you need to give or repay a small loan? Do you need to pay more attention to your spouse or kids? This is not a request to do the radical. It's a challenge to do something small. All the servants did was fill jars and deliver a beverage, but it made a huge difference. Don't overlook God's small orders. A miracle might be on the other side of your obedience too.

November 26

Give Openhandedly

Deuteronomy 15:7-8

God has a deep compassion for those who don't have much. This is reflected in His Law that He provided to Israel. (Deuteronomy 15:7-8) He desired that Israel be a community of faith that sought out the needs of the disenfranchised instead of avoiding them. They were not to wait for the government to bail out the needy or simply expect the rich to tend to their hardships. It was the role of every faith-driven person to care for the poor.

Even though you might have more than enough to survive in comparison to most of the world, you might find yourself to be "closed-fisted" to the poor. It's easy to find reasons why you shouldn't give. Maybe you've thought, "Well, they got themselves in that position!" Or, "They will waste what is given to them." That might be true on both accounts, but it doesn't take away the test you have with your wealth to give openhandedly. Yes, it's prudent to use wise judgment, but keep in mind it's better to error in generosity rather than stinginess.

<u>Closer Challenge</u>: Have you noticed a pattern of stinginess in your life? Do you often see a need but are negligent in meeting it even though you can? **Today**, practice openhanded giving. Instead of tightly hanging on to what you have, preserving it for self-interests, open your eyes, heart and hands to the ones around you in need of a special financial lift. When you encounter someone with a material need today, do your best to help meet it. It may not need to be much but practice openhanded giving. It will not only bless the one you're touching, but it will also bless you.

November 27

Return to Your First Love

Hosea 3:1-3

No person in the Bible might be less envied than Hosea. God called him to marry a prostitute, Gomer. In obedience, he submitted to God's orders, thinking Gomer might change and love him as a faithful bride. Unfortunately, she returned to her sinful ways and continued to lie with other men for money. Instead of God releasing Hosea from this relational torture, He called Hosea to *return* to her. (Hosea 3:1-3) Oh, the humiliation and embarrassment Hosea must have felt when he pulled out fifteen shekels of silver to pay for his wife! What could God possibly be teaching Israel through Hosea's life?

Well, Hosea's life with Gomer is a spiritual picture of mankind's relationship with God. Though God always remains faithful to us, we commit spiritual adultery when we turn away from Him by chasing after sins of our former self. And just when we'd think God wouldn't take us back, remarkably He upholds His end of the covenant by lovingly forgiving us. He even pays the price for our sins with the blood of Jesus! In return, we are compelled to return to Him as our first love.

<u>Closer Challenge</u>: It's possible that a sin from your former self has been reoccurring in your life. If that's the case, you are committing spiritual adultery by drifting away from your first love. **Today**, seriously consider your thoughts and actions to determine if you're betraying God with your affections for something else. If you are, return to your first love by repenting of that sin. Leave that lifestyle with full abandonment! Get help if necessary. Don't try to wage war by yourself. Speak to your pastor or a godly friend for guidance, but ultimately, return to God, because He'll take you back the moment you return your heart to Him!

November 28

The Sole Priority of God

Matthew 6:33

It's likely that at some point you've created a personal list of priorities with your time. These lists vary in size, but generally speaking for most God-fearing people, the list looks something like this: First, God. Second, Spouse/Family. Third, Relationships/Friends. Fourth, Ministry. Fifth, Occupation. Sixth, Hobbies/Entertainment. A list like this seems practical and beneficial, but the lines often blur, creating frustrations and unmet expectations. For example, it's not easy justifying a time when placing your job is a priority over your family. It can also be a challenge when your family is blocking you from obeying God. It's fair to say that these lists can cause a conflict of interests.

There is a better, more biblical approach to your priority list. Make it one item long. "But seek first the kingdom of God and his righteousness, and all these things will be added to you." When you simply set your mind and heart on God, the Spirit of God will direct you where and how you should spend the time you've been given on earth. Each day you should spend time seeking what is best for His Kingdom, and the rest will be added. The Spirit of God will keep you in a healthy rhythm between all these interests if you actively seek to hear His voice and obey daily. Listen closely to God, and He will direct your time wisely.

<u>Closer Challenge</u>: Do you feel pulled in several different directions of interests? Are you failing to manage your time well? **Today**, start with asking God for guidance with your time. Honestly pray, "God, show me how I can best use my time for Your Kingdom and glory." If needed, each morning properly schedule your day in accordance with God's direction. If you follow the Spirit, you will experience a full day of meeting needs beyond what you could've done on your own. Furthermore, you'll also waste less time. Seek first the Kingdom of God.

November 29

God Must Glorify Himself

John 12:28

If you know anything about God, it's that He *hates* idolatry. Just as much as He loves you, He has an equal emotion of hate when we turn our affection and attention toward other gods. Idolatry is replacing worship of God with anything else. It's substituting the real with something fake. God disdains idolatry because it shifts glory away from Him, and it robs us of the *best* in life, which is Him! For a precise depiction of God's hate for idolatry, read Psalm 106.

Therefore, since God hates it when His creation worships anything but Him, it would be inconsistent of God to glorify anything but Himself. He *must* glorify Himself and not another, for no other is greater! (Isaiah 46:9-10; Psalm 95:3) If He were to worship anything in His creation (i.e., the sun, stars, people, carved images, etc.), He would be settling for less, and He'd be misrepresenting what He calls us to do. This isn't arrogance; it's righteous for Him to do so. As a result, in the final hours of Jesus' life, Jesus calls out to the Father to glorify Himself, and the Father affirms that He already has. God's pursuit is for His own name to be glorified only, and it's perfectly appropriate and right that He seeks an increase of His own fame.

<u>Closer Challenge</u>: Is there idolatry in your life? You can know by answering this question: How do I spend my time, talents and treasure? If these are focused more on the world, you are practicing idolatry. **Today**, discover what your idol tendencies are by measuring how you spend your time, talents, and treasure. Wherever that trail ends, you'll find your potential idol. Rid it aggressively before it overcomes you. Remember, even God must worship Himself, so how much more should you?

November 30

The Measure of Your Love for God

---

1 John 5:1-3

God makes it very clear in His Word how we know if our love for Him is real. The measure is how we love others. (1 John 5:1) A person who overflows more hate for others than love proves his love is not for God but really himself. When Jesus was near the end of His life, He left a reminder for His disciples that His commandment was that they love one another as He had loved them. (John 15:12) Love takes more effort than expressing feelings; it entails demonstration. (Romans 5:8) If you don't demonstrate your love for others through sacrifice, you are not displaying your love for God. And as a result, you don't love God.

It's important to understand that our claims must match our actions. If not, we're actually living a lie. For our real beliefs are reflected in our behaviors. If you love others, your claim is true: You love God. But if you neglect loving others, then the Spirit of God is not ruling in your life, and there might be an absence of God's Spirit in you. There will be no question when you stand before Jesus if you loved Him or not. He will simply measure your life by the way you loved others.

Closer Challenge: When evaluating your life, do you often discover yourself refusing to sacrifice your desires to help others? If so, it's quite possible your love for God isn't real. **Today**, start with one simple act of sacrifice for another. Give generously, provide time to listen, help willingly in a practical way. Pay close attention to your circumstances; the Spirit of God will lead you. Let your motivation be God's love for you. This simple exercise may not seem like much, but it can lead to a healthy pattern. And most importantly, it will support your claim of loving God.

December 1

Follow Me: Leave Everything

Luke 5:27-32

Tax collectors were often considered renegade Jews. Not only were they cooperating with the progress of Rome, they handled business unethically. Because of their connection to Rome and crookedness in their dealings, they were often excommunicated from normal Jewish religious activities. Not only were they disliked, they were banned from common fellowship. But in an unexpected move, Jesus reached out to a despised Jewish tax collector and said, "Follow Me."

Now, when Jesus called Levi, it was an invitation to a completely new life. Jesus doesn't renovate by simply addressing a few areas to polish up, He demolishes a life and starts it over. It's a full reset. Levi had to leave behind everything he knew. Due to the crooked nature of tax collecting, he left his job, including his habits of thievery. His methods of wealth had to be released. He even had to let go of his idea of being rejected, because now he was accepted. Everything changed from this point going forward. And unlike the fishermen, who could return to their work if things didn't pan out, once Levi quit he couldn't go back to his job. It was Jesus or bust! This is the same type of attitude we should have when we accept the call to follow Him.

Closer Challenge: Have you truly accepted the call of Jesus to leave everything? **Today**, evaluate what it means to follow Jesus. Consider the things you must release. Write in your journal at least one thing you need to leave, and do it! If you are not willing to leave everything, you're not obeying His call. The call to follow Jesus isn't simply to rearrange a few bad habits; it's a call to completely leave it and let Jesus rebuild and redirect it as He sees fit to best glorify His name. This is the only way to live a Spirit-filled life and move forward honoring God.

December 2

Follow Me: Accept Your Story

John 21:15-22

When the resurrected Jesus spoke to Peter privately about his unique mission of suffering, instead of humbly accepting the call, Peter oddly asked about John's mission. "Lord, what about this man?" After this question, Jesus reminded Peter that it wasn't Peter's concern what John's mission was. Regardless of the calling, Peter needed to focus on this primary command of Jesus, "Follow me." It was paramount that Peter focused on *his* mission, regardless of what God calls others to do.

God has a unique story for you. It might be full of blessings or riddled with heartache and suffering, but it's your story. It might be crammed with adventure or preparing for one big moment, but it's your story. No one knows the mind of God. Why does He allow one person to face hurt and another to experience great success? Only with heavenly eyes can the reasons be seen. But one thing is certain, you've only been given one life to use for glorifying God, so make the most of it.

<u>Closer Challenge</u>: Have you often found yourself coveting the story God has for others? Are you fighting against your life's story? **Today**, instead of wishing for another person's life and mission, work through these steps to accept your mission. First, *thank* God for the life He's given you and for the life you're coveting. Both have significant purpose! Secondly, evaluate your story to see how you can use it for God's glory. Your giftedness, passions and experiences are all part of your story and can be used to glorify God. Delay no longer. Let *your* life, as God is shaping it, shine for Jesus!

December 3

An Advantage of the Spirit: His Presence

John 14:16

When the Holy Spirit isn't understood, Christ-followers miss out on His blessings. Jesus said it is to our advantage that He goes away. For if He doesn't return to the Father, the Helper will not come. (John 16:7) It's good that Jesus leaves because the Spirit is not confined to one place. As powerful and peaceful as Jesus was in the flesh, He was physically in one place at one time. Conversely, the Holy Spirit is everywhere at all times. He is the ever-present dwelling of God on earth. He resides both in you and around you to bring peace, protection, and pleasure.

As a result of this beautiful indwelling of God, the Holy Spirit is our Helper because He is *with* you as you suffer. He is *with* you as you celebrate. He is *with* you when you need protection. He is *with* you when you're in need of direction. He is *with* you when you need strength. The Spirit is your Helper because He is the holy presence of God WITH you at all times! As challenging as it may be for mortal man to understand God's presence through the Holy Spirit, when you *believe* in Him you are rewarded with a spiritual awareness that doubters seek desperately.

<u>Closer Challenge</u>: Have you truly believed in the Holy Spirit as your ever-present help? Do you recognize His involvement? **Today**, spend some time right now considering the Holy Spirit's role in your life. *Believe* He is helping you during your time of sadness, celebration or desperation. You are never alone! God is with you and He is here to help you. Turn to your Helper today and believe it is to your advantage that Jesus has returned to the Father so you can rest in the presence of the Holy Spirit.

December 4

An Advantage of the Spirit: His Teaching

John 14:25-26

Since the Spirit is present with you at all times (John 14:16), being the very mind of God, He is the dominant voice leading you to understanding in spiritual matters. Jesus said the Helper is the one who teaches truth and brings it to remembrance. (John 14:25-26) The Spirit buries doctrine in your soul, and when you need it in everyday life, He reminds you of that truth so you can follow Jesus and resist temptation. When you read or hear the Word of God spoken, He stirs your mind and connects you to that truth. Without the Helper, you cannot understand anything of God.

Even though you will have the distinct privilege of sitting under eloquent orators of God's Word, none of them have the ability to pierce your soul. None of them can be ever-present with you to remind you of a truth in a time of need. The Spirit is the One who awakens a sleeping soul to sound doctrine and timeless principles, leading that person to practical application. And in a moment of need, it is the Helper who will sound like an alarm, recalling a specific Word for that situation. Though you may not always be aware of His moving, the Helper is at work in your mind, filling you with the wisdom and knowledge of God. (John 16:13)

<u>Closer Challenge</u>: Are you believing in the Spirit as your primary teacher? **Today**, declare your trust in the Spirit as your Instructor. Thank Him for helping you know the veracities of God. Next time you find yourself in a setting where the Word of God is taught, pray silently that your Helper will teach you what is necessary for that day. Make this a pattern in your worship routine any time you read, hear or even speak the Word of God. No person can help you understand the truths of God as the Helper does. It is to your advantage that the Holy Spirit is your teacher. (John 16:7)

December 5

An Advantage of the Spirit: His Empowerment

John 15:26-27

In Jesus' last discourse with His disciples, He explains that the Spirit is coming to glorify the Son. Even though the Spirit is part of the Godhead, He is not seeking to be exalted; instead, even the Spirit sets His aim on glorifying Jesus. (John 16:14) For when the *Son* is lifted up, all mankind can be drawn to Him, believe in Him, and be given eternal life! (John 3:14; 12:32) It is the distinct role of the Holy Spirit to bear witness about Jesus.

Likewise, just as the Spirit aims to exalt Jesus, your mission in life is to bear witness to Jesus by drawing closer to Him personally and leading others to have a close relationship with Him too. (John 15:27) However, adequately extending the gospel story into the lives of unbelievers is an impossible task on your own. As a result, it is the Spirit who empowers you to bear witness. (Acts 1:8) Since the Spirit is the ultimate teacher, penetrating deep within the souls of mankind (John 14:25-26), only He can awaken the heart of the unregenerate. It's not your role to change a person. But as you are empowered to present God's redeeming message in word and deed, the Spirit of God will use your effort to seep into a life and bear witness of Jesus.

<u>Closer Challenge</u>: In your attempt to persuade others to follow Jesus, have you leaned upon the Spirit to empower you? **Today**, as opportunity presents itself, simply present the story of Jesus to someone. But before you set out on this adventure, pray *now* that the Spirit will empower you and bear witness about Jesus in the soul of the hearer. Trust in the Spirit to do His job, and watch the gospel message change a life. It is to your advantage that the Spirit of God has empowered you to share the message of the gospel. (John 16:7)

December 6

An Advantage of the Spirit: His Convicting

John 16:8

Turning hearts to God is not the work of man. Though believers are to present the gospel well, it's not their role to change a person. Yet throughout history, many are convinced that they can force transformation. So, they drive unbelievers to the brink of disgust in an attempt to convert them. As a result, they end up pushing away the unregenerate further from God instead of closer to Him. Christ followers must come to the understanding that no person can change the heart of another. You might be able to force them to *act* differently to pacify your nagging, but only the Spirit of God can convict the world of sin, righteousness, and judgment. (John 16:8)

Our spiritual responsibility in regard to leading people to trust in Jesus is two-fold. *Present* the gospel with clarity (1 Peter 3:15) and *pray* for the Spirit of God to change the heart. (Romans 10:1) *Present* and *pray*. And then after we do our part, we must trust the Helper to do His, which is to draw the wayward soul to Jesus through conviction. Only when the Spirit convicts the unbeliever will there be genuine and lasting change.

<u>Closer Challenge</u>: Have you attempted to do the work of the Spirit? Have you tried to take the place of the Helper? Who have you approached repeatedly about turning to Christ? **Today**, continue to *present* the gospel with love and compassion and earnestly *pray* that this individual would be saved. But ultimately, rely on the Helper to *convict* the heart and turn your wandering friend or family member to follow Jesus. As you do your role, trust in the Spirit to do His.

December 7

The Spirit-Filled Life

---•---

Ephesians 5:18

Due to misunderstandings of what it means to be *filled* by the Holy Spirit, many believers are uncomfortable even investigating His role in our lives. Unbiblical fanaticism has driven some to ignore the beautiful doctrine of the Holy Spirit. Yet, it cannot be denied that great events took place when God's people were Spirit-filled. So, what does it mean to be Spirit-filled? It means you are *passively* controlled and possessed by God. Paul writes that believers are not to be *filled* [controlled/possessed] with wine which leads to chaotic, uncontrolled living but be *filled* [controlled/possessed] with the Spirit. (Ephesians 5:18) Being Spirit-filled isn't just *having access* to the Holy Spirit for salvation; it's being *led* by the Holy Spirit in everyday living. You can receive the Holy Spirit for salvation but not be Spirit-filled. (Mark 14:27; James 5:19) This happens to backslidden believers. (Proverbs 14:14)

If there is a continual dominance of God in you, you're being Spirit-filled. Inside-out He is ruling your thoughts and actions. You'll still be tempted to sin, but God's hand is guiding you. That is why being Spirit-filled is not a one-time event. You must *keep* letting God influence you as a pattern of life. It's habitually surrendering control of your life to the wisdom, words, and works of God, resulting in attitudes and actions that mirror Him.

<u>Closer Challenge</u>: Are you living a Spirit-filled life? Is there a pattern of God ruling your beliefs and behaviors? **Today**, commit to living a Spirit-filled *day*. In every thought and action you make today, let *God* direct you. Yes, EVERY thought and action. Before you speak, look, or step, determine how God would desire you to move. If you live like this today and each one going forward, you'll experience the blessing of a Spirit-filled life. Choose to be Spirit-filled and watch God amaze you and others you encounter.

December 8

Not Left Without a Redeemer!

―――――•―――――

Ruth 4:14

The noble story of Ruth brings *hope* to all those who don't think they have a fighting chance at being blessed after great loss or even failure. Having lost her husband and being in a new land, Ruth didn't have much hope from a worldly perspective. She needed a redeemer. A kinsmen-redeemer in the Old Testament was responsible for protecting the interests of needy extended family members. When Boaz learned he was second in line to redeem Ruth, he took the necessary measures to claim her from the first in line redeemer. (Ruth 4:1-12) When it was properly transferred, Boaz married Ruth and cared for her. Oh the elation Ruth must have experienced when she first realized she had been redeemed and accepted by Boaz! She was not left without a redeemer. (Ruth 4:14)

Fast-forward close to the present. Today, you also haven't been left without a Redeemer. Jesus pleaded your cause and paid the price of your sin to claim you as His. You were not deserving of such great love, but He claimed you anyway. You have been granted the rights of royalty, being heirs of the Kingdom of Heaven! As a result, you can declare as Job did, "For I know that my Redeemer lives..." (Job 19:25)

<u>Closer Challenge</u>: Have you seriously considered the price Jesus paid for you? He redeemed you with His own life! **Today**, before you do anything else, bow down on your knees, and as Ruth declared to Boaz, call out to God, "Spread your wings over your servant, for you are *my* Redeemer." (Ruth 3:9) In that simple statement, you are declaring your neediness to God and His ability to purchase, protect and preserve you. Worship Him throughout the day in light of your redemption!

December 9

Love According to Jesus

---◆---

Romans 5:8

Over the last couple of centuries, people have reduced love to a romantic affair. Yet when love is based upon feelings, it becomes conditional. As long as people *feel* loved, they may return love; but as soon as that feeling changes, the deal is off! Jesus doesn't define love this way. For Jesus, love is clearly a *demonstration* regardless of the one being loved. "But God *shows* His love for us that while we were still *sinners*, Christ died for us." (Romans 5:8) The deepest form of love was expressed when God demonstrated His love for us even when we didn't deserve it. No love is lasting unless it is demonstrated through sacrificial action.

It should be no surprise that the greatest two commandments start with love. (Luke 10:27). To love God means to demonstrate your affections for Him in a sacrificial way. Likewise, to love people requires the same commitment. You can't say you love God or anyone else if there is no demonstration. Love is not a mysterious feeling with no expression. It's not even mere words; it's proven! Even if you don't feel like loving someone in the moment, it's a decision of the will to display it. And when you decide to love in a sacrificial way, it's amazing how the feelings will follow!

<u>Closer Challenge</u>: How have you defined love? Does it have more to do with passively following emotions or actively demonstrating it? **Today**, practice love as Jesus displayed and directed. First, love God. Don't just say you love God, sacrificially show Him with your time, resources, and strength. Secondly, love people. Pick at least one person who needs to experience your deep affection of love. Your statement of love will reach deeper if you sacrifice something dear to you. So display biblical love by practicing these two great commandments today.

December 10

Risking for the Outcast

Acts 9:26-27

Paul (formally known as Saul) was a supporter of killing Christ-followers. (Acts 9:1) He aggressively sought to halt the movement of the church. So, it isn't surprising that people were afraid of him after his conversion experience. (Acts 9:18) Was this a trick to get close to Christians, only to turn on them once accepted? Many were terrified. But one brave soul took a risk on Paul and accepted him as his personal responsibility to disciple. Barnabas, known as the encourager, went against conventional wisdom of protecting himself and pleaded Paul's case before the apostles. This bold move showed confidence in a man who would eventually be one of the most influential individuals in all Christian history!

Often, we tend to write off those who have opposed the forward movement of the gospel. It's easy to justify that we shouldn't get involved with such individuals for protection's sake; but in doing so, we might be missing a great opportunity to invest in the life of someone who could impact eternity greatly. What would the church be like without the writing contributions of Paul in the New Testament? Thanks be to God for Barnabas' willingness to see the potential in Paul and take the risk of partnering with him! May we all have a heart like Barnabas to see the potential in an outcast!

Closer Challenge: Are you quick to doubt the transformation in some new believers because of their defiant or contentious past? Maybe all they need is someone like Barnabas to believe in them so they can make a significant contribution for the cause of Christ. **Today**, think about those in your church or community who have recently converted to Christianity. Instead of being skeptical of their conversion experience, take a risk on them. This week spend some time with a new convert. Listen intently to this person's story and gently instruct him or her as needed. If you're struggling to find a new convert, pray now for someone who is combative to the gospel. Just as God changed Paul, He can call that person out of spiritual blindness. When that happens, risk developing that person spiritually, as Barnabas did for Paul.

December 11

Finding Hope After Failure

Laminations 3:21-24

Israel had it all. God had chosen them to be His favored people. He would bless all who blessed them and curse all who cursed them. (Genesis 12:2-3) As long as Israel kept the covenant, they would never be destroyed. (Deuteronomy 6:13-15) But, as history goes, they failed time and time again to remain faithful. They were enticed by the flesh to go their own way instead of being directed by God. (Jeremiah 10:23) Since they didn't heed God's warnings, Jerusalem had to be punished. God allowed enemy nations to rise up against them and overtake them. Yet, this wasn't God abandoning them; it was God disciplining them. For His love could never forsake them.

After being humiliated by the destruction due to their own sins (Laminations 1:9), Israel knew it was time to go back to the One constant in their lives. God's loving faithfulness had never waned. So they mourned; not over their losses, but over breaking God's heart. Repentance was the only action that could return them to God's favor. So, their only hope was to cling to God's mercy and His promise that He would never leave them nor forsake them. (Deuteronomy 31:6) They had to hope in God's faithfulness. (Lamentations 3:21-24) Our hope is no different today.

<u>Closer Challenge</u>: Have you been humiliated due to abandoning God's direction? Have you come to the point where you realize you're to blame? **Today**, if failure is bringing great sorrow in your life, cling to the hope of God's faithfulness. Repent over your sins. Don't mourn over your losses. Mourn over breaking God's heart because of your disobedience. (Psalm 51:4) Understand that God still loves you as much as He ever has. Though you may lament today, restoration awaits you as you return to the Lord.

December 12

The Kingdom of Heaven

Matthew 3:2

When Jesus speaks of the Kingdom of Heaven, many think of it as a place, an inward power, the universe or even the church. Certainly, those play a role in the Kingdom of Heaven.. But with careful evaluation of Jesus' words, the centerpiece of the Kingdom of Heaven is a *reign*. A reign marks an influence that goes beyond territory, people or methods; for a true reign is defined by the One who holds the supremacy. And in regard to the Kingdom of Heaven, that authority endures with Jesus' unchangeable sovereignty throughout the created universe. From the furthest star to the highest heaven back to the deepest crevice of person's heart, the reign of Jesus stands as the irrevocable government throughout all eternity!

Ultimately, every person will eventually admit the dominant rule of Jesus (Philippians 2:9-11), but the wise choose to be loyal to Him *now*. And the only way to come under Jesus' reign is to repent and believe. (Mark 1:15) For those who choose not to repent and believe, eternal destruction awaits them. (Psalm 92:7) But for you, who have yielded allegiance to the Sovereign King while in the body, the King has not left you without instructions. Keep seeking those teachings like a treasure and live by them fully!

<u>Closer Challenge</u>: Are you wisely living *under* the reign of the Ruler of the Kingdom of Heaven? Is Jesus your King? If so, it's paramount you know what the King expects of you as His loyal follower. **Today**, read in the Gospel of Matthew the different pictures Jesus provides about the Kingdom of Heaven. Do a word search on "The Kingdom of Heaven" by using a concordance, an online Bible study tool or app. Study at least three of these passages and apply how you should live based upon your King's creed. As a member of God's Kingdom, take seriously your role in honoring your good Ruler.

December 13

Prepare, Don't Provoke Your Kids

Ephesians 6:4

As parents, you have the God-given responsibility to raise your children according to Scripture, not as *you* see fit. But even with the greatest intentions to follow God, when moments of frustration and fatigue occur, the potential of dealing with your child in an improper manner increases greatly. When frustration and fatigue rise, be careful not to provoke your child to anger. Doing so can lead your child to resent both you and the Lord. Exasperating a child typically occurs when *your* anger is out of control. It's extremely important to keep your bitterness in check so your children don't become an outlet for your outrage!

Paul is clear that believers are to bring up their children in the discipline and instruction of the Lord. (Ephesians 6:4) This means you are to *model* biblical teachings with your life. When your child disappoints you, show mercy as God shows you. When your child needs correction, provide it, but speak the truth in love. (Ephesians 4:15) And if your child experiences the wrath of your unrestrained anger, be a model of repentance. Kids will test your faith and patience, but don't allow patterns of anger to control the way you parent. It can have long-lasting negative effects on your children.

<u>Closer Challenge</u>: Have you used your children as a target to aim your anger? Is there unresolved bitterness in your children due to your outbursts? ***Today***, if you recognize a pattern of provoking your child to anger, practice repentance before them. Share with your child specifically how you have been wrong. Ask for forgiveness and explain how you will act differently. Finally, if you have any lingering bitterness due to how your parents treated you, forgive them! Don't let their failures control your future. Practice forgiveness. After all, you were forgiven by the Father when you didn't deserve it.

December 14

The Best Part of Being an Heir

Romans 8:14-17

To think of heaven brings groans to the soul. (2 Corinthians 5:2) Scripture teaches there will be no tears, pain or sorrow. (Revelation 21:4) There will be a great reunion of all who have gone before you. Mansions, streets of gold, heavenly singing and so much more. But as good as that will be, nothing compares to the greatest part of being an heir...God Himself! The best gift of your inheritance is that you get to have a close relationship with the Creator. In fact, God adopts you as His own child! And as a child of God, you get to call Him your *Abba*. (Romans 8:15) You get to draw closer to a Daddy who is captivated by His love for you.

Sometimes we're misled when we think of being heirs to God. We may assume God will give us all we desire materialistically. We'd like to think of God as our Great Sugar Daddy in the sky, merely spoiling us with frivolous gifts. But, if that's how you view God, you've missed the intimate nature of being a called an heir. The greatest inheritance is *relationship* with Him. And as you sit with God, like a child craving nearness to his daddy, monetary gifts become an overflow of the Father's love.

<u>Closer Challenge</u>: Is your view of God based upon what He can give you with His unlimited resources? Have you forgotten that the true gift of God is God Himself? **Today**, don't ask God for anything regarding the things of this world. Simply say to God in the quietness of your soul, "I just want YOU. You are my portion forever; not heaven, not your resources or abilities, just YOU. You are my inheritance. And that's enough." (Psalm 73:25-26) When you can come to God like that, you'll better understand what it means to have an Abba. You truly cherish your position as an heir to God.

December 15

The Greatest Test You Will Ever Face!

Deuteronomy 6:10-15

It's tempting to think the most challenging test in life is when things are taken away from us, suffering great loss. As difficult as that is, there is a greater test. And the most alarming part of *this* test is that we don't often realize we're even being tested. Your greatest test in life is when you've been given *much*! God warned Israel that when they had been given the land they were promised, great cities they did not build, and homes full of good things, don't *forget* the Lord! For if He was forgotten, His anger would rise against them. Unfortunately, this is a test they failed on a regular basis.

When things are going well, there is a greater temptation for you to commend yourself for accomplishments, while forgetting God. You are enticed by the flesh to boast in your success and claim personal victory. But as one who fears God, run from this kind of perspective! It's critically important that when you receive God's favor, hold firm in your heart that He is your *portion* forever. (Psalm 73:25-26) A heart ungrateful for the blessings you've received can lead you down a path of ruin.

<u>Closer Challenge</u>: Have you recently thanked God for His favor in your life? *Today*, quietly walk throughout the home where you live, praising Him for specific items you've been given. *Never* forget it is the Lord who has provided you these blessings! For if you forget, you fail the test. Whether you have been given much or little, the Lord is your portion forever. (Psalm 142:5) He is enough! All the extras you have in life are a bonus. Be thankful for God's bountiful hand upon you.

December 16

Praying for God to Defend Himself

———————•:•———————

2 Kings 19:14-19

King Hezekiah did what was right in the eyes of the Lord. During Hezekiah's reign, God's people had already split into two kingdoms. The ten tribes to the north were called Israel, and the two tribes to the south were called Judah. In the sixth year of Hezekiah's reign over Judah, Israel was defeated by Shalmaneser and the Assyrians as punishment because they did not obey God. (2 Kings 18:10-12) The next king of Assyria, Sennacherib, then proceeded to overthrow Judah. Sennacherib sent a letter to Hezekiah and his people, mocking God and expressing his nation's superiority. (2 Kings 19:10) Hezekiah then turned to prayer. Spreading out the letter before the Lord in the Temple, Hezekiah cried out for God to defend His name. (2 Kings 19:15-19) God heard the prayer and the angel of the Lord struck down 185,000 Assyrians. (2 Kings 19:35)

It can be frustrating to witness the secular world mocking the Living God. Each day carries the potential of someone defaming God and accusing Him of weakness. The temptation is to defend God in *your* strength by speaking against such evil. Though there are occasions when you should stand for Him, never forget that God is powerful enough to defend Himself against any threat to His name. Simply call upon Him to do so as Hezekiah did.

Closer Challenge: Have you recently witnessed someone or a group of people mocking and defaming the name of God? **Today**, find a place without distractions where you can commune with God privately. Similar to Hezekiah spreading out this offensive letter before God, voice out loud in prayer any insults you've heard others make about Him. Ask Him to defend Himself and save you from any harm for *His* glory's sake. As you patiently wait for God to respond, continue to commune with Him in close fellowship.

December 17

Rescuing a Family Member

Genesis 14:8-16

Family has a way of bringing out the worst and best in you. You can be deeply offended by family in one moment but amazed by their love in the next. No matter how you currently feel about your family, you have a biblical calling to tend to your family's needs. (1 Timothy 5:8) So regardless of the past, your family is counting on you to rescue them in times of need.

Abraham and Lot had a rocky relationship, but when it counted the most, Abraham came to Lot's aide. After a dispute led Abraham and Lot to part ways, Lot found himself in the crossfire of several kingdoms. He was captured by the enemy nations. Abraham was notified of Lot's captivity and immediately assembled his trained men, chased down the enemy, and rescued Lot. Even though they parted ways in a dispute, Abraham didn't refuse his role as the kinsman of his nephew, Lot. (Genesis 14:14)

Closer Challenge: Do you have a relative in need of being rescued? Maybe this family member is held captive by an addiction, an abusive relationship, or a debilitating illness. **Today**, assume your role as the rescuer for this family member. Model the commitment Abraham had for Lot. Abraham forgave fully, pursued fervently, sacrificed freely, and battled ferociously. Forgive your family member for any wrongdoing. Pursue him or her with great conviction. Sacrifice what you must to save this person. Battle hard to overcome this challenge. Don't take lightly your role to rescue a family member in need. God will be well-pleased with your love.

December 18

Rebuking a Wayward Believer

Titus 1:9-13

Unfortunately, not all believers stay on the right path. Some become persuaded to believe myths, false doctrines and erroneous philosophies. When this happens, God has called faithful believers to turn them back. The Cretan circumcision party was a group that combined Jewish law and the Christian faith. Mixing faiths is never good. As a result, Paul instructed Titus and the leaders of the Cretan church to *rebuke* swiftly such error.

Rebuking is often perceived as a challenging practice in the Christian faith. So instead of addressing error, passive individuals often ignore it, thinking they are *keeping* peace. But this is not peace-keeping; it's allowing error to spread, and it delays healing. Please understand that rebuking biblical matters should only take place between believers. You cannot rebuke non-Christians because they don't have a biblical worldview; it just leads to unhealthy arguments. (Proverbs 23:9) That person must first be led to belief in Jesus. But in regard to people claiming to be Christ-followers, you have a responsibility to correct those in error.

<u>Closer Challenge</u>: Is there a *believer* in your midst who is spreading false doctrine? **Today**, take the proper steps in rebuking that individual or group. First, *look inward*. Before you say a word, look at *your* heart to make sure there is nothing blatantly erroneous. (Matthew 7:4) Secondly, *look upward*. Make sure you are aligned with God's truth and your motives are pure. (Ephesians 4:15) Rebuking aims to be curative, not vindictive. Finally, *look outward*. If there is no cooperation after attempting to resolve it one-on-one, bring other believers with you to rebuke. (Matthew 18:16) If you humbly rebuke another, great healing can occur. As a believer, you have a responsibility to correct the wayward. Rebuke with love and grace.

December 19

Worship with Your Mind

Colossians 1:15-19

If you're not careful, you can routinely show up to your weekly church gatherings and miss why you really worship. This happens when Christians fail to engage their *minds* in worship. Biblical worship is more than stirring up an array of emotions that lead to raising hands, bowing heads, or shouting praises. Biblical worship is even more than giving out generous gifts to needy persons. After all, non-believers do that! Worship certainly includes those things, but biblical worship initiates from a *belief* that Jesus is supreme and sufficient in comparison to all other gods.

So, what can you mentally know about Jesus? According to Colossians 1:15-19, Jesus is supreme over all gods because He is the fullness of the Deity, even the face of the invisible God. He is supreme over creation because all things are made by Him, through Him, for Him. He is supreme over time because He is from the beginning, making Him eternal. He is supreme over all believers because He is the Head of the church. He is supreme over death because He is the firstborn of the resurrection. He is completely sufficient because He is the One holding all things together. There is no god or anything in creation that can claim His superiority! And based upon this knowledge, all your worship flows.

<u>Closer Challenge</u>: Has corporate worship become routine for you? If so, it's quite possible you haven't been engaging your mind. **Today**, along with Colossians 1:15-19, read a few more of the great Christology passages. (Philippians 2:1-11; John 1:1-18) Let these passages strengthen your beliefs; for it's your beliefs that lead to your behaviors. Next time you participate in corporate worship, be mindful of what you are singing, reading, hearing or praying. For these powerful words of God can influence your perspective and purpose! Worship God with all your mind.

December 20

When the Unexpected Comes

Matthew 1:18-25

Joseph was excited! He was betrothed to be married. Life was in a good spot for him. But then, something unusual happened. Mary, his soon-to-be wife, became pregnant. Disappointed, Joseph sank to a low point emotionally. He certainly had no plans for remaining with her. What could he do? He could expose her to public disgrace and even have her stoned. But, he loved her too much, so he decided to divorce her quietly. Yet while struggling with his loss, an angel came to him in his sleep and instructed Joseph to continue in the marriage, because the child Mary was carrying was from the Lord. Unsure of what the future would hold, Joseph took a leap of faith and married her as the angel said.

Joseph thought his life was planned out, but when the unexpected came, he had to adjust. When facing unexpected situations, people tend to respond in one of these three ways. They might *pout in pity*, feeling unloved by God. They might *shout in anger*, fuming against God's plan. Or, finally, they *sprout in faith*, trusting in God even when things don't go as expected. For Joseph, he chose to sprout in faith. Though life didn't go according to *his* plans, disappointment faded as he saw God's perfect plan unfolding before his eyes!

Closer Challenge: Have you been met with unexpected turns in your life? Is disappointment controlling you? **Today,** put your disappointment on hold and choose to look at your situation from God's perspective. Write in your journal several possible ways your unexpected turn of events could result in good as you continue to love God. (Romans 8:28) Not one mortal person who has walked this earth has been able to perfectly map out his or her life. We've all had to adjust. But the ones who prevail are the ones who trust God in spite of the unknown.

December 21

When You Lose Control

Luke 1:38

Mary had her life mapped out. She was to marry a good man, Joseph. Her father and mother had already approved, so she was betrothed. All they were waiting for was the big day. Nothing would seem to hold them back. But, things changed in a flash. An angel came to Mary and informed her that she would have a child conceived by the Holy Spirit. (Luke 1:26-35) And this wasn't just any child, He would be the long-anticipated Savior! Even though she was shocked at the news, Mary ended her questioning with amazing trust. She bravely stated, "Behold, I am the servant of the Lord; let it be to me according to your word." (Luke 1:38)

Life made sense to Mary up until this point, and then the bottom fell out from underneath her! She lost control. Everything she assumed certain was unraveling. What would her friends think when she was seen pregnant? How would her parents respond? Would Joseph stay with her? It was all unknown to her, but regardless of their responses, she yielded to God's direction. A loss of control doesn't mean God has abandoned you. Often it's a sign He has you right where He wants you, but you have to look at things differently.

<u>Closer Challenge</u>: Are the plans you had for your life unraveling before your eyes due to reasons beyond your control? How have you responded? **Today**, instead of fighting against the direction where God is steering you, submit to His leading. Name one thing you have refused to submit to. Write it in your journal. Now, take one tangible step toward submitting. Share with a friend or spouse your decision. Finally, as Mary displayed trust, pray to the Lord, "Behold, I am the servant of the Lord; let it be to me according to your word."

December 22

Uninhibited Praise

―――――•―――――

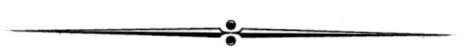

Luke 2:20

Of all the people God could have used to announce the arrival of the Savior, why did He choose shepherds? Why not use the mayor of Bethlehem, the Jewish ruling body, Caesar, or even a country Rabbi? Why not use someone with more clout? Well, it's hard to know for certain, but a strong case can be made that God used these shepherds to display uninhibited praise. (Luke 2:20) After they encountered the angelic chorus of the multitudes and beheld the face of the Savior, all they could do was unleash an amazing outburst of celebration. Anyone of clout might have been too dignified or may have felt threatened by this child, but the shepherds had nothing to lose and everything to gain because hope had come. So praise was their instinctive response.

We've made Christmas into a lot of things, but one thing we've often failed to do at Christmas is express uninhibited praise. We talk about peace, love, and hope at Christmas, and rightly so. But as a result of these, there ought to be an outburst of praise and celebration. If you truly understand the message of Christmas, that the Savior has come, your immediate response must be an eruption of praise! The shepherds modeled this for us.

<u>*Closer Challenge*</u>: Are you full of praise this Christmas? If so, let it be expressed outwardly like these shepherds. **Today**, any time you pass by a manger scene, use it as an opportunity to express pure joy. When you see the child in these manger displays, say out loud, "Praise God, the Savior is born!" If you're at a restaurant, department store, church, home, or wherever, let out a shout of praise! Let unspeakable joy flow from your soul because of the hope this Child brings. Don't let Christmas become too composed; burst forth with uninhibited praise because the Savior has come!

December 23

When You Believe Again

Luke 1:63-64

We've all said things we've quickly regretted, but few have had immediate consequences from their words like Zechariah. Zechariah was selected to burn incense in the Holy Temple. And while performing his task, Gabriel the angel suddenly appeared with a prophecy. He informed Zechariah that he and his wife, Elizabeth, would have a son, and they would call him John. In disbelief, Zechariah protested, citing that he and Elizabeth were too old. Once those words escaped his mouth, it was too late. His failure to believe cost him the precious gift of speaking until the child was born.

You can learn a lot when you're unable to speak. He probably became a much better listener during this time. He was able to observe and ponder the ways of God moving in their situation. And so when the time came for them to name the child after his birth, Zechariah took a simple step of faith toward believing again. When asked what the boy's name would be, he wrote on a tablet, "His name is John." With this seemingly small act of faith, his tongue loosed and he was able to speak again.

<u>Closer Challenge</u>: Has your disbelief placed you in an unfavorable situation? Have you spoken foolishly when you should have trusted God? Often, the quickest way back to favor with God is one small step of obedience. **Today**, recall a current struggle of faith. What is causing you disbelief? Now, regardless of how bizarre or surreal God's will is upon your life, prove your belief in Him with the next chance to act in this matter. One right step can refocus your life and bring amazing perspective. Learn from Zechariah that failure to believe isn't the end. God is merciful. He can redeem you as soon as you take *your* next, simple "His name is John" step.

December 24

Preparing for the King

―――――⋅―――――

Matthew 2:10-11

Though many traditions exist about the Magi coming to Jesus near His birth, several unanswered questions remain. What were their names? What town did they come from? How many were actually there at Jesus' birth? These answers, among many others, are unknown. But instead of focusing upon what we don't know, there is great significance in what we do know. They were a symbol of hope for all Gentiles. When the Magi laid eyes upon the Lord, Jesus became "a light of revelation to the Gentiles," just as Simeon prophesied. (Luke 2:30-31)

But there's more we can learn from these men. First, when coming to the King, they didn't come *empty-hearted*. They were filled with excessive joy! (Matthew 2:10) Their affections were directed to Jesus. Secondly, they didn't come *empty-headed*. They understood the significance of this Child and bowed before Him. (Matthew 2:11) Finally, they didn't come *empty-handed*. They brought precious gifts of gold, frankincense, and myrrh. (Matthew 2:11) When coming to the King this Christmas, model these wise men who reverently approached the Savior.

<u>Closer Challenge</u>: How are you coming to the King this Christmas? Are you too distracted by worldly influences to even notice? **Today**, plan your Christmas celebration similar to the Magi. Don't come empty-hearted. Embrace the moment with your affections. Don't come empty-headed. Know what this Child represents. Carefully read and study the Christmas story. Finally, don't come empty-handed. In some way, offer a gift to someone in need to honor Jesus. (Matthew 25:40) If you embrace coming to Jesus like this, you'll come to your King wisely.

December 25

The Sweet and Sorrowful Cries of Jesus

Luke 19:44

As with every newborn child, Jesus relied upon His mother. Humbling Himself, He submitted to her feeding Him, changing Him and tending to His every need. Never lose sight of the fact that He was fully man. And since He was fully man, it's fair to assume that He cried as we do. As a baby in His mother's arms, He cried with sweet tears of love. But there was one cry in Jesus' life that was sorrowful, signifying the reason for His coming.

When Jesus entered Jerusalem the week of His eventual death, He was cheered; He was adored; people loved Him! But, it was for the wrong reasons. They didn't understand the true reason for His coming. They were amazed by His power, but they wanted it to overthrow Rome. They sought a conquering warrior, not a spiritual sacrifice. They failed to see they were separated from God because of sin. They missed it! And so shortly after hosannas were proclaimed, Jesus wept. He sobbed. He didn't cry sweet tears, but instead, tears of sorrow because they missed the purpose of the manger. (Luke 2:11; Luke 19:44)

Closer Challenge: Have you missed the purpose of Jesus' coming? Are you caught up in the modern distractions of Christmas? If so, Jesus *weeps* for you. **Today**, honestly decide what is most important to you. Your greatest need isn't a list full of presents checked off; it isn't a house full of guests and perfectly cooked food; it isn't even spending time with family. Your greatest need is forgiveness of sin. If you refuse Jesus, He cries for you on this day and every day you quench the Spirit. There is one message at Christmas that can't be overlooked: Jesus came to save the world, including you. If you haven't already, choose this day to accept Him as *your* Savior.

December 26

The Veil Is Gone!

Mark 15:38

What appeared to be the most demoralizing day in all human history actually turned out to be the grandest. While hanging on the cross in His last few moments of life, Jesus cried out in a loud voice, giving Himself up to the Father. (Mark 15:37) Oh the defeat, many thought! But simultaneously, the curtain in the Temple that was veiling the Most Holy Place was torn from top to bottom. The curtain symbolized the separation between God and mankind; but when it was torn, it was a sign there was no more separation. If you believe in Jesus, you can now draw close to God with no restraint.

In light of the veil being torn, the author of Hebrews urges us to confidently draw near to the throne of grace. (Hebrews 4:16) This can only be possible with the work of Jesus on the cross to justify our position before God as approachable. Without the blood of Jesus, the veil would remain and our sins would be unatoned for. But now that the veil is gone, you can run into your Abba's arms, unafraid to approach Him in all of His holiness! On the contrary, if you fail to approach Him, you're wasting the privileged access you've been graciously given.

<u>Closer Challenge</u>: Are you hesitant to come before the Father because of His holiness or your sin? **Today**, without losing reverence for His position, draw closer to God with confidence. Come to Him with any request you might have, knowing He welcomes you. One of the greatest delusions believers have is that they believe and behave as if the veil remains. It's gone! Just as your sin has been removed, so has the barrier between you and God. Unflinchingly approach your Father today as a child would his Daddy.

December 27

Roll Your Stone Away!

John 11:38-41

Sad new came to Jesus. His good friend Lazarus was very ill. But instead of immediately making His way to Bethany to heal him, Jesus delayed four days. Lazarus died. When Jesus finally arrived, Martha was disappointed that He didn't come sooner. Mary was crushed that her brother had died, which led to Jesus weeping with her. Then, in a demonstration of compassion, Jesus led them to the tomb. When they arrived, Jesus instructed them to "take away the stone." He very well could have removed it Himself, but He wanted *them* to do it. Martha resisted, saying the odor would be too strong because he had been dead for four days. But in an act of faith, *they* removed the stone, and Jesus brought Lazarus back to life!

Each of us faces impossible situations, leaving us paralyzed by our own disbelief. And as a result, a lot of "stones" are left untouched. Miracles are left undiscovered because we lack the faith to remove the stones blocking the wonder. Jesus didn't ask them to raise Lazarus from the grave. All He requested was that they have some participation in faith. They were to remove the stone. That's it! And when they did, they were able to witness one of the most amazing events in human history.

<u>Closer Challenge</u>: Are you facing an impossible situation? Maybe today the still small voice of God is asking you to participate, even though doubt clouds your vision. **Today**, determine what "stone" you need to remove for God to work in your life. It may seem small. It may seem too late. It may seem foolish. But remove it! Participate in this small act of faith so you can leave room for God to display His glory. Remove your stone!

December 28

Walk in the Spirit

---◆---

Romans 8:8-9

Now that you are no longer condemned because of your sin (Romans 8:1) and are justified before the Father because of the work of Jesus on the cross, you are *freed* from the flesh! (Romans 8:2) In fact, you have no obligation to the flesh at all. You owe the flesh nothing. If you are in Christ, there is now a deep compelling from within to be controlled by the Spirit. (Romans 8:8)

Most believers hold firmly to the doctrine that once you believe in Jesus, you are no longer *condemned* to death because of His work on the cross. It's a marvelous truth that should be celebrated. However, many believers stop short of the full freedom He has provided. Not only are you no longer condemned to death, but as a Christ-follower, you are no longer *constrained* to sin because of the Spirit's ongoing work to sanctify you! You are no longer a slave to the flesh; and if you continue on that path, you cannot please God. (Romans 8:8) It's time to walk according to the Spirit!

<u>Closer Challenge</u>: Is there a fleshly struggle that has been holding you back from experiencing freedom in the Spirit? Your problem might be as simple as accepting the truth that the Spirit of God has already set you free. **Today**, instead of rehearsing your fleshly struggle over and over again in your mind, firmly fix your eyes on Jesus. (Hebrews 12:2) You are not meant to continue in the flesh, so why do you keep going there? When you become tempted by a fleshly struggle, immediately replace that thought by reciting *Romans 8:9* throughout the day. Do this as often as needed to remind yourself you are freed. You are no longer *constrained* to sin!

December 29

What Do You Want?

---

1 Kings 3:9

If God asked you to request anything of Him and He would give it like He did for Solomon (1 Kings 3:5), what would your request be? A new car? World peace? A thinner waistline? What would be the first thing that comes to mind? Would it possibly be a discerning heart?

Many of us aspire to lead great endeavors and impact many lives for God's Kingdom. But have we weighed the cost of being this kind of leader? Have we understood the wisdom it takes? If you desire to lead, you must desire godly wisdom. To try to change the world on your own will be a miserable attempt. But it is possible to change your world with God as your mind and heart. There is no wisdom apart from God, so to seek it from an outside source is simply unattainable. God is wisdom, and as you draw closer to him, you are penetrating the very wisdom of God and planting it into your own life.

<u>Closer Challenge</u>: Do you want to be a leader? Do you want wisdom? **Today**, spend time seeking out God's wisdom. Do a word search in the Bible on "wisdom." Call up a person who you think is full of God's wisdom, and allow this person to share what he or she is currently learning from God. Over time, seek out biographies of godly men and women who have walked this Christian life before you to see how they gained the wisdom of God. Be proactive in your attempt to gain wisdom, and remember to display humility, because if you don't, wisdom will escape you. If you want wisdom, ask God and He will show you the riches of His wisdom!

December 30

A Longing for Heaven

Ecclesiastes 3:11

This world offers many appealing alternatives to God. You can pursue hobbies, careers, relationships, material possessions and more. You can even seek after good things, such as a family, service and being generous. But as good as these are, they cannot fill the hole in your heart fit for eternity. Solomon wisely said God has placed eternity in the hearts of mankind. (Ecclesiastes 3:11) We groan for our eternal dwelling. To see God in all His fullness and to witness the greatness of heaven is the yearning of our souls.

However, when we exchange the real for something fake (Romans 1:25), our hearts cannot be satisfied. For a short time, there will be some enjoyment from the offerings of the created world, but that will soon fade when reality settles in. Paul wrote that while we are in our earthly tent, we inwardly groan for our heavenly dwelling. (2 Corinthians 5:1-5) This is by design. You are not made for this world. You are made for God, to worship Him, love Him, and pursue Him with all your heart. Never exchange Him with anything else!

<u>Closer Challenge</u>: Are you inadvertently pursuing something other than God? Maybe you haven't even realized it, but you're spending much of your time, resources and strength on things that don't pertain to your future dwelling. **Today**, carefully gauge what rules your heart by asking three close friends what they observe is most important to you. Direct them to be honest. Receive their advice as love. (Proverbs 27:6) If they observe your passion is something other than things pertaining to eternity, make a decision to change course. The truth sometimes hurts, but it is good medicine for the soul. God has placed eternity in your heart. Don't fool around with things that are not pointing you in that direction, for you'll never be satisfied.

December 31

Spiritual Remembrance Day

Psalm 143:5

In the Old Testament when God's people encountered blessings, sorrows or even wrath, they often set up altars to worship and remember God. Noah built an altar of praise when he came out of the ark. (Genesis 8:20) Abraham constructed an altar after receiving the promise of being the father of many nations. (Genesis 12:7-8) Moses built an altar, calling it, "The Lord is My Banner" after Aaron and Hur held up his arms while Joshua and the Israelites defeated the Amalekites. (Exodus 17:15) As illustrated in these examples, it's important to pause and worship God before continuing on to your next stage of life.

As you come to the end of yet another year, it's healthy to reflect upon what God has been to you before moving on to the next year. (Psalm 143:5) Whether your year was filled with great blessings, challenging trials or heartbreaking losses, God is still worthy of praise. (Job 1:21) So before you take one step into the New Year, stop and bless His name.

<u>Closer Challenge</u>: Which characteristic of God best describes His interaction in your life this past year? Has He been your salvation? (Psalm 13:5) Fortress? (Psalm 18:2) Healer? (Psalm 30:2) Refiner? (Isaiah 48:10) Strength? (Psalm 73:26) Provider? (Psalm 65:9) Faithful? (Psalm 89:8) If you had to choose one characteristic of God that represents the way He expressed Himself to you this past year, which would it be? **Today**, pause and praise Him! Kneel to the ground, thanking Him for His closeness to you. Make this a spiritual marker of praise. Through joy and pain, God longs to be near to you. Never doubt His love. Keep drawing *closer* to God.

Appendix 1

One on One Disciple-Making Plan

Hello Disciple-Makers,

First of all, I'm praising God that you're considering being a *One on One Disciple-Maker*! You may have already been discipling others for years. For that, I applaud you. So, if you have a plan, continue to do what best fits you and those whom you disciple. But for those who do not have a personal plan, I'd like to share with you how I've been discipling. My aim is to give you some tips that can help you. I use these three objectives, which I call the **3 C's to disciple-making**...

1) <u>**Call**</u> **someone to follow you for one year**. Don't be bashful. There are people who want you to ask them to come with you as you seek after and draw *closer* to Jesus. It's not about being better than them; it's about taking leadership to point people to Jesus. When you show you're ***interested***, it normally motivates that person because they feel loved. I suggest you call someone who is new in the faith or weak in the faith due to lack of personal touch. It can be someone in the church or someone who isn't even a believer. An unbeliever would be great! After all, Jesus discipled many people who weren't very religious. You can too. Just let the Spirit guide you and ask someone to join you on this adventure. You can start any time of the year, but January gives you a nice one-year commitment. (By the way, I think this is obvious, but keep it a *same gender* partnership.)

2) <u>**Challenge**</u> **your disciple**. You and your partner can be challenged in many different ways, so be creative. With the men I've discipled, here are my guidelines:

1) We meet **face to face** once a month at a coffee shop, restaurant, home or my office. (As the discipler, *you* need to take initiative to schedule these meetings consistently!)
2) We follow a daily Bible study **plan**. I've used many different devotionals and Bible study plans, but I'd suggest using this book as your guide. It's a great resource because it has 366 entries. It will keep you both engaged in God's Word daily. Plus, you can use the

Closer Challenges as talking points. If either of you happens to miss a day, just keep pace with the current day. Don't be overly concerned about the days you missed. Progress is most important. But, the aim is to spend time with God daily.
3) During the meeting, we often discuss some or all of these **questions**: What did God teach you from the devotional/Bible study or church this past month? What is God teaching you in life circumstances over the past month? How have you been able to share Jesus? How have you ministered to your family? How have you served God? We don't always touch on every question, but these are good questions to get your discussion flowing. Just be Spirit-led.

3) **Copy this experience next year.** We must make spiritual copies of ourselves. From the beginning of the partnership, spiritual cloning must be communicated. You and your disciple can certainly consider meeting another year together, but also encourage him or her to start discipling as soon as possible.

Finally, this is not meant to be a church *program*; it's aimed to be a *lifestyle*. I can tell you from experience, this has been a wonderful blessing and adventure for me. I pray you will see the great spiritual value in this for you and the ones you disciple. You will be a blessing, and you'll also be blessed by those who partner with you.

Drawing Closer to God with You!

Louis W. Heard

Appendix 2

Topical References

Abilities (Gifts) – Sep 2
Accountability – Jan 5
Anger – Oct 15
Apologetics – Apr 3
Assurance – Jun 11
Authority – Apr 15
Believing – Aug 28
Believing – Dec 23
Betrayal – May 20
Bitterness – Jul 24
Bitterness – Oct 17
Blessings – Nov 11
Boundaries – Jan 23
Brokenness – May 3
Brokenness – Aug 21
Calling – Nov 17
Calling – Dec 2
Caring – Jun 30
Childlike – Feb 10
Choices – Aug 8
Church – Feb 17
Church – Oct 19
Church – Oct 24
Church Change – Jul 19
Closeness – Jan 1
Communing – Jan 2
Compassion – Mar 15
Compassion – Nov 2
Complaining – Jan 8
Complaining – Mar 31
Complaining – May 6
Confession – Mar 8
Confidence – Oct 16
Conflict – Apr 17

Conflict – Jun 6
Confusion – Nov 18
Consecration – May 31
Consistency – Sep 9
Control – Aug 20
Control – Dec 21
Conversion – Jun 25
Cooperating – Nov 6
Correction – Apr 30
Correction – Sep 13
Coveting – Feb 1
Death – Mar 3
Death – May 22
Deception – Sep 27
Decisions – Jun 20
Decisions – Nov 1
Deliverance – Aug 1
Dependence – Feb 4
Dependence – Apr 8
Dependence – May 30
Dependence – Jul 4
Dependence – Nov 4
Dependence – Nov 23
Depression – Aug 7
Devotion – Aug 25
Devotion – Sep 10
Disbelief – Sep 25
Discipling – Dec 10
Divisive People – Aug 3
Doubt – Nov 13
Drifting – Nov 19
Elderly – Oct 11
Encouraging – Jun 19
Encouraging – Jul 10

Endurance – Jul 6
Enjoying Life – Feb 20
Equality – Mar 20
Esteem – May 29
Evangelism – Jan 3
Evangelism – Feb 13
Evangelism – Mar 21
Evangelism – Jun 17
Evangelism – Jun 26
Evangelism – Jul 21
Evangelism – Aug 11
Evangelism – Sep 20
Evangelism – Nov 10
Evil – Oct 31
Failure – May 23
Failure – Dec 11
Faith – Jan 24
Faith – Mar 4
Faith – Apr 21
Faith – Jul 20
Faith – Oct 18
Faith Action – Feb 8
Faith Action – Dec 27
Faithfulness – Jun 18
Fake Ones – Nov 20
Family – Jan 28
Family – Apr 13
Family – Jun 7
Family – Oct 2
Family – Dec 17
Fasting – Feb 18
Fasting – Sep 23
Favoritism – Jan 22
Favoritism – Apr 18
Fear of Death – Aug 4
Finishing – May 24
Finishing – Oct 30
Followship – Aug 10
Forgiveness – Jan 15
Forgiveness – Mar 17
Forgiveness – Jul 28

Friends – Jun 24
Friends – Jul 1
Future living – Aug 9
Giving – Jul 9
Giving – Sep 21
Giving – Nov 26
Giving Back – Jul 2
Giving Mercy – Feb 24
Giving Mercy – Apr 2
Glory – May 25
Glory – May 26
Godless Chatter – Sep 18
Godly Living – Apr 26
God's Care – Mar 30
God's Jealousy – Jul 17
God's Presence – May 1
God's Presence – Jul 15
God's Will – Feb 12
God's Will – Mar 23
God's Will – May 16
God's Word – May 27
God's Word – Oct 5
Gossip – Jan 19
Gratitude – Feb 11
Grumbling – Jul 3
Guilt – Feb 29
Guilt – May 14
Habits (Bad) – Jun 23
Hearing God – Mar 2
Hearing God – Aug 5
Heaven – Feb 26
Heaven – Nov 14
Heaven – Dec 12
Heaven – Dec 30
Heirs – Dec 14
Helping needy – Jan 17
Helping others – Oct 23
Holiness – Jul 31
Holy Living – Apr 28
Holy Living – May 4
Holy Living – May 7

Holy Spirit – Dec 3
Holy Spirit – Dec 4
Holy Spirit – Dec 5
Holy Spirit – Dec 6
Hope – Jul 18
Hope – Oct 7
Hope – Nov 24
Hosting – Feb 2
Hosting – Oct 25
Humility – Jan 20
Humility – Mar 16
Identity – Feb 23
Idolatry – Nov 29
Idols – Aug 17
Idols – Nov 8
Impact (Fruit) – Apr 16
Integrity – Apr 5
Interruptability – Jan 14
Joking – Apr 1
Judging – Sep 12
Justification – Jun 12
Knowing Jesus – Oct 29
Laughter – Jun 14
Laziness – Aug 30
Leaders – Jan 31
Leaders – Apr 12
Leaders (church) – Sep 5
Leadership – Jan 13
Leadership – Mar 9
Leadership – Apr 15
Legalism – Mar 7
Loneliness – Nov 9
Lordship – Jan 4
Lordship – Feb 5
Lordship – Jun 28
Lordship – Oct 14
Love – Feb 14
Love – Mar 14
Love – Apr 27
Love – May 2
Love – Nov 27

Love – Nov 30
Love – Dec 9
Lust – Apr 19
Marriage – Feb 3
Materialism – Feb 7
Meekness – Aug 22
Memories – Jul 12
Mentoring – Jan 9
Mentoring – May 5
Mercy – Sep 15
Mercy (God's) – Jun 22
Mercy Giving – Aug 24
Mind Battles – Aug 18
Miracles – May 9
Miracles – May 21
Missions – Feb 27
Missions – Mar 6
Missions – Apr 24
Missions Prayer – Sep 19
Money (Debt) – Apr 6
Money – Jun 1
Money – Jun 2
Money – Jun 3
Money – Jun 4
Money – Jun 5
Mothers – Jul 7
Music – Jun 8
Names – Aug 14
Neighbors – Aug 13
New Life – Jul 11
Obedience – Jan 6
Obedience – Jan 29
Obedience – Mar 12
Obedience – Oct 28
Obedience – Nov 25
Obedience – Dec 1
On Mission – Nov 15
Opportunities – Mar 1
Opposition – Mar 24
Opposition – Sep 7
Overflow – Jul 14

Parenting – Dec 13
Parents – Nov 5
Patience – Feb 28
Patience – Jun 10
Peace – May 28
Peace – Oct 9
Peacemaking – Mar 19
Peacemaking – Aug 26
Perfection – Sep 1
Persistence – Oct 21
Persecution – Aug 27
Perseverance – Sep 3
Perspective – Mar 11
Perspective – Oct 22
Perspective – Nov 14
Plans – Sep 17
Praise – Feb 6
Praise – Dec 22
Prayer – Feb 9
Prayer – Mar 28
Prayer – Apr 29
Prayer – May 13
Prayer – Jun 16
Prayer – Jul 26
Prayer – Sep 22
Prayer – Oct 4
Prayer – Nov 3
Presence – Mar 26
Pride – Mar 29
Pride – Sep 28
Priorities – Mar 5
Priorities – Mar 25
Priorities – Apr 14
Priorities – Nov 28
Purity – Feb 22
Purpose – Feb 16
Purpose – May 12
Purpose – Jun 21
Purpose – Oct 8
Rebuking – Dec 18
Repentance – Oct 1

Reputation – Sep 6
Rest – Feb 15
Recognition – Nov 7
Reconciliation – Jan 12
Reconnecting – Jun 29
Redemption – Dec 8
Reflect God – Apr 22
Refreshed – Oct 10
Relationships – Mar 27
Remembering – Apr 23
Remembering – Sep 24
Remembering – Dec 31
Restitution – Jul 8
Rewards – Jul 13
Righteousness – Jan 21
Righteousness – Aug 23
Romance – Aug 19
Sabbathing – Jun 13
Sacrifice – Oct 12
Salvation – Jan 7
Salvation – Jan 27
Salvation – Aug 6
Salvation – Dec 25
Second Chance – Jul 16
Self-Worth – Oct 3
Service – Jan 25
Service – Apr 7
Service – Jul 29
Service – Nov 12
Shame – Apr 4
Shameless – Sep 4
Sin – Jan 11
Sin – Jan 18
Sin – Apr 20
Sin – May 18
Sin – Jun 27
Sorrows – May 19
Speaking Up – Jan 26
Speaking Up – May 10
Speech – Mar 18
Speech – Nov 16

Spiritual Warfare – May 8
Spiritually Dry – May 17
Spirit-filled – Dec 7
Spirit-filled – Dec 28
Steadfastness – Sep 30
Strangers – Oct 27
Strength – Aug 15
Strength – Sep 16
Struggles – Jan 30
Submission – Jan 16
Submission – Feb 25
Suffering – Jan 10
Sympathy – Mar 13
Temptations – Apr 9
Testimony – Mar 10
Thankfulness – Nov 21
Time with God – Apr 11
Time with God – May 15
Tough Love – Oct 26
Tragedy – Sep 11
Transformed – Aug 12
Troubles – Sep 26
Trust – Jul 23
Truth – Apr 10
Truth Seeking – Sep 14
Truth Telling – Feb 19
Underprivileged – Aug 31
Understanding – Jul 27
Understanding – Sep 29
Undivided Heart – Sep 8
Unexpected – Dec 20
Uniqueness – Jun 9
Unity – Nov 6
Using Stories – Oct 20
Vengeance – Dec 16
Warnings – Jul 22
Weaknesses – Aug 2
Wisdom – Jul 5
Wisdom – Dec 29
Wonders – Oct 13
Worldview – Oct 6

Worry – Jun 15
Worship – Feb 21
Worship – Mar 22
Worship – May 11
Worship – Dec 19
Worship – Dec 24
Zeal – Aug 29